AF243711

MARBLE CAMP AND ME

A City Child's Life in Arizona Territory

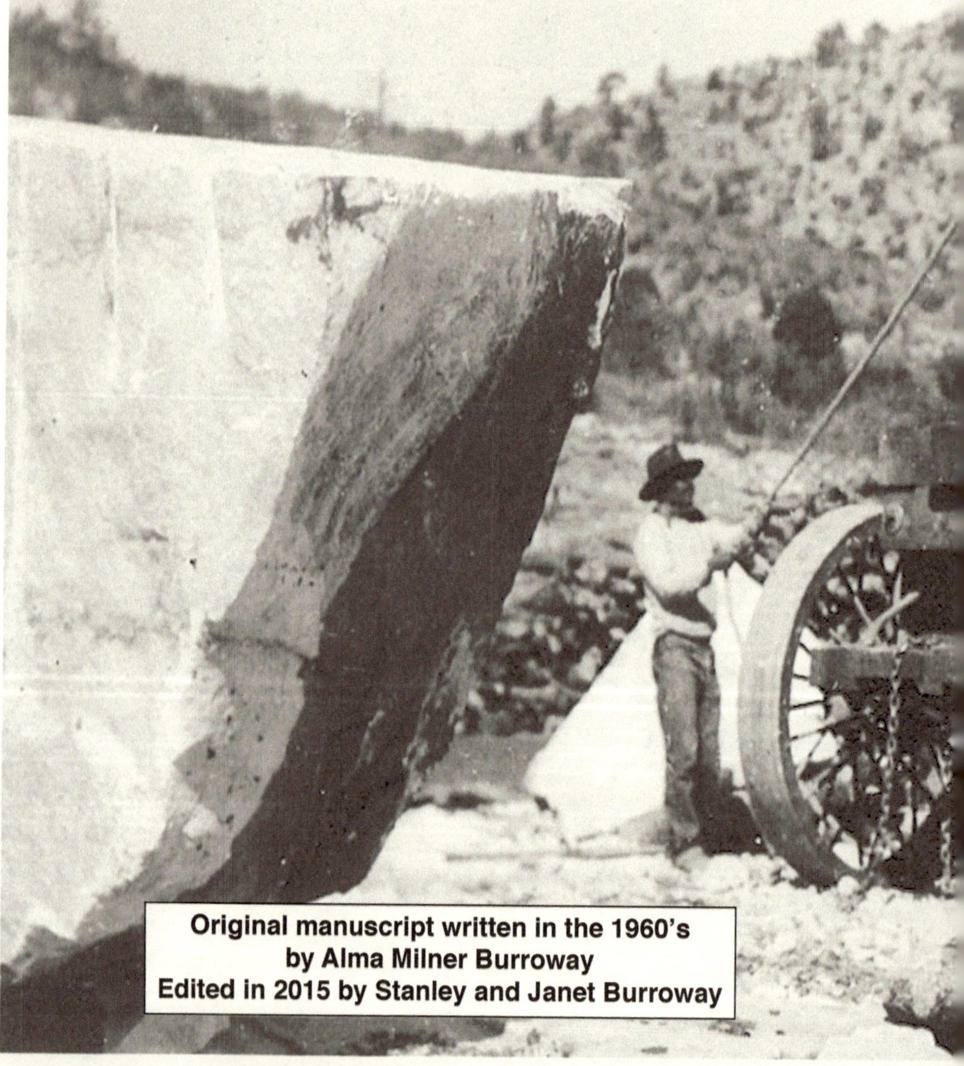

Original manuscript written in the 1960's
by Alma Milner Burroway
Edited in 2015 by Stanley and Janet Burroway

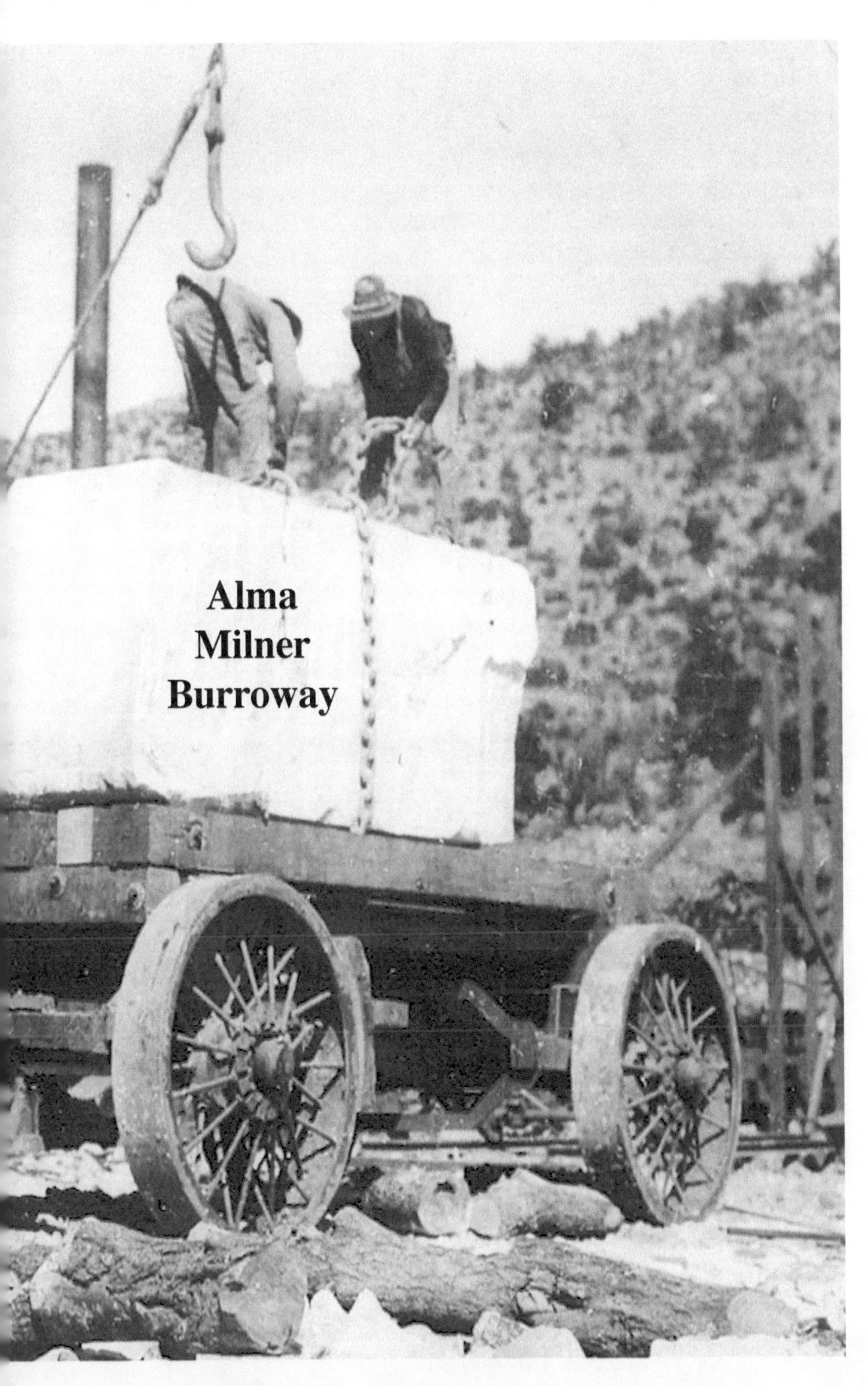
Alma
Milner
Burroway

Published by *The Country Side Press*, North Powder, OR 97867
Printed in the USA

Book Design and Layout by Debby Schoeningh/The Country Side Press

ISBN: 978-0-9907798-0-3
Library of Congress Control Number: 2014915789

ACKNOWLEDGMENTS

I wish to acknowledge the invaluable support, encouragement and insight of my sister and co-editor, Janet Burroway. I would also like to thank Jenna Hubert for turning old manuscript pages into computer copy and old album pages into scanned and restored photographs. And I am especially grateful to Debby Schoeningh, publisher of The County Side Press, who did all of the above and a great deal more to save this story from obscurity. — *S.F.B.*

A NOTE ON THE PHOTOS

Dana T. Milner — "Papa" in this story — possessed a Kodak Camera, either his own or the property of the Arizona Marble Company, and he is, so far as we know, the photographer for all of the pictures in this book except the few in which he appears.

It's probably worth noting, because the adults in these photos often seem stern, that facing a camera in the early 1900s was still a fairly infrequent and formal occasion so subjects usually tried to look "serious."

Full Disclosure: The photo on the cover is a composite of two that appear in original form in the text. The mill was visible from the spot where the picture of the fawn was taken but to include it would have meant photographing from behind the child and obscuring the fawn's head.

TABLE OF CONTENTS

ABOUT THIS BOOK

In the 1950's and early '60s, my mother, Alma Milner Burroway, then approaching her own sixties, set down the story of her life from age four to age ten, when she and her mother left a bustling little Ohio city on Lake Erie to follow her father to a rough mountain camp at a marble quarry in the Arizona Territory. When she wrote, Mom was the only person still alive who had been at Marble Camp from its early days until it closed.

The manuscript was not so much lost as neglected, and it has never seen print until now, so the story it tells, from 1908 to 1914, is a little more than 100 years old. When we were youngsters, my sister, Janet, and I used to listen as Mom entertained us with many of these stories from her childhood, so we believe that the events in the book happened just about as she put them down, though of course the conversations are recreated from her memory. In editing, my goal has been only to shorten the book slightly and make some references clearer to today's readers.

"Tom Sawyer" is set on the banks of the Mississippi, "Little Women" in Concord, Mass., but the stories they tell reveal at least as much about time—the middle years of the 19th Century—as about place. This book is about Marble Camp but, almost in passing, it says a lot about life and attitudes in the early days of the 20th Century, also a time worth remembering.

Mom never thought of herself as a adventurer—after all, she arrived in her corner of the West in a Pullman car, not a covered wagon. But she and her family were among the last of the American pioneers, and her mother was one of those women who brought cotton prints, piano music, sugar doughnuts, and polite manners to a very hard place.

— Stan Burroway

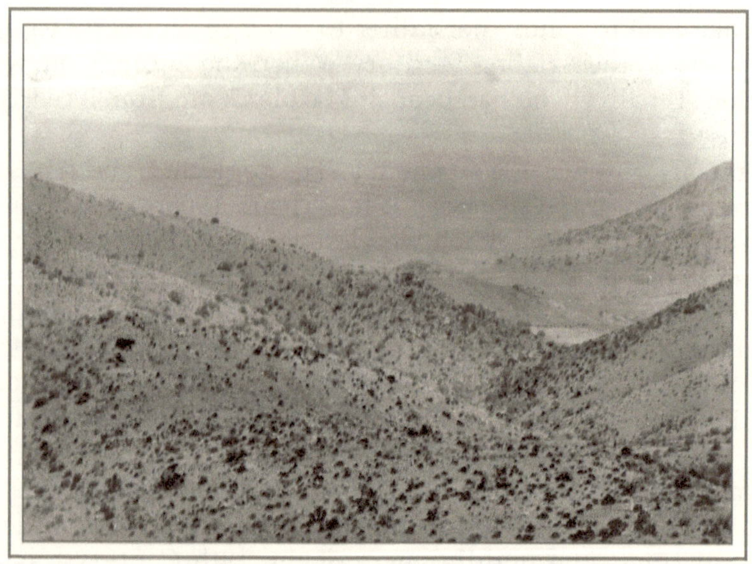

In the Chiricahua Mountains

1.

Papa's Disappointment

The first time we went up to Marble Camp, over a road that hadn't been built yet, Mama rode all the way sitting on a box of dynamite.

She didn't know it, of course. Papa was too smart for that.

When a stylish young woman leaves the tea parties of a town like Lorain, Ohio, in 1910 to ride up a mountain on a lumber wagon, you don't necessarily tell her that the explosives are under her side of the seat.

I was struggling to hold onto the kitten that was determined to get to the big ham in the back of the wagon and worrying about what Johnny Kaiser, the teamster holding the reins next to me, was muttering about my cat. And Papa was busy trying to out-guess Daisy, my new burro, which he was leading behind the wagon on a rope. I was a little anxious about Daisy. At five I could hardly handle my first kitten and Papa had bought me my first burro.

As we bounced, joggled and strained up the side of the Chiricahua Mountains in the southeastern corner of Arizona Territory, I looked back over my shoulder at the little town we had left in the valley below. Bowie, with its two gangling water tanks, its adobe shacks and white-washed cattle-shipping corral, looked interesting enough, but it certainly wasn't Lorain. I closed my eyes and tried to remember how green and busy Lorain had been when we left. Here it seemed as though time was standing still, and we were the only things going any-place except for the squirrels. They ran with a rippling motion up the mountainside, but you knew they'd soon be back where they started. This wild country was their home. No matter how hard I tried, I couldn't see it as our home too.

How did we ever get in such a place, I wondered glancing back at Papa, who was leading Daisy a few feet behind the wagon. I hoped he couldn't read my mind. It was on account of Papa that we had ended up in Arizona Territory.

It all began just after my fourth birthday party in January of 1909.

Papa hadn't been well and Mama had finally coaxed him to go and see Dr. Cox.

"It's nothing but a bad cold," Papa said. "The doctor will laugh at me for making him visit for a case of sniffles."

"It's more than sniffles the way that cough hangs on," Mama said firmly. "I'll make an appointment for you to see him today, on the way home from work."

Late that afternoon Mama and I were waiting when Papa and Dr. Cox came out of the consultation room. Papa was looking very serious. The doctor had his nose glasses in one hand and pulled on the black ribbon attached to them. He dropped the ribbon and tapped the palm of his hand with the glasses as he told Mama, "Maud, I think you and Dana had better make plans to go West."

Mama and Papa looked at each other. They hadn't been expecting anything like that. "Might be consumption in the lungs," the doctor added soberly.

Mama said "Oh!"

"Mind, you, I don't say there is for sure, but we'd better not take a chance."

That had been six months after the day the bank had opened. Papa had been working long hours helping to organize a new bank in the busy steel town of Lorain. It had concerned Mama that Papa was working so hard, but he passed it off saying, "Hard work never hurt anybody. I don't mind burning a little midnight oil when it will mean a good job."

The doors of the Bank of Lorain were set to open for business at ten o'clock on May 25, 1908. Mama had put extra starch in Papa's collar to be worn at the opening. I watched him as he stood before the bathroom mirror brushing his hair smooth with a military brush in each hand.

"I must look my best," he said, "when they call me into the office of the President. How will you like it to be the wife of a bank cashier, Sweetheart?"

Mama was smiling. Papa was only twenty-six, pretty young to be cashier – and not just a teller – of a promising new bank! She reached out her hand to brush a fleck of dust from his coat. Then we followed him outside to stand on the porch and watch him as he disappeared around the corner on his way to work.

All day there was a little thrill of expectancy in the air. At five o'-clock Mama and I went to sit on our front porch step to watch for Papa.

I could tell something important was supposed to happen though I had no real idea what a "cashier" was.

When Papa came in sight Mama and I stood up quickly, and started down the walk to meet him. He seemed shorter than usual and very tired.

Always when Papa got home from work the first thing he did was kiss Mama and me. He seemed to have forgotten about it this time. In a daze he walked up the steps and opened the screen door for us.

Mama didn't say anything till we got inside, then she just said, "Oh, Dana!"

"Mr. Phinzy's nephew, Frank, is going to be the cashier." There was a stunned look in his eyes.

"There, there," Mama said as he gave a great sob. She threw her arms around him and they clung to each other. I stood miserably watching them. Not getting to be *cashier* must be very bad.

No one knew if it was the disappointment or the over-work that gave Papa the cough and caused him to lose weight in the next months, but when he left, the bank had to hire three men to take his place. Years later when X-rays showed no signs of scars from lung trouble, we all wondered if maybe Dr. Cox hadn't been pulling a fast one to get Papa a change of scenery. Dr. Cox was good at diagnosis, and it was hardly likely he'd have been that far wrong, but we never knew.

All we did know was the doctor we trusted wanted Papa to go out West. There never was any question about taking his advice.

2.

A Big Jump

For a week after Papa's visit to the doctor, we all poured over maps and travel books. I could only read by colors, and the pink sections on the maps looked best to me.

The more we studied, the more Papa and Mama seemed to favor a place called "Denver" and they kept coming back to it. Mama ran her finger along on the map from Lorain to Denver and said with a sigh, "Well it certainly is 'West'. Let's go there, Dana." Suddenly she slipped her arms around his neck and he drew her close.

"Denver it is, then, sweetheart," and Papa pushed the maps away.

I was glad it was settled. "Denver!" It had a nice friendly sound.

Oddly, all our friends must have thought we were leaving for good because they seemed so concerned. Mama belonged to the choir and the Maccabees, and a sewing club, and besides she had been born in Lorain.

Grandpa Pierce had been a carriage maker, a respectable member of the community. Six feet four when he was young, as he grew older he stooped to a mere five feet nine inches, probably to get down closer to Grandma, who was a little trick. Grandpa Pierce had been neither a religious nor a very sociable man, but Mama always said, "Pa was good moral man. Besides," she added, "Grandma had enough religion and sociability for half a dozen Grandpa Pierces." Grandma baked pies for church socials, took trays to the sick, gave handouts to the poor, helped pack missionary barrels, sat up with the feverish, and often served as a midwife. She loved to have too much going on, and Mama took after her. The only thing Mama would have liked better than a three-ring circus would have been a four-ring one. People would really miss her while she was away.

All day long friends called up on the telephone or came to say how sorry they were we were going. Few of them had ever been out of Ohio and I guess Denver seemed a long way off. Some of the women were crying. From all I could learn we were going to go on a train, and that was not a thing to cry about.

For the first six year after their marriage, Mama and Papa had lived with Grandma and saved every cent toward a home of their own. Now we lived in it, a new two-story house with gables and gingerbread porch. The last rose bush was planted in the front yard. The living room could have come out of a picture book. It had oatmeal wall paper and a border of pink roses at the ceiling. In the center of the room was a prized heirloom, a table given Mama and Papa by Grandma as a wedding present. The wood base was dark mahogany, which matched our piano. The top was mottled grey and white marble and so highly polished you could see your face in it. Originally it had belonged to Mama's Great Aunt Ann, a stylish little lady people said Mama took after.

Everyone called it "That Table," but I couldn't see why Mama was so proud of it. Every morning when she cleaned the house, she'd lift the small starched tidy and vase of artificial flowers and the family Bible, and run a slightly damp cloth over the marble surface. No trinkets or knick knacks were allowed on the polished surface of "That Table" to detract from its graceful elegance – just the vase of flowers and the Bible. Personally, I thought it was over-rated. It looked like just another piece of furniture to me.

The living room couch, now, was something special. It was green plush and carved wood, and the arms let down at each end on a sort of ratchet to make a single bed for company.

We hadn't even had any company yet to try sleeping on it.

The couch held white velvet pillows with huge roses, hand-painted on them by Aunt Kit, and yellow checked gingham cushions with wide ruffles. Some of the room's chairs were not at all comfortable for a little girl, but I had a little rocking chair that was just the right size.

There were lovely old shade trees in the yard, planted when the land was only a cow pasture. The grass would be green, and our new rosebushes would bloom for the first time in the Spring. Some of the trees were not too big for a little girl to climb on a hot day.

Mama said, "It's a shame to have to leave it all before such important things can happen."

She was careful, though, not to say anything like that in front of Papa because she was too worried about his health. When he was around, she always talked cheerfully about things as though she was afraid he might back out and decide not to leave Ohio.

Grandma had her own ideas about what we'd find in Denver. "It's almost like you were going to Africa among the cannibals, going West like this into Indian country. I won't sleep a wink at night, thinking of you being in mortal danger. Why they might even scalp you!" She looked anxiously at Mama and me as though she were seeing us for the last time unscalped.

"Oh, the Indians are friendly now," Papa said laughing, "Besides, most of them are on reservations. I doubt if there are any to speak of in Denver."

Grandma didn't believe that for a minute, and she shook her head and wiped her eyes fiercely with a corner of her apron.

Mama hated so much to part with the brand new furniture it was decided we'd ship it to our new home. All but the piano and the marble topped table, which were to go to Grandma's house for safe-keeping until we returned.

"The piano is so heavy it will be expensive to ship, and the table might get broken in the shipping," Grandma said. "Great Aunt Ann would turn over in her grave if she knew 'that Table' was out of Ohio and among strangers. I'll keep it for you, and you can have it when you get settled here in your home again."

Papa was going to Denver ahead of us, and the transfer company would get our things ready for shipping.

On the last night, after all the good-byes had been said to the rest of the family, Papa and Mama and I went for a walk down our street. It was a warm, clear night. When we were past the street lights, we could see the stars shining. The city was digging a new sewer a block or so from our house, extending the line for new houses – new houses for people like us, people who might someday have to take down their curtains and pictures and leave their marble-topped tables and their grandmothers, and move away to some unknown place.

The sewer tile had been delivered that day, and stacked along the ditch at intervals. We sat side by side on the tile and watched the moon come up.

"You can smell the lake tonight," Mama said.

You could always smell the lake and it didn't seem different from any other night to me. She just noticed because we were leaving it. If you thought about it, the lake really didn't smell too good — a blend of fog, fish, smashed lake flies, and smoke from the tug boats on Lake Erie and the Black River. But we had gotten so used to it we would miss it when it wasn't there.

We all took a good deep breath of "the lake." Suddenly Mama's shoulders began to shake with sobs and Papa put his arms around her. It was always good to have him put his arms around Mama. It made such a "together" feeling, even if it was only because she was crying. He got out his handkerchief and wiped her eyes.

Suddenly Mama exclaimed, "My goodness, that child is still up. We'd better get home."

Papa helped Mama off the tile and took my hand as we started back. When we drew near our house, it seemed to be waiting hopefully for us in the moonlight and we stood and looked at it for a long time. A gas jet was burning in the living room, and the light streamed through the ruffled curtains at the windows. I felt as though the house were reaching out its wooden arms to us, and I wanted to crawl into them and let them cuddle me. We didn't dream it was the last time we were ever to look at the house together.

"It won't be for long, sweetheart," Papa said softly. "I promise to get well soon. Before you know it, we'll be living back in our own home again."

To a four-year-old girl, the promise sounded very binding, and for years I kept wondering when we'd go back "home" to Lorain.

3.

Unexpected Intruders

The next day Papa boarded the train for Denver. It was no trouble to rent a house that still smelled of new lumber and fresh paint, but Mama was anxious to choose the tenants carefully. "I want good renters so that it will be in livable condition when we come back to it," she said. "It's bad enough to let strangers wear off the newness without getting somebody in who might make a wreck of it."

That alarmed me. They had wrecked a house near Grandma's, and I hated to think of ours like that, with its windows and shingles off.

It was almost a month before we were ready to leave. Papa wrote that he found a temporary job as an office clerk in Denver. "It isn't a very good job," he said, "And I am still hunting a better one. I have rented a house for us and I'm anxious for you to come."

Mama and I were staying at Grandma's house then, and the day before we were to leave, Grandma made a startling decision. Peering into her closet, she lifted her new alpaca off the hook and laid it on the bed by her wicker suitcase and said, "I've been thinking, Maud. I believe I'll go along to Denver. It won't take me long to pack my suitcase." She drew her Sunday shoes out of their calico cases and lifted the lid of the suitcase, which was half full—evidently she had been silently planning it for longer than she let on. "I've always wanted to see the West, and I can help you get settled. I'll feel a lot easier if I can picture you in your new home."

Grandma was always "picturing" things. Then too, she wanted to see for herself about those Indians.

The main thing I remember about that trip to Denver was about my legs. They were too short to suit grandma, or else maybe the seat was too deep. She kept pulling me forward so my legs hung down and pushing me back in the seat so they stuck straight out.

"It's a shame," she said. "How can a child be comfortable when the seats don't fit her? Such a long way to go with no seat to fit a child!"

Grandma's concern got in the way of my looking out the window. I'd just see something interesting going by when I'd feel myself being pulled forward to make me "fit" better or pushed back to make me more "comfortable." When I looked out again, the little boy in the red suit or the funny smoke stack by the track, or whatever I had wanted to see, was gone. I never sat still long enough for comfort to be a big problem.

It was reassuring to see Papa standing on the platform in Denver. The family was all in one piece again, but the feeling didn't last very long. Mama knew right away that Papa had something on his mind. As soon as he had greeted us, she put her hands on his shoulders and said, "What is it Dana? You have something to tell us. Out with it!"

Papa grinned sheepishly. "Can't fool you can I, sweetheart? Well, I think I may have a line on a really good job. I answered an ad in the Denver Post. It was for a bookkeeper and auditor."

He sounded as though there was something he was afraid to add.

"What else?" Mama asked.

We could feel Papa's hesitation. "It said, 'The applicant must be willing to leave Denver'."

There was another silence, and then Papa went on matter-of-factly.

"I made an appointment with a Mr. Kerr, the man who advertised, it's a job in Arizona."

Papa waited again for Mama to speak, but she was silent. Arizona! That *was* the land of the Indians, and they could have it for all Mama cared.

"They're opening a marble quarry there and it's a chance to get something permanent. Do you mind very much moving again, Sweetheart? The salary is good and they'll pay our train fare." He searched Mama's face anxiously.

I distinctly thought I heard Grandma groan, but Papa appeared not to hear and had a determined look. He was usually mild mannered, but when Papa made up his mind about a thing, there was a stern look about his jaw that was all out of proportion to his size.

"Let's go to the hotel now," Mama answered as she picked up her hat box. She was smiling, not happily.

Later that night, when Grandma and I were sleeping in a room adjoining Mama and Papa, I awoke several times. The door was ajar and the folks were talking in low voices.

I heard Mama say, "How can we be sure we'll like it?"

Papa answered in a half whisper. "Well, you won't have to go for a while. Anyway, the houses are not built at the quarry. We'd have to stay in a little railroad town near the mountains or live in a tent up there."

In the dark I thought I could feel Mama shiver. "I'll go on and look things over," Papa added. "You can follow later if I decide it's a good thing."

Still Mama didn't say anything. I wished she'd speak up and say whatever Papa wanted to do was all right. It would make Papa more comfortable, and me too.

Papa went on, "You and Ma can get settled in the house I've rented here and stay till I send for you from Bowie. That's the name of the town. It's spelled with a 'w' but Mr. Kerr says everyone there pronounces it 'Boo-ee.'"

You could tell by his tone that Papa really wanted to go. The idea of being a pioneer in a new venture fired his imagination. He had been raised on a farm in Kansas, and though all his family had moved to Lorain, his roots were not deep there as Mama's were.

They talked some more, and then I heard Mama say with a sigh, "Well, we'll always wonder what we missed if we don't go. Now that we are this far, it's not so hard to keep going." Then she added, "But do you know, I never would have been so willing to leave Lorain if I'd known we were going to land in Arizona?"

I could hear the smile in Mama's voice and I was relieved. It was all right now to go back to sleep.

Papa's train left at three in the afternoon of the very next day after we arrived. He said we didn't need to go to the depot, as we would want to get started unpacking right away. He'd say goodbye to us before he left the hotel.

In spite of his short stature, he seemed tall to me that day. A man of travel on his way to climb the steps of another train. He looked stylish too in his best suit and derby hat. There was no tobacco smell about Papa, just good clean shaving soap and fresh linen. With Quaker grandparents who spoke softly when they said, "Thee must do this, Dana", or "Thee must do that", or "Thou art a fine upstanding lad." you somehow didn't fall into worldly ways.

He kissed Mama and held her in his arms a long time. She hugged him as if she didn't want to let him go. I don't think she wanted to see him get on another train.

But as soon as he was out of sight, she and Grandma gathered our suitcases from the hotel and we climbed on a streetcar to go to our new home. Mama wasn't the kind to waste much time feeling sad if there was work to be done.

"You'll find the keys at the house next door to the east," Papa had said. "The people there own the house we are renting. Their name is Kilinsky, and they seem like nice people. You'd better get acquainted with them if Ma doesn't stay long and you and Alma are to be there alone."

It was a little scary to think of Mama and me all alone in a strange city at night with both Papa and Grandma far away.

Our house was an ugly red brick bungalow with unkempt yard. Mama took one look at the yard, and said with a wry smile, "Well, I know what to expect inside."

When she turned the key in the lock, the door swung open on squeaky hinges.

Grandma frowned and then said grimly, "We'll fix that first thing. A drop of oil will do it."

She and Mama stepped in carefully. They hardly seemed to breathe until the got the windows open.

"You stay in the doorway, Alma, till we get some fresh air in here," Mama said, unlatching a window.

She and Grandma pinned their long skirts up over their petticoats. The house did smell a little musty. Grandma peeked in a bedroom, "It's not as bad as I expected really. We can set up a bed here in the living room and wait till morning to clean it good."

Our boxes, barrels and furniture were sitting in the middle of the room. Papa had uncrated the furniture and taken the lids off the barrels of dishes. Mama was looking things over, "It's a good thing Dana had time to do that. We'll only have to put things in place as soon as the house is clean."

Quickly she and Grandma opened a trunk and got out sheets and pillows and a couple of blankets.

"When we get the bed ready to sleep in, let's walk to the grocery. Dana said it wasn't far," Mama said, tucking a pillow under her chin to slip on its embroidered pillowcase. Mama would have thought us poverty stricken if we'd used plain pillowcases. All of ours were embroidered, and many had lace edges added.

While she went next door to ask directions, Grandma finished making the bed.

The gas lights wouldn't be turned on till the next day, so at the store we bought a couple of candles and a box of matches. We ate our supper at a little delicatessen and restaurant so we wouldn't have to leave the house again that evening.

Grandma said, "We won't have any light but these candles, so as soon as it's dark, let's go to bed."

"It will give us a fresh start in the morning," Mama agreed.

Grandma put the candles and matches on a chair by the bed. Mama and I got in first. Grandma blew out the one candle we had lighted and crawled in beside us. It was a little crowded with three in a bed, but we were so tired we went to sleep in no time.

I have no idea what time it was that I woke up. It must have been about midnight, and I was itching from head to foot. Mama said impatiently, "Lie down, Alma, and go to sleep."

"I can't Mama, ants are biting me," I answered, as I scratched myself first in one place and then in another.

Mama's and Grandma's feet hit the floor at the same time as they both bounded out of bed.

In her excitement, Mama knocked the matches off the chair, and she and Grandma bumped into each other as they felt around for them in the dark. Mama found them first and hastily struck one and lighted a candle. She handed it to Grandma and lighted the other one. They threw back the bed covers and looked dismayed at the sheets.

"Do you see anything, Mama?" I asked.

She didn't say a word, just pointed horrified at some little specks.

Just then something else caught her eye.

"Ma, look!" she fairly shrieked, pointing at the wall. Grandma looked where Mama was pointing and nearly dropped the candle.

"Maud," she said in horror, "It's an ARMY of bedbugs!"

There were certain words that Mama and Grandma and their friends seemed to speak only in whispers. They were words like "consumption," "corset," and "cancer," and last, but certainly not least—that word "bedbugs." Whenever they mentioned any of those words they looked around first to see who might be listening, and then dropped their voices. When Mama whispered "bedbugs" she always lifted her skirts and gave them a brisk shake as though she was afraid some might be lurking in the folds. This time Grandma had almost shouted, and now Mama lifted her gown and shook the tail of it.

A solid black line of bedbugs stretched end to end from a crack in the ceiling angle, down the wall, and over to our bed. They must have had a long dry spell and thought they were on their way to a feast.

"Quick Maud, hold my candle too above this barrel of dishes!" Grandma said excitedly.

Mama held a candle in each hand while Grandma hastily dug into the barrel. After unwrapping a few pieces of the well-packed dishes, she pulled out four deep saucers. Mama and I watched her, wondering how she could use dishes to fight an army of bedbugs. She made trips to the kitchen and filled them with water at the sink, then came back to the bed and Mama lifted it while she put one under each leg.

"Now," she said, "We'll take turns holding the candles while we smash the bugs that are already in the bed."

Although Mama and Grandma were too ladylike to say the word "bedbugs" aloud, they certainly waded right into the job of smashing them.

When they were reasonably sure they had killed them all, Grandma said, "Now let's all take off our nighties and shake them good."

With one accord we pulled our nightgowns over our heads and

shook them. Mama gave mine an extra shake. We left one candle burning when we got back into bed, and none of us slept much.

When the sun finally came up and Mama could see me, she shrieked, "Look at that child!"

I was a sight. Even mosquitoes poisoned me, and with those bedbug bites, my eyes were nearly swollen shut.

It was a bad beginning, and Mama would have been homesick if she and Grandma hadn't been so busy. As it was, they started scouring and cleaning at daybreak. As soon as the store opened, they got kerosene for the woodwork and formaldehyde candles to burn. Mama said, "The fact that the store carries such things proves it's a 'buggy' neighborhood." Certainly not one bug could have survived that campaign. In fact, we didn't see another one while we lived there.

Grandma only stayed a few days. She had things to do back home and she could see there weren't any Indians to worry about in Denver, but after she left Mama and I felt really cut off from the world. Letters from Papa were the most important things in our lives, and we watched every day for the mailman.

Some of the things Papa said were encouraging because Mama would smile, but some of them seemed to take her breath away and she would look worried and act as though she had forgotten I was there.

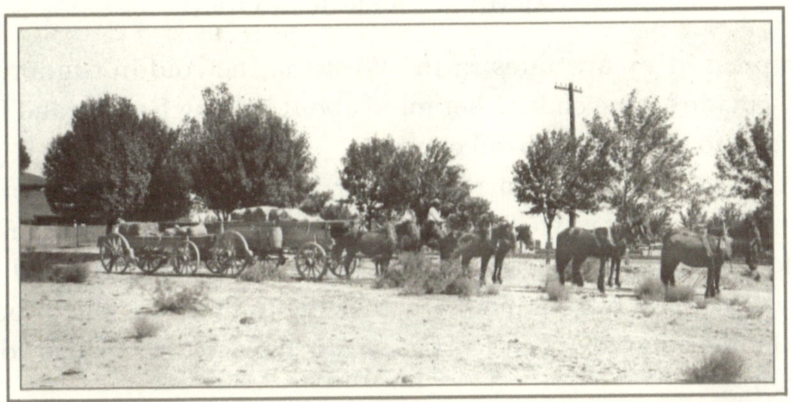

A big load, ready to leave Bowie for Marble Camp.

4.

No Flowers for Juan Flores

After one particular letter Mama sat looking off into space for a long time and the look on her face made me a little frightened. "What's Papa say in his letter?" I finally found courage to ask.

It was a few seconds before she answered, and then she looked at me in the queerest way and said, "Oh, he was telling me about a man named Juan. He had an accident."

Abruptly she changed the subject. "Let's have our supper now. We'll eat a little early and I'll read the new book Grandma sent you before bedtime."

Years later, when I read that letter and Papa filled in some more details, I could understand why Mama was so upset.

It was something that happened one day near Bowie.

Juan Flores had fallen off a lumber wagon and the left rear wagon wheel had run over his head. There was no need to send for a doctor to be sure he was dead.

Papa shouldn't have written Mama about it, but he was honest and so impressed by attitudes in the West that he couldn't ignore it. It nearly made Mama change her mind about leaving Denver and following Papa to such uncivilized country.

That morning the quarry teamster, Johnny Kaiser, Jim Short, a laborer, and a Mexican worker, Juan Flores, had started off to camp with a load of lumber. Before they left, Papa and three men stood on the dusty street and talked about whether the lumber was piled too high. Juan Flores had only been working a few days and was eager to prove himself.

"Thees load, he ees not too high," he said. "See, I seet up here. He sprang lightly to the top of the load and sat down.

Probably the glass or two of tequila he had at Dad Kellum's saloon made him extra brave.

Jim Short, a tough-looking little fellow wearing blue overalls and shirt and a bright red necktie, his concession to a trip to town, climbed up beside Juan. He untied his necktie, folded it neatly, and put it in his shirt pocket beside the package of Bull Durham tobacco. His visit to town was over and it was time to lay aside his dress-up clothes. He, too, had had a glass or two of tequila for his breakfast that morning.

"Naw, the load ain't too high," he said.

The teamster climbed up to the seat and Papa looked once more at the lumber piled on the wagon. These men know their business, he decided, and gave a nod to Johnny. Johnny passed the signal on to the horses. "Le's go boys." The horses strained slightly to test the effort necessary, then gave a huge lunge to start the wagon moving along the dusty street.

"I watched the wagon out of sight with some misgivings," Papa said, "then went back to work in my temporary office."

It was a sunny morning and the drone of voices came from the Chinese restaurant adjoining the office. Papa had been working on the ledger for about an hour when there was a knock at the door. Jim Short stood on the doorstep. By the look on his face Papa knew something was wrong.

"Mr. Milner, he fell off. Juan—he went to sleep. He fell right under the back wheel." Then probably thinking Papa would blame himself for allowing the load to be too high, he added, "It wasn't the load. It didn't shift a bit. I guess Juan was a little drunk."

Papa asked quickly, "Is he hurt bad?"

"Hurt bad! His head is—yeah. He's dead."

"Oh!" Papa said. "Well, do you know what we do next?"

"Yeah, we gotta get a coroner 'fore we kin do more."

Mr. Hendrix, the postmaster, was also the coroner. He and Mr. Bunch, the storekeeper, McDaniels, the barber, a railroad brakeman and Papa all climbed into a rig from the livery stable. For a while nobody said much as they jolted along. The road from Bowie wound around catclaw and mesquite bushes, and up and down gullies, following old cow trails to the scene of the accident. Jim Short, who had been there when it happened, seemed reluctant to talk about it.

Papa wrote, "I wondered why Mr. Hendrix took along a pick and a couple of shovels, but I was so busy thinking about how I could get in touch with Juan's family that I didn't give it a second thought."

Finding Juan's family, Papa reasoned, could be a tough task. There was a fast turnover among the laborers. Every week Mr. Kerr, the quarry manager, had Papa hire and fire a man or two. Some were lazy, some drank too much Tequila and Mescal whiskey, and some just didn't care to work at all.   In the Arizona territory there were no labor laws, so no records had to be kept of the men's families or past, and some of the men wanted as little known about themselves as possible.   Papa wondered where Juan's Mother was. Perhaps he had a wife some-where. Where would the family want him buried? It would be up to Papa to find out.

The livery rig jogged along the twisty road to just beyond a deep arroyo. The bright sunshine beat down on the desert, and Papa thought, no one in Ohio would dream this was April. It seemed more like June. Directly ahead lay the mountain range that contained the marble deposit, the object of all this activity with the teams and wagons, and labor and material.

Finally the men began to talk about the weather and politics, and they'd laugh occasionally. Papa thought it seemed callous not to be more quiet as they drew near the place a man had been killed. Life was certainly cheap in Arizona.

As they rose out of the arroyo, the road turned to the left, and made a half circle around a mesquite bush so that the wagon piled high with the lumber came suddenly into view. Johnny, the teamster, was standing by the horses' heads, as far away as he could get from the body of Juan lying by the rear wheel in the dust. The coroner drew the rig along side, and with a murmured "whoa" and a pull on the reins, brought the horses to a standstill. He was the first to climb out of the rig.

He went around to the side where Juan lay and stooped down beside the body. The other men climbed down and stood silently watching him. When he stood up, he said, "Yep, he's dead all right."

Without a word McDaniels and the brakeman grabbed the pick and one of the shovels the coroner had brought, and started to dig beside the wagon. Papa stood watching them in amazement.

"For the life of me," he wrote, "I couldn't believe there were going to bury that Mexican there on the desert. I've been kidded a lot about being a tenderfoot so I just kept still and waited. The digging was hard below a few inches of sand, and we all took turns. As soon as we had dug a narrow place about five and a half feet long and three feet deep, the coronor said, "That's good enough boys. The coyotes won't dig him up that deep."

The men climbed out of the grave and put down their pick and shovels. Johnny and the barber walked over to the body and leaned over to pick it up. Johnny brushed a big red ant off Juan's shirt, then took hold of his shoulders. Together they carried him over and laid him beside the grave. Then they crawled down in the hole and lifted Juan down.

"I felt paralyzed," Papa said, "I couldn't move till I saw the men pick up their shovels and I knew they were going to cover him up. Then I said, "Hold on boys!"

"I got a gunny sack from under the seat of the wagon and laid it over Juan's head, or what was left of it. I wanted to ask them to let me say a prayer, but I could see they were all in a hurry to get it over with, so I said a hasty one to myself."

"While the men were rounding up the grave," Papa went on, "I found a piece of wire in the wagon and made a cross out of two sticks. The men had climbed in the wagon and were waiting before I finished."

"I'll show you the grave when you come. It's really rugged here,

Maud. I wonder if you can stand it."

No wonder Mama was upset. She never used to cry when we lived in Lorain before Papa got sick.

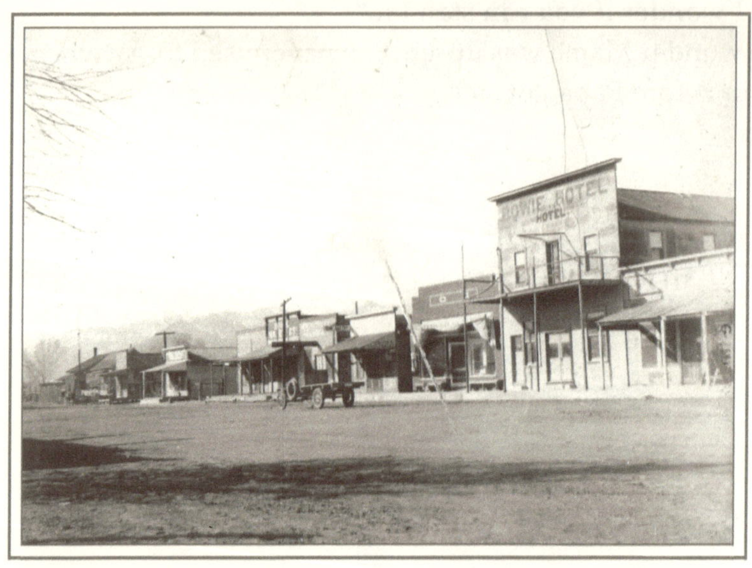

The west side of Bowie's wide Main Street, looking south toward "our" mountains.

5.

New Territory

Mama looked pensively out of the train window. The Arizona desert was sliding by to the clackety-clack of the wheels on the rails.

I turned to press my nose tight against the glass. Close to the tracks strange, ugly, grayish bushes were bent low in the hot noonday wind.

When you are five — and I now was — you are not so interested in scenery as in people and living things; and suddenly I said excitedly, "Look, Mama! There's a hoppy thing!"

The little wrinkles on Mama's young forehead smoothed. "I see it," she said. "That's a jack-rabbit I think. You know, Papa wrote they were coming right into the yard where he lived."

This was a big rabbit, and he suddenly stopped his hopping and froze, his long ears back, beside a cactus. I pressed my nose tighter against the double pane of the Pullman window, but he disappeared. Just the dusty bushes again. Nothing else moved.

Back home in Lorain, Mama used to let me make a playhouse by putting a blanket over chairs. Here the big mountains off to the south reminded me of the bumps the furniture made under the grey blanket. Close to the tops were stripes of dark trees and brush, like the border near the blanket's edges. There was one sharp peak that could be a bump made by the back of a tall kitchen chair.

The sky was deep blue here, and the sun was so bright it hurt my eyes. I shut them to keep them from watering, but when I opened them again, the glare hurt worse than ever.

There was a sudden rushing noise as the conductor opened the door and came in from the car ahead of ours. A blast of hot air came in with him, and Mama began to fan herself with her white lace handkerchief.

With a quick glance at Mama, he hesitated by our seat.

"Kinda hot for May, isn't it?" he said pleasantly, speaking more to the dark polished wood above the windows than to us.

Mama nodded silently.

He seemed to notice us for the first time. "How far East you folks from?"

"Ohio," Mama answered. "Lorain. We got a nice breeze off Lake Erie this time of year, but here—goodness!"

The conductor leaned down to look out the window.

"Nothing but greasewood along here for a ways." Then, as if to defend the country we were passing through, he added, "Sure is a pretty sight, the desert, when it rains."

"Does it ever?" Mama asked softly.

"Yep!" Comes down pouring when it lets loose. Seen all them gullies running full sometimes. Washes the tracks right out some places. We have to go mighty careful through here when it's raining now I'll tell you."

I watched him, fascinated, as he stroked his bushy grey mustache, parting it with his thumb and forefinger, then pulling down the ends to curve it toward the corners of his mouth. It was not at all like the way the man who sold coffee in Lorain rubbed his mustache, and it was almost as interesting as the way his trainman's cap, at least a half size too large, rested on his very red ears.

"It seems like wild country," said Mama.

"Oh no Ma'am," the conductor told us. "This is 1910! The Indian tracks old Cochise and Geronimo left through here have been cooling for twenty-five years. See over there, in those mountains off to the south? That's where they used to ambush each other. Some Denver bankers are building a regular little town up there now. Going to quarry marble. Mountains are full of it they say."

"Oh, is that where it is?" Mama asked with new interest. "That's where we're going to live!" She stopped fanning herself and leaned forward to press her nose against the glass.

"You don't say!" The conductor parted his mustache again. "Didn't know they were planning to have women and children up there. This little girl going all the way up in those mountains, is she?"

I nodded uncertainly.

"Well, now, how far do you suppose those mountains are?"

"I don't know," said Mama.

"Aw, take a guess."

Mama squinted intently at the desert. Dry gulches reached in twisted paths toward us from the mountain range. In the bottoms of the ones close by the tracks I could see cracks baked by the hot sun. They looked to me like the cracks in the attic ceiling of Grandma's house. The greasewood was beginning to disappear, but bushes and an occasional bunch of wildflowers struggled through the soil and bent low in the hot breeze.

"Well, it's a mile," said Mama. "Maybe, a little more."

"Hah!" said the conductor, very pleased with the answer. "Well, I guess! That's what a couple of fellas on the train thought one day last year. We come to Bowie and they found out we was going to stay twenty minutes so they decided to hike over to 'em for the exercise." He chuckled as he thought about it. "The train had to go off without them. Station agent told me they come into the station puffing just after we pulled out. Hadn't got anywhere near the mountains. It's nine miles of course."

"Mercy!" Mama said. "What makes it seem so close?"

"Dry air," said the conductor. He lifted his too large hat to scratch his head, then settled it squarely on his ears.

"There is one thing you might have to be a little careful out here," he said, pointing a forefinger at Mama warningly, "the country's full of snakes and centipedes."

Mama was very white, I thought.

"Oh, of course," the conductor went on hastily, "if you don't bother them, they won't bother you, I always say. Just keep out of their way if you can."

He pulled a large watch from his vest pocket, looked at it, and squinted at the desert once more.

"Well, you folks better get ready to get off," he said, and turned to the rest of the car. "Bowie! Next stop!"

Bowie! Bowie in the Arizona Territory — that was where Papa was. I wished I could remember what he looked like. It had been eight months since he had said goodbye to us, and at five your memory of a face hardly stretches back that far.

Mama began hastily to gather our things.

When the suitcases were out from under the seat and our coats were on the seat beside us, she straightened my sash and tied my blue polk bonnet as we looked out at the unpainted shacks that lined the railroad. We were pulling into Bowie.

Mama grasped my hand and hurried me down to the end of the car to stand by our suitcases. The train slowed down and we began hunting eagerly for Papa in the motley group of men at the depot. There was not a single man with a white shirt, and Papa always wore white shirts. One tan, husky man smiled in our direction, but Mama gave him only a passing glance. Like several of the others, he wore a brown khaki-colored shirt and pants, heavy work shoes and puttees. There were a half-dozen Mexican men in blue shirts and baggy overalls.

Could it be that Papa had not been able to come? Mama was squeezing my hand so tight it hurt. The train came to a grinding standstill, and the porter opened the door. As we climbed down the steps, the man who had smiled at us through the window strode forward and scooped me up in his arms. Mama looked at him in astonishment.

"Why, Dana Milner, you are as brown as an Indian."

She glanced around timidly to see if there were any Indians within earshot. That would have been a good safe remark in Lorain, Ohio, but here --. Papa laughed and held me tight for a minute.

Then he set me down, and it was Mama's turn.

For a few seconds she seemed to entirely forget her misgivings, she was so happy to be in Papa's arms again. I wanted her to let go so I could have a second turn, but she clung to Papa like she'd never let him go.

Finally he said, as he picked up our suitcases, "Come this way. We'll go to the house as soon as I show you the depot-hotel. It's the finest building there is in town and the best eating-house between Tucson and El Paso." His tone was as proud as if he owned a half interest in the depot and restaurant.

He was still looking at Mama and smiling. "It's not far to walk and there's no street car." He chuckled at that, like he'd made a joke.

Except for the hot, oily, railroad smell by the tracks, the air was fresh and pure.

Papa walked with such a quick, firm step, Mama and I could hardly keep up with him. He carried our heavy suitcases like they were empty.

Papa was right. The depot-hotel was a remarkable building for a town the size of Bowie. It was two stories high and, from the cafe and restaurant on one end to the freight and storage rooms at the other, it must have been over half a block long. Papa led us to the door at the end that housed the hotel and had us peek in. The lobby had huge black leather upholstered furniture, and we could see neat waitresses in black uniforms and starched white aprons standing at the marble-topped counter in the cafe.

It didn't look as fine to me as the Brown Palace Hotel we had seen in Denver, but it was better than we could expect in a town the size of Bowie.

"We'll stay here overnight when we come down from Marble Camp," Papa said. "Let's get to the house now. It's down the street a way."

We walked strung out Indian fashion down the middle of the very wide, sandy road.

At right angles to the railroad tracks, directly south toward the mountain range we had been watching, stretched a few scattered small high-front buildings just like those of the towns Mama and I had been passing through. None of them were painted except in front. Each building had a sign above the front door; "Post Office", "Barber Shop", "Livery Stable."

Papa turned down the street back of the railroad houses that lined the tracks.

"That's the office," He said, "right by the Chinese restaurant." The building he indicated was a tumble-down shack with broken wooden steps. It was set a couple of feet off the ground on piling and had never seen a coat of paint. There were two front doors, one no doubt to the restaurant and one to the marble quarry office. Nothing about it reminded us of the bank where Papa had worked in Lorain.

"It's not so bad inside," Papa said hastily. "We won't stop now. We'll get rid of these suitcases first thing." That was the signal to put down the luggage again to give Mama another hug.

"What will the people think?" Mama asked, peering over Papa's shoulder in the direction of the dilapidated restaurant and office building.

Papa chuckled. "They'll say there's a man who is glad to see his family, and they'll be full of sour grapes." But he let Mama go and picked up the suitcases again.

We were drawing near a whitewashed adobe house with a picket fence around it. There were several big shade trees in the yard, bare except for a few sprigs of grass. Between two of the trees was a stretched red and white hammock. It all looked cool and inviting.

"This place is called the Skinner house. I've rented it till the camp is completed. We may be here a month or two!" Papa said as he dropped his burden to unlatch the gate. "Shall I carry you over the threshold?"

Mama laughed, "Isn't it a little late for that?"

"Maybe so," Papa agreed. "Come, have a drink of Bowie's famous water."

He led us over to a red clay jar that hung from a tree by wires. "This is an olla," he said. He pronounced it "oya." There was a tin cup in the fork of the tree, and he filled it and handed it to me. It was cool and had a dandelion taste.

When he handed it to Mama, she started to drink, then drew back and pointed to little brown specks floating in the cup.

Papa laughed. "Oh, they're just little particles of wood from the inside of the redwood water tanks down by the depot," he reassured her. "They won't hurt you."

Mama looked doubtful, but she resolutely put the tin cup to her lips and swallowed.

All the while she was drinking, she was watching Papa over the edge of the tin cup. What she saw must have pleased her, for when she stopped drinking and handed it back to him, she had the look of contentment that she always used to have before we left Ohio.

After our cool drink, we went inside to look over the house.

The owner must have really liked blue because all the walls in the house were painted that color. The house was meagerly furnished, but Mama said, "It has everything we need to keep house till we can go to Marble Camp." It sounded as if she was anxious to get on with the adventure, and for a city-bred young woman to be dropped suddenly in the middle of one of the ruggedest parts of the West really was an adventure. I had a feeling I was peeping around Mama's long skirts at this new strange world, scared but still hopeful about what I might see.

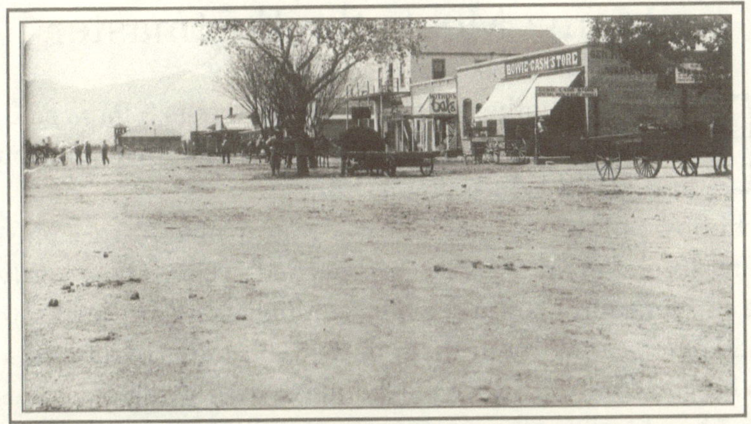

**The east side of Main Street looking north
toward the railroad**

6.

Mama Meets the Postmaster

"Before you bother to unpack your things," Papa said, "let's go see the office. Fong, the Chinaman, owns our building and I'll introduce you to him."

A chubby fellow wearing a little round black cap came to the restaurant door to greet us as we approached. He walked softly in his Chinese slippers and I could see he wasn't wearing any socks, the first man I had ever seen without them in the daytime. He flashed a broad smile as he said "Ha! Do!" then waxed into a long string of Chinese ending with "Amelika."

Papa explained after we left that Fong had only been in America a year and he always made a speech like that when he met anyone new.

I was wishing Fong would take off his little hat so I could see if he had a long braid under it. In my storybooks Chinamen always wore queues.

We left him and went to the office side of the building.

Papa was not proud of the building but he wanted us to see the fine equipment the company had bought.

"This filing cabinet is oak, he said, "nothing finer anywhere, and this is a new typewriter." He walked across the floor to where two desks sat side by side. The floor sagged so badly that a block of wood had been slipped under two legs of one. "This one is mine — solid oak."

He could see Mama was comparing it to all with the bank and its furnishings in Lorain and he was anxious to take her attention from the building itself, which was close to falling down. The floor sloped so that it made me seasick to walk across it. Sniffing the air, I wondered how Papa could stand the sour odor coming out of the restaurant next door. It seemed to float right through the thin wall between the two rooms.

"What smells like that?" I whispered.

Papa sniffed. "Oh, I don't even notice it anymore. I think it has something to do with the Chinese vegetables Fong uses in the soup. Part of it is the smell of grease on oilcloth on the tables. He uses cold water to wash the restaurant dishes, pots and pans and they all have a coating of grease. You ought to see them, Maud."

Mama frowned as though she wouldn't care to.

"The smell is unpleasant if I stop to think about it," Papa went on, sniffing again, "but I'm so used to it I hardly notice."

"Does anybody eat at the restaurant?" Mama asked in a low voice.

"Oh, yes! On account of the pies. Fong's pies are known far and wide, and the customers put up with the grease and bum soup for the sake of them. Anyway, it's a busy restaurant. Now look at this set of books." He opened the ledger on his desk, "Mr. Kerr said I could set them up to suit myself. It's the first time I ever had a chance to try some of the things I've figured out. They work fine, just like I thought."

There was pride in Papa's voice and Mama nodded. She was watching his face, and she must have liked what she saw there.

Papa had bought a supply of groceries and when we got home Mama cooked our supper, humming a little tune as she worked. In Lorain she had always hummed when she was happy and things were going right. It made the bacon and eggs taste extra special tonight.

The next afternoon we took another walk and met Mr. Hendrix at the post office. This time before we started out, Papa said, "Now remember, you can't believe everything Mr. Hendrix says. He knows you're a tenderfoot and he'll try to horrify you."

Mama said she'd remember and not let him see she was being impressed.

All of the business buildings in town had the same high board fronts that we see now in Western moving pictures. As we walked, Mama said, "I guess they put those fronts on to distinguish the business places from the homes, but I don't think they help the looks of them much. They just look like somebody forgot to cut the boards off at the roof.

On each side of the main street there was a boardwalk about two hundred feet long. Sand drifted over it so you could only see part of it, but the walk in front of the post office was swept extra clean.

"Mr. Hendrix sweeps it here," Papa said. "He likes to be outside where he can nail somebody to talk to."

When we arrived at the post office, I was ahead and Papa opened the door for me. I started to go in, then stepped back suddenly.

Papa chuckled and said, "Oh, they won't hurt you, they're all dead and then stuffed."

Along one wall of the post office lobby were the goggle-eyed heads of a buffalo and two big cinnamon bears. Above a partition of mail boxes sat a lifelike squirrel nibbling a walnut. His glassy little eyes looked at us quizzically. I stepped in gingerly and Mama and Papa followed.

A man standing at the mail window was sorting a handful of letters. He was a large man with little eyeglasses that pinched on his nose like the ones Dr. Cox wore in Lorain. When he saw us come in, he laid the letters down and came through a door beside the mail boxes to greet us. His smile made me think of pictures I'd seen of Teddy Roosevelt. They both had big white teeth, as well as those wild animals.

"How do ya do, Mrs. Milner?" he said in a booming voice. That man of yours sure was anxious to have his family get here. Reminds me of a feller come here about six years ago. Come here for his health, same as your husband. He was awful anxious to have his wife and kids come too. He got him a job here as a brakeman on the railroad, and after he got enough money together, he sent for his family."

Mr. Hendrix hesitated as though this was the end of the story, then took off his glasses and added as if it were a minor detain, "Too bad about him! He was sleepin' in a hammock of Skinner's yard (Papa had told us we were staying in the Skinner house), and a tarantula crawled in with him and bit him on the neck!"

Mother said, "Mercy!" then bit her lip and glanced at Papa. He appeared not to notice. We had no idea what a tarantula was, but it sounded ominous.

"Yep," Mr. Hendrix went on while replacing his glasses, "sure did! Bit him right on his joogular vein. He must'a died in his sleep because they found him dead in his hammock next morning. His wife and kids got here that day, and they sure didn't know they wuz coming to a funeral. You want to watch out for them tarantulas, Mrs. Milner. They ain't nothing to fool with." He looked at Mama sternly over his nose glasses.

Mama murmured something about being careful.

Papa said if there was no mail he guessed we'd be going. Mr. Hendrix appeared not to hear; at least he didn't look in the quarry's mailbox, just kept looking at Mama and me.

"I hear snakes and centipedes is plentiful up there where they're building that camp. Fellow in yesterday, works on the road throwing rocks out of the way, says there's a centipede or scorpion under mighty near every rock he turns over. Probably the same on up a piece where they're building the houses and things. All virgin country. Nobody ever bothered them mountains but the Indians and that was quite a spell back."

Papa said firmly it was time to go, and could he have the afternoon mail, please? Mr. Hendrix removed his glasses and went right on. He had Mother's ear and was enjoying himself. He knew she was shocked.

"Speaking of snakes..." He hadn't really been speaking of snakes, but no one interrupted him to say so, "If you or the little girl ever should git snake bit, I'll tell you what to do." Mama couldn't suppress a shudder. She took hold of my hand and pulled me close to her. "Just cut a cross where the bite is. Use your pen knife or —" He looked thoughtfully at mother. "Guess you wouldn't have no pen knife handy. Well, if it was close to home, you could use your butcher knife."

Mama looked helplessly at Papa. Papa was looking out of the window. "Then you get a hen, a setting hen is the best, they say, you cut off its head and if you're bit on the hand or foot, plunge that place that's bit into the hen."

Here Mr. Hendrix replaced his glasses and demonstrated with a jab of his right arm. "I don't know why ya do it, but I've seen fellows do it and I never seen one die yet from a snake bite if they done it in time."

Mama closed her eyes and looked a little sick.

"Of course, if yore bit higher up on the leg — "

"Mr. Hendrix, we've got to go," Papa broke emphatically, "we'll come back again some other time. May I have the mail now?"

Mr. Hendrix looked a little disappointed but he went to the Marble Company's box and fished out a half dozen letters which he handed to Papa. "Take care of that wife of yours, young feller," he said in a stage whisper. "She looks a little puny for this country."

Papa opened the screen door of the post office for us and we walked down the boardwalk to our own sandy street. We were all quiet till we reached our own gate, and then Papa spoke, "Don't worry about what Mr. Hendrix said. We —"

That was as far as he got for all of a sudden Mama began to laugh and cry at the same time.

"There, there," Papa said, holding her tight, "I was afraid of that. You're not the first woman he's given a case of the hysterics. I tried to warn you. Consarn him!" That was as close as Papa ever came to swearing.

I always hated the post office after that. It seemed like that place was full of snakes and centipedes as well as all those wild animals hanging on the walls. Mr. Hendrix was all that Papa had said about him — and more.

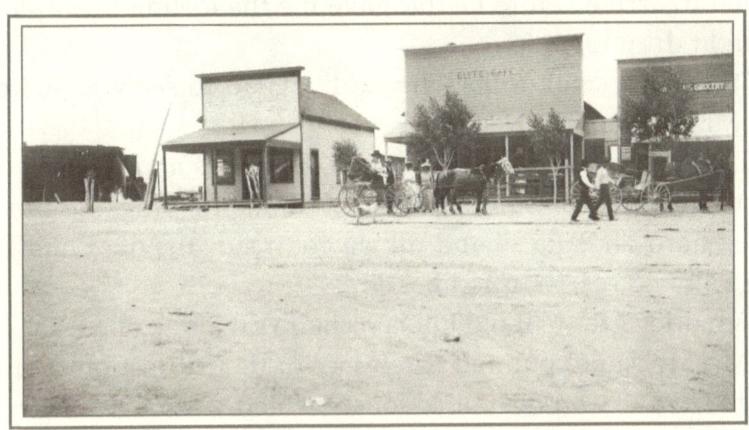

Street scene in Bowie

7.

The Barber's Pets

The next day we met Mr. McDaniel, the barber, and found that he was an awful talker too, but Mr. Hendrix and he rarely spoke to each other, Papa said.

"They don't try because neither of them likes to listen, so they just don't start anything."

The barber shop was open any time you could catch "Old Mac." It was around the corner from the Post Office, on a side street, a frame building with the usual square front and tin roof. The walls were clapboards nailed on the outside to two-by-fours. As we walked by in the late afternoon, Mr. McDaniel was standing in his doorway. He was a very tall man and he leaned forward as he walked out to greet us. He had a shock of bushy black hair and a handlebar moustache. Somehow his head reminded me of the lion in my animal book, and the way it seemed to arrive before he did gave me the feeling that at any minute he might drop to all fours.

"Step in a spell, folks," he said. "Glad to see your wife got here safe, Mr. Milner."

There weren't any customers in the chairs and it was a chance for him to get hold of some listeners. Remembering the post office, I tugged hard on Papa's hand till we got inside the door and I could see there were no scary stuffed heads.

A motley group of old kitchen chairs sat along one side of the room and Mr. McDaniel pointed carelessly in their direction to indicate we should be seated. He climbed loose-jointedly into the barber chair and turned it to face us.

The floor was worn, unpainted wood. The ceiling was the bottom side of the galvanized tin roof. Each exposed two-by-four of the walls had a big nail driven in it to make a hat rack for the customers. On one of the nails hung an old sweat-stained cowboy hat. There were three or four untidy white enamel spittoons scattered around the room, around which was some evidence that not all Mac's customers were good shots. The odor of oily hair sweepings, hair tonic, and steaming bath water hung in the air, and on top of a pot-bellied stove in one corner a tea kettle was steaming. The fire was kept going to heat water for barbering, no doubt; it was a warm day and there certainly was no other need of a fire.

In the back of the room was a door in a partition about the height of a man. A splashing sound came from the other side of the partition, and Mr. McDaniel explained.

"A customer. I sell baths here; twenty-five cents apiece and cheap at half the price."

He wagged his enormous shock of hair and stroked his mustache.

"It's a lotta work. I hafta heat water in the tub in the back yard; bring it in bucketsfull. I got it fixed so's the water runs out a hose. Waters the trees I got planted in the back yard."

He paused to let the full import of his strategy soak in. Then, not getting any response, he went on.

"I get sort of mad the way some fellers leaves the tub dirty. It makes it hard for the next feller. Has to clean the tub 'fore he can get in. 'Course some of them don't bother. They just make a new ring and go on. Me, I like a clean tub when I take a bath."

Mama nodded. Every once in a while she would steal a glance at Papa. His face gave no indication that he was amused. It would never do to let "Old Mac" know they might be laughing at him.

Mr. McDaniel seemed to know all about everything. At least he would talk on any subject that happened to come up. He always started with, "Now, I'll tell you that I think!" He sounded so sure that I thought he must be a very smart man.

On a rickety table in one corner were three or four old magazines. I went to look at them. One was about cows, probably some *Stockmen's Report*, one was a *Geographic* we'd seen a long time ago, and one was an old *Ladies Home Journal*. I'd seen it too so it didn't look like there was anything very interesting at the barber shop for me. I wished we'd go home soon.

I was looking at the hole in the barber chair where the stuffing was coming out between "Old Mac's" legs, when I heard Mr. McDaniel say in a whiny voice, "Now you git back in there! I thought that catch was fastened."

He lumbered over to a shallow box on the floor by the stove. I hadn't noticed it before. The lid, a flimsy frame covered with screen, was moving and suddenly a little head that looked like it might belong to a mean snake came sliding out. I clutched Mama's knees.

Mr. McDaniel said, "I'll just let 'em out a little while. They need exercise the same as people."

Lifting the lid, he tipped the box and out slithered two horrid orange and back striped gila monsters about 18 inches long. Mama couldn't suppress a little gasp, and she squeezed my arms so tight they hurt. The gila monsters looked like giant lizards. They waddled around the room for a while and we all kept our eyes glued on them.

I slid off my chair and climbed on Mama's lap. She had her feet up on a rung of her chair, poised for flight.

"Ain't they cute?" asked Mr. McDaniel, as he sat down to enjoy them.

After a bit, he walked over to the box again and picked up each of them by the neck and laid it gently back in the box.

"That's enough now, just git back in there little feller. Want to see them eat their supper?" he asked us.

Papa nodded, but not enthusiastically. Mama was not able to speak. We sat as if we were frozen in the customers' chairs. Mr. Mc-Daniel went to a little room in the back and brought out two eggs. He opened the cage and broke the raw eggs into two flat salmon cans.

"Eggs is 'bout all they'll eat in captivity," he said.

After Mr. Mac fastened the catch on the lid, we all came closer and looked at them in the box.

They were standing with their heads in the cans and seemed to be eating very slowly. Mr. McDaniel kept up a running patter to us and the gila monsters.

"Gotta eat plenty, little fellers. Mrs. Milner, these reptiles are right friendly to humans if they feel like you love 'em."

Mama looked at Mr. McDaniel, then at the gila monsters, and then at Papa, and you could see she never would.

It was fun to watch Mr. Mac's pets, now that they were back in the box, but Mama said, "Dana, don't you think we'd better go?" and Papa said yes, it was time to start fixing supper.

When we got outside, Mama said, "I'd just as soon have a snake in my house, Dana. Those gila monsters look dangerous to me."

Papa said, "They can be dangerous I guess, but Mr. Mac has strange friends. You ought to see the mean old eagle he has in a cage out in the yard behind his shop. Mr. Mac calls it 'such a sweet bird,' and every-body knows eagles are as mean as can be."

Mama said, "Well, I'll tell you this, Dana Milner, if I've got to love gila monsters to live in this Godforsaken country, I don't think I'll stay long." Papa laughed and said he didn't think he could learn to love them either, and how would Mama and I like to go for a ride out in the country soon? He knew somebody he wanted us to meet.

I guess Papa thought it was about time he introduced Mama to some people who weren't characters.

8.

The Riggs Ranch

In fact, the Riggs family were the first people we met who seemed like "back home" folks. The very next Sunday, Papa took us to see their ranch. Early in the morning, right after breakfast, Mama and I heard a noise out at the front gate and when we went to look, there was Papa sitting in a dilapidated buggy holding the reins of a pair of lazy looking horses.

He grinned and said, "It's not much, but it's the best they have at the Bowie Livery Stable. How quick can you girls get ready to go to Riggs ranch? Mrs. Riggs has invited us for dinner."

We scurried around to do the breakfast dishes. If Mama had left the work undone she wouldn't have enjoyed a minute of the outing. When we were ready, Papa lifted me up to the buggy seat.

Mama hesitated about getting in, and Papa looked a little stern and said, "You might as well get used to it Maud. It's the only way there is to get to camp." He took hold of her arm to help her. We had always traveled by streetcar before, and this was my first buggy ride. You'd never guess, seeing other people ride, how thrilling it was to sit behind two switching horses' tails. One horse was black and one was brown, which reminded me of the time Grandma made a mistake and put on one black shoe and one brown one. It didn't occur to me that the horses would also look better if they were the same color. I was fascinated by the way the black one kept flicking the flies away from his sides with his motley plume and the way the brown one kept his left ear forward and his right one turned back like he wanted to be sure to hear from all directions. The buggy needed a coat of paint and the seat sagged tiredly on one side. Daylight came through several small holes in the top, but to me it was better than Cinderella's Pumpkin Coach.

We jogged out of town, with Papa holding the reins like an expert. For a few minutes I felt a little anxious knowing Mama didn't think horses were safe, but Papa seemed confident and as we trotted along in the warm sunshine, I began to feel brave. I decided this was the ideal way to travel, much better than streetcars or even trains. It was a wonder we hadn't come from Denver this way. It could certainly have been a lot more fun.

The early June sun began to beat down on the roof of the buggy. The road wound and twisted through the valley like an injured snake. Whoever first laid it out must have thought it was easier to go around the big mesquite and catclaw clumps than to dig them out. Or maybe they just followed cow trails. Papa said the cows made paths through the valley to the water holes. He pointed out one mother cow with two calves.

"See that," he said. "The cow is taking care of another's calf while she goes to water. When the mother gets back this cow will take her turn. They don't go every day. It depends on how far away the water tank is and how often it rains."

Imagine having to go a long way just to get a drink of water! Water had been so plentiful in Lorain.

Every once in a while we'd ride through a steep gulch. There was deep sand at the bottom of each one, but not a drop of water. I began to feel a little thirsty.

After a while Mama seemed so engrossed in the things Papa was pointing out that she forgot about the horses.

"Straight ahead on that little green knoll is the Riggs ranch," he said, pointing with the buggy whip. "See the house nestled in a clump of trees?"

If its gables had been turrets, it would have been a real castle. As it was, I had a feeling there ought to be a moat, like my story books told about, at the foot of the hill. The house was painted white and set against a background of old green shade trees. A tall chimney rose out of the left center of the house. A green carpet of grass covered the hillside from the house to the road below.

"How in the world do they cut all that green lawn?" Mama asked.

Papa chuckled. "Whenever the grass gets high they just turn in the horse. It's a good arrangement. Cutting the lawn was never one of my favorite jobs." Mama smiled, then looked sober for a minute. Maybe she was thinking about our fresh new lawn in Lorain and wondering how it looked on this bright June morning.

The road curved around a mesquite and Papa lifted the whip to point off to the right of the ranch.

"Old Fort Bowie is up that canyon. That was the fort that guarded the stage coach route through the Apache Pass. Ever so often the chiefs, Cochise and Geronimo, would go on the warpaths and attack settlers or the stage coach."

Mama was smiling again, "If we had been here then, I guess Ma would have had a right two worry about us getting scalped." Papa nodded and went on, "It's from springs up that canyon that water is piped down to the Riggs Ranch." I was glad to hear that. At least I could get a drink when we got there. "The spring is near the fort," Papa went on, "there's watercress growing on the banks of it. Some day we'll go there on a picnic and we'll pick our own salad right on the spot."

Mama and Papa had picked watercress and dug sassafras roots in the woods in Ohio while they were courting.

Just then the horses shied a little away, and Papa's tone changed as he said, "That's where we buried Juan."

The cross looked very lonely standing at one end of the mound of dirt. It had leaned to one side so Papa stopped the horses and climbed out of the buggy to straighten it up. When he got back in, we drove along in silence for a while. I felt Papa's arm steal around Mama and me as though he meant to protect us from things, lots of things we didn't even know about yet.

As we drew near, we could see the house was a rambling two-story affair with a long wide porch across the front and a lean-to at one side. I shut my eyes for a second to hold on to the castle we had seen from the distance. A barbed wire fence ran around the bottom of the knoll. There was no moat.

As Papa drove the horses up to the gate and jumped down to tie them, a half-grown shepherd dog came down the path at a lumbering walk. He was barking loudly but with an announcing bark, not a threatening one. When we got to the bottom of the hill he stopped barking and came up to the buggy to nuzzle Papa's hand, wagging from his head to his graceful tail. Papa patted him with one hand and with the other he slipped a rope through a ring in the harness of one of the horses. He was tying it to the fence post as a door opened up at the "castle" and Mrs. Riggs stepped out and came down the path to meet us. She was a tall blonde woman with a very pretty face and blue eyes that, young as they were, had little wrinkles at the corners. Her nose turned up saucily and she was smiling to welcome us. She was carrying in her arms a little wisp of a girl in a full starched blue calico dress, and the material in both of their dresses was the same. Both wore white organdy pinafore aprons, the little girl's a tiny copy of her mother's.

Mama was looking at Mrs. Riggs and I was sizing up the little girl as Papa watched us both. Mrs. Riggs reached us, she set the little girl down and put out a graceful hand to Mama.

"You're Maud and I'm Anna Mae, spelled with an "e". It's more stylish that way don't you think? Let's not bother with that "Mrs." business. I know we're going to be good friends."

Mama took her hand and nodded. "I'd like that, and I do think an "e" is more stylish. I always wished my mother had added one to my name.

Of all the things Mrs Riggs could have mentioned at greeting Mother, "style" was probably the wisest. Mama was the stylish one in her family. Everyone said she could even tie a bow so it looked like an artist had done it. She could take an old dress and pull it in here and let it out there, and by adding a bit of lace or a new linen collar, make it look brand-new. All the family used to ask her advice about remodeling their clothes, so Mrs. Riggs had touched a vital subject that was to be especially important with us isolated in a mountain camp with no one to talk to or admire Mama's efforts.

I was looking at Mrs. Riggs, thinking how pretty she was when she took a few steps toward me and laid her cool hand on my head.

"You are Alma," she smiled at me, "that means 'soul' in Spanish, you know."

I hadn't known, and I had no idea what "soul" meant in English, let alone Spanish, but it must be a nice word as she pronounced it like a benediction. The way she looked at me made me feel much older than five. Just then a little mountain breeze ruffled her fluffy blond hair and she looked so pretty I decided right then that here was the lady I wanted to be like when I grew up.

"Come on up to the house," Mrs. Riggs said as Papa fastened the gate behind us. "Tom will be home soon. He went to see about some trouble on the telephone lines up the canyon. Come along, Shep."

As we walked up the worn pathway to the house, I was wondering which of the two front doors was the right one to enter. When we reached the porch, Mrs. Riggs opened the one on the left and we entered a monstrous kitchen that smelled very much like Grandma's in Lorain. There was a huge iron frying pan of chicken sizzling on the range, and on the drainboard a tempting, freshly-iced five-layer cake. The ride in the fresh air had made me so hungry I could hardly wait till time to eat. I forgot for the moment about being thirsty.

"I hope you like chicken," Mrs. Riggs said as she walked quickly to the stove and lifted the lid of the frying pan. We are out of beef and I got up early and killed some chickens. We'll be ready to eat as soon as Tom gets back. Take off your hat in the bedroom, Maud."

As she spoke, she was moving things around on the stove like she was playing a game of checkers, this pan forward, that one moved up to take its place. Every move was sure, and she didn't take a second to consider what she should do next.

As Mama and I stood wondering which direction to go, Mrs. Riggs glanced up from her kettles and said, "Oh, Pauline, you can show them where the bedroom is so Aunt Maud can take off her hat." She had called Mama "Aunt Maud." It was beginning to seem more like "back home" all the time. Mama had been "Aunt Maud" to so many nieces and nephews in Lorain, and it was one of the things we had missed without knowing it.

Like a flash Pauline darted out of the room with Mama and me following at a dog trot to keep up with her. She raced through the living room and down the hall to a giant-sized bedroom. There was an enormous blue bow on top of her head and its loops bobbed along like huge rabbit's ears.

It was surprising that she had let her mother carry her down the path to greet us, as she had refused my hand when we started up the path to the house. It was going to be a challenge to play with a child two years younger than I, but one who had such definite ideas.

Mama went back to the kitchen and Pauline led me from room to room showing me her treasures. She talked plainly and her daintiness gave me a feeling of gawkiness that I was never to quite overcome.

She was as quick as a wink and would pull out her toys and shoe boxes of trinkets and spill them on the floor so I could see them better. Then as quickly she would lose interest and, while I hastily tried to put the things away like Mama had taught me, she would hurry off to another box or cupboard saying, "Come on, there's more."

Most of the things were broken or torn, here a doll without a wig, there one without an arm, a book with the top cover missing, an empty bottle of paste, and an old thread spool that the dog had evidently chewed. The last was the only thing that she seemed to think called for an explanation.

"Shep," she said, cocking her head on one side, "he chewed that. Too bad!" She picked it up and slipped it in the pocket of her apron.

I somehow couldn't echo her concern about a discarded spool being chewed, but I soberly nodded agreement. I was picking up that "batch of junk," and she was leading the way pell mell to a woodshed attached to the house. I hurried to catch up with her.

"None of my things in here, just Mama's wood and things to eat."

There were things to eat all right, enough food to stock a small grocery. There were cases of canned goods and sacks of potatoes, onions, flour, and beans, as well as the wood stacked in stove lengths along the walls. The shed opened off the kitchen and was handy to the big kitchen range that swallowed up the wood stored in there. We only stayed a minute as Pauline was off again to show me the two upstairs bedrooms.

As we flew through the living room, I noticed it had the other front door. In all the times we visited at the ranch though, I never saw anyone enter the living room door. The kitchen was the center of activity at the Riggs Ranch and no wonder! From the big range by the woodshed door came the most heavenly smells and flavors, whether it was homemade bread, angel food cake, piccalilli or apple butter being made from apples from the trees in the back yard, no one could resist the kitchen. Even if you didn't hope to taste whatever was cooking you didn't want to get very far away from it.

The upstairs rooms were finished, but there was no furniture unless egg crate cupboards containing more of Pauline's stuff could be called furniture. Suddenly, as she fingered a miniature doll buggy with a missing wheel, Pauline stopped still and listened. With a bound she was at one of the dormer windows.

"My daddy!" she exclaimed and rushed down the stairs without waiting for me.

I hadn't heard a thing, but I watched her from the window as she ran down the path toward the corral. Mr. Riggs was unsaddling his horse, and I saw her throw herself in his arms as soon as he had slipped the bridle over the horse's ears.

Now I remembered that I was thirsty so I went down to the kitchen for a drink of water. With a minimum of motion, Mrs. Riggs was moving from the stove to the woodshed, to the sink, and back to the stove again.

Tom and Anna Mae were a happy example of a May and December marriage. He was bald-headed and stocky and not as tall as his wife and was at least twenty years older than she, but the minute you saw the way they looked at each other, you knew the difference in their ages didn't matter in the least. There was an easy air of contentment about him. He greeted us like he was really glad we had come.

"So you are young Dana's wife?" he said to Mama and he shook her hands. "No wonder you were in such a hurry to get her out here, Dana! I'd a been the same way."

Mama blushed and gave a pleased little smile. People in the West really said what they thought.

Mr. Riggs looked down at me, "And this is the youngun. Perty little girl! Nice for you have a new friend, huh, Pauline?"

Now Pauline reached out a hand to take mine. It was very pleasant to have a new friend who wanted to hold your hand.

"Tom get washed up," Anna Mae said briskly, "Dinner'll be ready in a minute."

"There she goes," Tom said with a look of pride that belied his words. "Always hurrying me! That's what I get for marrying such a young wife. Used to dangle her on my knee when she was a baby. Shoulda' known then she'd be a whirlwind when she grew up. Never would sit still." Even I knew he was boasting, not complaining, as he went to clean up for dinner.

The bathroom, a leanto at the back of the house, was large enough to be a small bedroom. It had evidently been added as an afterthought, probably Mrs. Riggs' idea.

There was no dining room, but the big square table in the kitchen was set with a snowy linen cloth.

"Most of the time we use oilcloth, but today we'll use linen," Mrs. Riggs said as she and Mama set the table.

At the kitchen table, Mr. Riggs picked up the heaping plate of chicken and passed it to Mama. It was the only time I ever remember anyone apologizing for serving chicken.

"Too bad not to have some good beef for you folks. We'll be killing a calf tomorrow," he said. "You're just a day early." Anna Mae laughed, "Tom doesn't think much of chicken," she said. "He thinks even bacon and gravy are better, but I tell him lots of people like chicken, so I often have it for company." When the plate came to me I was amazed at the number of drumsticks, my favorite piece. There must have been legs of six or eight chickens on the immense platter. Mr. Riggs laid two drumsticks on my plate.

Fresh biscuits and honey, relish, and well-seasoned vegetables followed the chicken. I even tasted the frijoli beans — seasoned with some hot stuff and onions. They weren't too bad but it would take a little while to get used to them.

Near the end of the meal Mr. Riggs looked at my plate and noticed it was empty.

"She polished off both of those chicken legs," he said with approval. "How about another?"

I shook my head, too full to speak.

Mr. Riggs was smiling, then suddenly he looked real sober. "Poor little girl," he said, "everything she eats goes right to her stummick."

He looked so serious that I had a moment of alarm, but then he suddenly slapped his knee and began to laugh. Mr. Riggs was often liable to act real sad and say something funny, so I learned you had to pay attention.

He always kept things lively at the table. Sometimes Anna Mae would say, "Now, Tom!" with a shade of disapproval when Tom was teasing Mother or telling a tall tale, but mostly she had a look of contentment. Besides having a doting husband, a measure of wealth, and a finer home than most of her friends, she had that rare gift of self-assurance that gave you the feeling her life was just as she had planned it.

Mr. Riggs owned cattle, bees, and the local telephone line. The cattle business was second nature to him, as he was one of the "Riggs Boys" who built a huge cattle dynasty on the other side of the range in the Sulpher Springs Valley. The bee business was his hobby. Later it was the only thing I didn't like about the ranch. The bees often swarmed on their porch, and one sometimes took a fancy to me. When the lilac bush by the front porch was in bloom the bees were at their worst and you couldn't get near to enjoy that heavenly lilac smell.

Mr. Riggs supplied telephone service to all the ranchers around. The lines ran helter-skelter over the mountains. They were not always in a straight line, for Mr. Riggs liked to use any convenient tree or tall bush as a pole. "What does it matter if the lines aren't straight, just so you can hear over them?" he said.

Actually, most of the poles were made by putting juniper posts in the ground and then wiring oak saplings to them for height. Mr. Riggs' lines covered almost two hundred miles from the small towns on the railroad to remote ranches in the Chiricahua Mountains. He had dug nearly all of the post holes himself and had erected the poles, using a team and wagon to deliver posts, wire, and insulators to the site. If you thought about it, it must have been a tremendous job and you couldn't blame him for taking advantage of any convenient "posts" nature threw in his way.

One strange thing is that forty years later, long after Mr. Riggs had passed away, those far-away ranchers were not served by any telephones at all. Mr. Riggs provided a service far ahead of his time, one that was lost in the years ahead.

Often, during a bad storm, service was disrupted. The next day

Mr. Riggs had to follow the lines over the hills on horseback to find where they were down or broken and put them back up or splice them. Usually he carried a big roll of wire on the saddle horn and a few tools and insulators in the saddle bags. It was a joke among the ranchers. "If Tom forgets the wire, he'll cut a piece of barbed wire from one of his fences, or ours, or use an old piece of baling wire to fix the line," they would say.

The telephones were huge monsters that hung on the wall just high enough for me to reach the crank. Everyone had his own ring, and there were to be at least a half-dozen parties on the Marble Camp line. The connection was never too good so you had to shout to be heard. Later, when we moved to camp, Mama called Mrs. Riggs often. The Riggs' ring was "two shorts and a long". Mama and Mrs. Riggs could hear "click"–"click"– "click all along the line as the listeners took their receivers off the hook and joined them. After they were through talking and had hung up the receivers, Mama could lift ours softly and hear her own topic of conversation being weighed and discussed on the line by two or more other parties.

"Did you hear that, Mary? Mrs. Milner is making another new dress. Seems like her man would get tired of her highfaluting ways."

"I know, but I guess she misses a lot of things back home. Maybe you can't blame her. Have you got your cucumber pickles done yet?"

"No, I been helping brand the calves. I may get at them tomorrow."

Mama would replace the receiver softly, sorry she had listened.

As they cleared the table after we ate, Mama and Mrs. Riggs' chatted like old friends. Mama had on one of Mrs. Riggs' big ruffled aprons, and she started washing the dishes while Mrs. Riggs worked with some fruit jars Tom had brought with him from his trip up the canyon.

"Tom takes my jars of sour cream in the horse saddle bags and that way I don't have to do the churning. When he comes home the butter has churned in the jars." She held it up to show Mama.

Mama looked at the jar in Mrs. Riggs' hands. "It's a good idea, but don't the jars ever break?" she asked.

"Mercy no, I never thought about it!" Mrs. Riggs laughed as she poured the contents into a wooden bowl. "That would make a mess wouldn't it?" She poured off the buttermilk, washed the butter in cold water, and began to knead salt into it.

All the way home we were basking in the glow of a pleasant afternoon. Mama seemed happier than she'd been since we'd come to Bowie. "You know, it seemed like I'd known her always," she said.

Papa gently slapped the reins against the horses' backs. "I felt sure you'd feel that way."

As we jogged along in the twilight just before the moon began to light the landscape, Mama said, "You know, Dana, Anna Mae killed those chickens herself — just chopped their heads off this morning and cleaned them and cut them up. I can see I'm not going to be able to depend on a butcher to do it."

Mama didn't intend to chop any chicken heads off. In fact, as long as we were to stay in camp, whenever Papa was going to kill a chicken, she and I would run in the bedroom, shut the door, and cover our ears with our hands so we couldn't hear the ax come down on the log, and we stayed till we were sure the chicken had finished flopping. But once when Mama picked up a very still-looking chicken it gave a last flying leap and nearly scared us to death.

When we arrived home that evening, it felt like we had opened another chapter in our new life. The Riggs Ranch was to be a very important oasis for us, and since it was about halfway between town and Marble Camp, it was just right for a resting place coming and going on our monthly trips to town.

This time Papa had introduced us to some real friends.

9.

A Wonder in the Sky

Only a few days after we arrived in Bowie, everyone began to talk about something special that was going to happen. When Mama and I went to the grocery, Mr. Bunch, the storekeeper, said, "It's a fine thing you arrived in Arizona when you did. A fine thing." He nodded his black fringed bald head. "Couldn't find clearer air for looking at a comet."

He didn't say what a comet might be and, since it was a new word, I went out on the front porch of the store to see if I could figure it out by taking a good look at the clean air.

Two little Mexican boys were scuffling in the dust. The front porch of the store was high off the ground so I sat down on the edge and dangled my feet. At home in Lorain you walked right in the stores without even a step. Here, the low end of town was in danger of quick flash floods, so five high steps from the ground were needed to be sure the flour and beans were dry the year around.

The two boys stopped writhing in the dust and came close to the edge of the porch. Maybe they knew what to expect of a comet.

"The air sure is clear," I volunteered. They looked at each other and grinned, still panting from their struggle.

"I bet she no can speak the Spaneesh good like me and you can speak the English," the dirtiest boy said.

The other boy rolled his little marble eyes. I tried again. "There's going to be a comet." I looked hard at the boys.

The words didn't seem to mean anything to them. "Papa says we're going to get up in the middle of the night to see it. Did you ever see a comet?"

The boys acted indifferent. There was no use to show their ignorance to a little gringo when a return to wrestling would change the subject. Without another word they went back to their struggle in the dust.

Mama came out of the store with two packages of groceries. "Here, you carry the small one, Alma. We have to go by the post office."

As we crossed the railroad tracks in the clear air we could see a train coming down the rails — far away.

"Is a comet like a train?" I asked. Usually Mama was very helpful, but this time she seemed to be preoccupied. "Mercy no! I've never seen a comet, but it's not like a train." With a wave of her free hand she dismissed the subject.

No one seemed willing or able to say what to expect of the thing everyone was talking about.

Early the next morning the alarm went off and it seemed like we had just gotten to sleep. Papa lighted the kerosene lamp and looked at the clock.

"One fifty-five. Time to get up. Shake your shoes, Maud." Already he was getting us used to shaking our clothes and turning our shoes upside down to shake out any scorpions that might have hunted a cozy bed there.

I was too sleepy to care about getting up so as soon as Papa got dressed he said, "I'll roll you in a blanket and carry you, Pet. You don't want to miss this."

Mama held the screen door open and Papa carried me outside.

Papa knew the direction we should look and in a moment he said, "There it is — Halley's Comet! We're none too soon. We almost missed it."

By that time I was half awake. There was no moon but there were many stars shining. I looked off in the direction Papa was pointing. One of the stars had a tail.

So that was what they were all so excited about! A comet was nothing in the world but a star with a tail! I took one good look and closed my eyes and snuggled into the blankets. As I drifted off to sleep again I thought, "I'll bet those little Mexican boys missed seeing the comet. Lucky boys."

Then Mama said, "Do you suppose it will be clear enough for them to see it in Lorain, Dana?"

I woke up. Imagine that! This was a thing they could see all the way to Lorain! I stuck my head out of the blanket and took another look. Still the same star with a tail, but now it looked different.

We had been days traveling by train from Lorain to Denver, and then later from Denver to Bowie, and now we were looking at a star with a tail hanging up there in the sky and Grandma could see it too at the very same time. This was more important than I thought. A comet was worth getting up in the middle of the night to see. It really was!

Those poor sleepy Mexican boys!

10.

Dad Kellum's Congregation

When we had been in Denver, there was one thing that Papa had written to us that really worried Mama. He said there was no Protestant Church in Bowie. A few women held Sunday school in the town's two-room schoolhouse and once in a while, if the ladies promised him a congregation, a circuit preacher of some denomination would come and preach a sermon. Mama couldn't imagine a town of three-hundred souls not having a regular preacher; about the only time she had ever missed Sunday school and church in her life was when she had la grippe, or someone in her family had been ill and quarantined. She knew there would be no more church up at the quarry, but this meant there would not even be a chance to attend church when we were in Bowie.

One Saturday while we lived there, a traveling preacher did come to town. He said he'd stay over Sunday and preach a sermon after Sunday school the next day if the ladies wanted to drum up a crowd. On Sunday morning when Papa and I went out early to get the company mail at the post office, we met "Old Dad Kellum," the saloon keeper, on the street.

Papa must have been awfully anxious to get a crowd together to please Mama, because when he saw the barkeeper he stepped up to him and said, "Mr. Kellum, Bowie has a school house and a saloon, and it ought to have a church. They're having a preaching services this morning. Would you care to come?"

Old Dad was a plump cherubic man with a wispy fringe of graying hair around his tanned bald spot. He looked a little startled at Papa's invitation, but he folded his arms over his bar apron and answered, "Hell, I sure would! I'll close up my place and bring my customers. Come along with me, Mr. Milner, I might need help to get 'em out."

Papa looked at me and hesitated, then he resolutely took my hand and we followed Mr. Kellum. Papa knew that Mama wouldn't have approved of him taking me into the saloon, but he didn't like to say no after inviting its owner to church. It was probably the first time since Old Dad had been in Bowie that anyone had dreamed of offering such an invitation and it was certainly the first time he had thought of bringing his customers along.

The saloon with its high square front had a flowery sign, "Dad Kellum's Saloon," with scrolls and curly cues painted above its swinging doors. It must have been the work of a sign painter passing through, probably for a few drinks on the house. There wasn't another as fancy in town.

The large room we went into had a bar running its length. There were depressions in the unpainted floor by the bar rail, worn by men putting their weight on one foot as they rested the other on the rail. Brass spittoons were placed at irregular intervals about the room and it was clear some of the men were no better shots here than in the barber shop. The room had a swept-out look and the stale smell of beer, cheap whiskey and dried tobacco juice. At one end, looking down saucily, was a huge picture of a pretty girl in a ruffled bathing suit. If Mama had seen the picture she would have said, "a dame", with a righteous little sniff, but I thought she was really pretty. I had a chilly little feeling running up my spine, though, that I shouldn't be here, so I stayed as close to Papa as I could.

A door at the rear of the big room led to dad Kellum's living quarters. "Sleeping quarters" would be better, for Old Dad spent all of his waking hours in the saloon, except when he ate every day at the depot. He always wore his apron, but now he took it off in honor of the occasion. "Boys, it's Sunday morning and come 'leven o'clock they are goin' to have preachin' services over to the school house. Mr. Milner here has asked me to go and I aim to take you all with me. Most of ye ain't clean as ya might be. They's a faucet and a wash pan an' soap in the back room. Use the towel hangin' up on a nail. Thet's clean enuf fer you varmints. Now, git goin'. Here's a comb if you ain't got one!"

The half dozen men looked at Dad Kellum in amazement, but they filed past him into the back room. They walked slowly, but Papa and I were surprised at how meekly they followed his directions. As I realized much later, his power over them was probably his control of their whiskey supply.

Papa and I went on to Sunday school, and just before eleven o'clock we saw the men coming down the road, walking single file like a bunch of convicts, with Dad Kellum in back of them like a Sheriff's deputy. The men's faces and hands were clean, their hair was combed, and they all had "I haven't had a drink for a month" expressions on their faces. Their hats were placed squarely on their heads, and not at the usual careless angles.

The few people who regularly came to church when there were any services craned their necks and tried to cover their surprise at the men who entered with noisy boots. Old Dad stood just outside the door and kept up a running patter of orders in a stage whisper.

"Take off your hat. Spit out your tobacco chaw, over there," pointing quickly in the direction of a mesquite bush. "Don't make no more noise than you have to. Charlie, you ain't as clean as the others, don't sit close to no ladies. Here, set in this little seat." He pointed at a small school desk off to the side.

There was one long bench at the back of the room, probably for use when both school rooms had an assembly. The women had also been at work gathering a congregation, for all of the back seats were full, and the men had to walk to the front of the room where the smaller seats were.

"Your hat, Jim," Dad Kellum pointed accusingly at the offender. "Take it off!"

The men hung their heads in embarrassment. They were not used to being seen in church. Papa and I sat by Mama up in front near the men.

When everyone was seated and they began to sing the first song, Old Dad sang louder than anybody. It was the first time anyone could remember seeing him in church, and they were surprised at how well he knew the hymns and the ritual. I opened my eyes and peeked at him during the Lord's Prayer. He spoke it unfalteringly in his deep voice. When the men fidgeted a bit during the sermon Dad Kellum "gave them the look" and they got quiet again.

After the service was over he marched ahead of the men back to the saloon. He pushed through the doors, which he had not bothered to lock, and they all trooped behind him like the mice following the Pied Piper.

That afternoon, as Papa and Mama and I took a walk, Papa said with a grin, "You see we can have church here even if we have to drag the men out of the saloon to make a crowd!"

When we passed Old Dad's place we found him standing in the doorway sunning his bald head. He had on a clean apron for once and his fringe of hair was combed. There was a peaceful look on his face and we heard him humming to himself. After we passed, Papa glanced at Mama and said "Did you hear what he was humming?"

Mama had a twinkle in her eye. "Shall We Gather at the River," she said softly.

11.

Johnny and Daisy

Late one afternoon after work, the camp teamster came to the house to see Papa about something he needed to take to camp the next day. Papa called Mama out to meet him and I tagged along.

"This is Johnny Kaiser, Maud. He came from Denver, too," Papa said.

Johnny nodded bashfully and took off his hat. He had a head of silky hair so jet black it looked as if he might have stuck his head in Papa's inkwell. The hair was soft and it packed tight, so that when his hat was off, where it had rested there was an indented ring like a marcelle around his head.

He was clean-shaven and his skin was dark and smooth. It seemed to me he squinted a little crankily when he looked at Mama. But when he looked at me a strange thing happened. Little wrinkles came around his eyes and they fell into a smiling pattern, like the way the pieces of glass in my kaleidoscope changed the picture when I turned it. I decided he liked me and it was nice to have a grown-up man, among all these strange new people and things, who approved of you. He certainly didn't look as stern when he smiled as he did when he just squinted. After he left, Papa said Johnny came of "Sturdydutchstock." I wished I'd looked at him more closely. I asked Papa if that was why he squinted so and he laughed.

"No, I guess Johnny is just near-sighted. But he's a fine teamster and the company is lucky to get a man who loves horses like he does. He has probably gone to the livery stable right now to keep the horses company. He sleeps on a cot in a stall so as to be near his two teams.

You notice he has a kind of horsey smell about him? He's hardly ever away from them."

I had noticed it and I thought it was very pleasant. Johnny was going to be nice to know and I was anxious to see those horses he liked so well. Papa said they were much better than the pair we had driven to the Riggs' Ranch, but I really couldn't see how any could be better than those.

Bowie had it all over Lorain as far as interesting animals were concerned. First there were the gila monsters of Old Mac, then the livery stable horses, and now after Johnny had left, we took our usual walk and became acquainted with burros. At the time they seemed to be best of all.

"Let's go to Mexican town for a change," Papa told us as we started out. "If Canute is at home he'll show us around. He's an old Indian and Mr. Hendricks says he is over a hundred years old, but he works hard every day as a wood cutter. He looks his age, but I'm puzzled by the Mexicans—their hair doesn't turn grey very early and a young woman looks about the age of her mother. It's the same with men. Two Mexicans will come to apply for work at the Quarry and one of them will say, 'This my boy. He good for work, too,' I'd swear it was the man's brother, maybe even his twin."

Walking north, we had crossed the tracks and then turned to the right to follow them for two or three city blocks. There were a couple of pepper-tree-shaded houses and a few unkempt small houses between the tracks and Mexican town.

As Papa finished talking, we came to a little shack. It was so low I couldn't see how anyone could stand up in it. Papa went down two steps and knocked on a door.

The most wrinkled man I ever saw answered the knock and ducked his head in the low doorway to come outside. He looked like pictures of old Indians in my story books. In fact he reminded me of the Indian who often chased me in bad dreams.

When I dared take my eyes off him, I peered down through the open door into the house. It was hard to see much, and no wonder. There was only one burlap-covered window, partly open.

"This is my wife and little girl, Canute. You told me you'd show me how the Mexicans build their houses. Do you remember?" Papa asked.

Canute bobbed his head once and I expected him to say "Ugh". Instead he spoke in English, broken but better than many of the Mexicans I had heard. He was short several teeth and in between his words he kept running his tongue into the holes in his jaw so that it gave you the impression he might be chewing gum. Like most Indians, he went right to work without any foolishness.

"This wall mud," he said, laying his hand on the adobes. "See, got straw," he pointed to little pieces of straw poking out of the bricks where they were worn by wind and rain. He led us over to a number of wooden frames by the woodpile. They were filled with half dried mud. Beside them was a hole in the ground and it was evident he used the dirt to make the bricks, 'dobes' as he called them. He picked up one of the frames in one hand and a stick in the other and gave the frame a sharp tap.

The block of mud that fell on the ground was about the thickness of an ordinary brick, but much longer and wider.

We followed him as he stalked back to the house.

"Put mud, put 'dobe, put mud, put 'dobe," Canute's hands worked slowly as he showed us how he laid up a wall.

He kept up his pantomime for a minute as we stood watching.

The door of the house was a wooden frame with burlap tacked on and it was hinged to the door frame with pieces of leather, probably the tops of an old shoe. For a doorknob there was only a big nail to grab.

The flat roof was made of old railroad ties laid on top of the wall and covered with mud and straw. We could see now the reasons the building looked so low because it was two steps below the ground, built over a spot where the dirt had been taken out to make other adobes. This made less wall to build and should make the house cooler in summer and warmer in winter just like Grandma's basement in Lorain.

"Does the water ever run down into the house," Papa asked, looking at the steps down to the doorway.

Canute ran his tongue into the holes between his teeth. "Seguro", he said. "Sometime come hard rain. Run down steps. The woman have to put the keed and the beans up on the table. Water all over floor."

Canute was demonstrating, lifting the kid and the beans, and then stepping high on tiptoe as if trying to keep his feet dry, pantomiming the adjectives he couldn't find to make his point.

Mama had been very quiet, listening but now she said, "The yards are so clean. Do they sweep them?"

"Seguro, if the yard dirty you no can see the snake. Maybe bite the baby. All the people sweep the yard," he hesitated and looked thoughtfully at Mama. "Sometime the snake he crawl in your house."

Even this old Indian wanted, apparently, to get in some licks on frightening Mama, who lifted her skirts and shook them as always, but shaking snakes out—not bedbugs this time.

Papa thanked Canute and we walked on. There was a little group of Mexican women collected near another house like Canute's. Each woman had a bucket or a pitcher.

"That's the faucet where they get their water, "Papa said. "There's just one for all the people who live in Mexican town."

Mama gave Papa an odd look and started saying something, then stopped. I wondered if she was going to ask him how far we'd have to carry water at Marble Camp.

Just then I noticed half a dozen little Mexican kids playing some sort of game with two burros. They'd climb on them and slide off of the burros' rumps. The one who got off his burro first was slapped on the back as the others shouted, "Bueno Juan!" or "Bueno Jose!" When they saw us watching them, they didn't yell quite so loud, and one said, "Good Juan!" The others all giggled at him for showing off his English in front of us. "Ándale! Ándale! (Hurry! Hurry!) Is my turn!"

They kept scrambling on and off.

After we'd watched them for a while, Papa asked, "Do you boys know anybody who has a burro to sell?"

The boys stopped their game and looked at each other. Then one of them poked a companion in the ribs, "Andres, the burro of Andres."

The other boys went into gales of laughter. We wondered what was so funny about Andres having a burro to sell. The boys' laughter trailed off and all but one of them went back to their game.

"The burro of Andres, he sell him to you. She live over by the tracks. I show you."

It was the smallest of the boys speaking and he struck off at a run in his bare feet to take Papa to the "house of Andres," Papa and I walked fast to keep the boy in sight. Mama followed more slowly.

There were three burros with their front feet hobbled, nibbling at a catclaw bush as we arrived at the shack. The youngster pointed at them and was about to leave us at a run when a Mexican came up the steps from a shack just like Canute's and shouted something in Spanish. The boy came back reluctantly. I knew just how he felt about wanting to get back to his game. Even in Lorain I hated it when Mama called me from play just to have somebody see how fast I was growing.

"This boy tells me you have a burro to sell," Papa began.

Andres looked questioningly at the youngster who turned to Papa and said, "He no speak English. I tell him what you want."

Turning to Andres, the boy spoke long and earnestly. Andres grunted several times and then said, "Diez pesos."

The boy hesitated, then looked at Papa. "He say ten dollars for the one by the gate with the white belly."

He said it apologetically as though he thought it might be more than the burro was worth, but Papa didn't seem to think it was too much. At least he walked over close to the burro to examine it. Mama stood her distance and didn't show much enthusiasm.

Daisy had longer hair than the others. She was light tan but almost white on her belly. Her ears, though, were rimmed with black and stood up very straight to give her an alert, interested look. Papa couldn't know that once in a while she'd lay her ears back, and you'd never know exactly what had displeased her, but you'd have an uncomfortable feeling that you'd better do something about it quick.

Her eyes didn't have the patient, docile look that many burros' eyes have, but since Papa didn't know what to look for in burros, he paid the man and handed the boy a nickel. The little Mexican's eyes danced.

"I show thees to Juan y Manuel. They weesh they come show you the house of Andres."

Papa grinned, "Ask Andres if he'll keep the burro till I can get a place for it. Tell him I'll pay for the feed."

The boy spoke again in Spanish and Andres nodded, "Si, Si, Esta bueno!"

"He say, 'yes'" the youngster said in obvious haste to get back to his friends. "I go now, Si?"

"Run along," Papa said, and without another word the boy clenched the money in his fist, turned, and ran as fast as a jack-rabbit back to show his nickel to his friends.

Mama wasn't a bit happy about the transaction. "Don't go too close, Alma. That burro may tramp on you or bite you, or whatever it is that burros do." She turned to Papa. "What are you thinking of, Dana? There won't be a doctor within fifty miles of Camp." It wasn't often she used that tone of voice.

Papa said jokingly, "What do we need a doctor for? The burro's not sick."

Mama looked provoked at him. "You know what I mean. If that child fell off and broke a leg what would we do?"

Papa looked sober and said, "Well, the burro isn't broken to ride yet and if we go at it slowly, Alma and the burro can learn together."

Mama sniffed. "You mark my word, something dreadful will happen!"

The tension between Mama and Papa somehow spoiled the fun of having a burro of my very own. I almost wished Papa hadn't bought her.

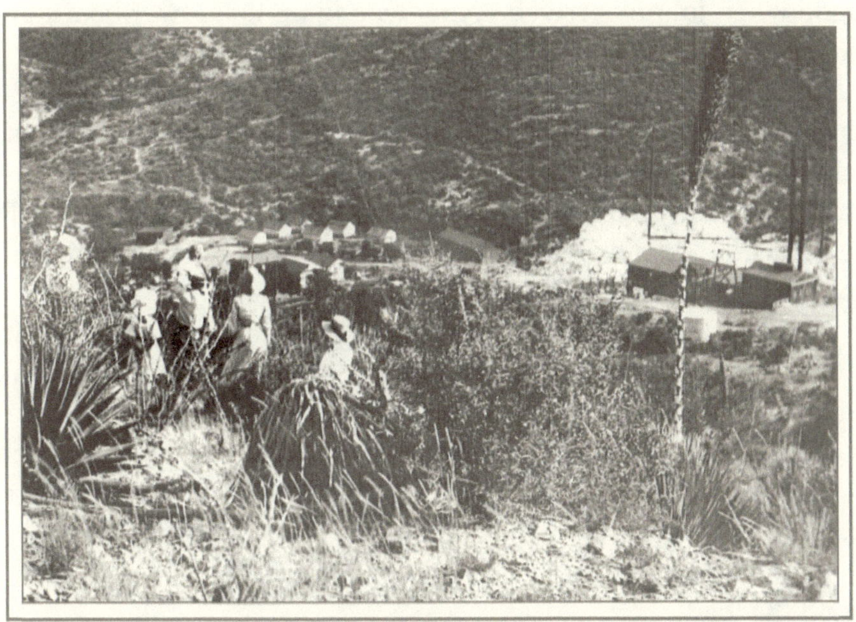

A group on a picnic above Marble Camp. Earlier, riding on the lumber wagon, Mama and I first saw the camp from about where this photo was taken.

12.

Marble Camp

It was early on a morning in June when Johnny drove the big lumber wagon to the front door of our house in Bowie. The day had finally arrived when we were to move to our new, unseen, home in Marble Camp.

I had been waiting for him. The wooden front gate at the Skinner place was well-balanced and firm on its hinges. It was fun to stand on the lower board and swing on it.

"You be the gatekeeper," Papa had told me as he and Mama began to carry our things out and lay them down just outside the gate. Everything but our trunks and the sewing machine was ready to load on the wagon when Johnny arrived. Now I stood on that lower board on the inside of the gate and looked over the team and wagon.

The horses were big black work animals, and I had to admit they were better than those from the livery stable. They had such broad backs though that I was sure if I sat on one, my feet would stick straight out. Grandma would have a fit if I rode a horse like that. Anyway Papa had said this team was not riding horses. These were extra big and strong to pull the heavy loads to Camp.

The wagon was painted forest green and there was a word painted on the side in bright red. Later I learned the word was "Studebaker" and Mama said it was the same kind of wagon her father used to sell in his carriage shop in Lorain. Comets and wagons from Ohio to Arizona!

A huge yellow umbrella stuck out of a pipe just in front of the seat, throwing its shadow on the ground in the early sunlight.

I climbed off the gate and stood by Mama while the two men discussed the load.

"We better put one trunk just back of the seat," Papa said. "I'll use it to sit on because we won't have room this time for the back seat."

"Yeah, me and Mrs. Milner and Alma can sit in the front and you can watch Daisy and the load," Johnny said, hoisting one of Mama's straw suitcases over the side of the wagon. We were to find it was an unwritten law that if Johnny was on the wagon no one drove the horses but Johnny. He was the official camp teamster. Papa was going to be busy that day anyway, taking care of Daisy.

When our things were all loaded, Papa tied the burro securely to the back of the wagon. Johnny climbed up and took his place in the driver's seat. Papa took Mama's arm to help her then lifted me up to Johnny.

"Straddle it," Johnny said as he sat me on the seat.

I had no idea what that meant and Mama said quickly, "One leg on each side of the umbrella pole, Honey."

So that was how I was to ride! I slipped one leg around the pole and grasped it in both hands. It was rather like riding a stick horse.

The umbrella shaded the three of us in front, but Papa had to ride out in the sun. He didn't mind. It never seemed to get too hot for Papa, and every few days since we arrived he'd say with relish, "Smell that good fresh air, girls. Dry as everything and hot as an oven." Mama and I thought it was pretty hot sometimes, but when Papa talked like that we'd take a deep breath and have to agree that it was dry and hot as an oven, and — good too.

The last thing Papa did before he got on the wagon was to hand up a kitten that a lady had given me. I had promised to hold it on my lap all the way if Mama would only let me take it. It was a boy kitten, white with tan spots, soft and furry.

Johnny frowned a little when he saw it, but he didn't say anything.

Papa swung up to his place on the trunk and Johnny unwound the reins from the whip socket. With a little click of his tongue and a gentle "Les' go boys!" we left the house to go to the store for a few last minute provisions.

A big ham had been ordered for camp. Also a sack of beans and a couple of bales of hay still had to be added to the load. Except for a covered box under Mama's side of the seat, Johnny had thought it best to load our stuff first so he would know how much room he had left. There were always things waiting to be taken to camp, and he'd just fill up the wagon with whatever he could take after our belongings were loaded.

It was lucky Mama didn't know that the box under the seat was dynamite. She would have had a fit. Under a hunk of canvas it looked as innocent as a case of milk.

Johnny threw a wet gunny sack over the ham to keep it cool, and at last we were ready to start on our first trip to Marble Camp. Picking up the reins, he clicked again to the horses. The rear wagon wheel had settled into a hole in the road and the horses had to give a lunge to start. Mama and I weren't expecting it, and as the horses gave a mighty heave, we nearly turned a somersault over the low back of the seat.

Daisy wasn't expecting it either, or else for some other reason she must have decided she wanted no part of the trip. When the horses leaped forward she stood her ground. The rope parted and Daisy stood looking at us mournfully.

Johnny brought the horses to a halt and Papa jumped down and went back for Daisy. He pulled on the piece of rope still around her neck, but it was no use. She wouldn't budge. He cut a switch from a mesquite bush by the front door of the grocery store, and coaxed and switched her alternately, in an effort to get her back to the wagon so he could retie her. She just looked sad and still.

Papa and Johnny both looked at the whip in its socket at the same time. They caught each other's eye, and without a word Johnny grasped the whip and handed it to Papa. Papa hesitated then took hold of it and then as though talking to himself he said, "I always hated people who beat animals, but I can see—" his voice trailed off, and he strode back to Daisy.

Mama and I shut our eyes and I covered my ears with my hands so I wouldn't hear as Papa brought the whip down hard four or five times on Daisy's back. If Daisy was hurt she didn't show it. She just stood still and eyed Papa stubbornly. Papa came back to replace the whip in the socket. He looked beaten. "It's no use," he said. "We'll just leave her here."

It seemed that Daisy was the boss today.

Just then Johnny said, "Look at that crazy critter."

Papa turned and there she was standing by the back of the wagon patiently waiting to be tied again to the load. She had moved up by herself and stood mournfully eyeing Papa as if to say, "What are we waiting for? Let's get going."

Papa reached under the seat to get a new length of rope and fastened her again to the back of the wagon.

This time when we started, Mama and I were braced for it and Daisy trotted docilely along as if she could hardly wait to get wherever we were going.

The dusty road stretched ahead of us to the South. Up on its grassy hilltop the Riggs ranch, half way to camp, was the only friendly thing we could see for miles ahead of us. Some of Mr. Riggs' cattle looked like little dots standing in the thin shade of the mesquite. We hadn't ridden far from town before "Meow-waw"—the kitten had smelled the ham in the back of the wagon and he dug his claws into my arms and hands trying to get to it. I had to hold him tight and at the same time hide the scratches from Mama because I knew she hadn't been too enthusiastic about taking a cat along. "He's liable to scratch you," she had said. But I begged so hard she finally consented and here was the cat doing exactly what she had predicted.

Johnny grumbled to himself. I could barely catch a word now and then, but I understood. "Darn cat, – know better – take a cat – when meat – wagon." It made me afraid of what he might do, and I cuddled the kitten fearfully, watching Johnny out of the corner of my eye.

At first it seemed as though we were sitting very high, but as we drove out on the plains and could see a long way, I felt nearer to the ground. It was a clear day and the Riggs ranch looked close.

The sun rose higher and began to bear down and the steady jog of the horses sent all of us, including the cat, into a kind of lazy stupor. Even the view became less clearcut and more hazy. By sitting forward and resting my feet on the dashboard, and then pushing myself back and dangling my feet, I was able to change my position more often than Mama. She sat silent most of the way and seemed to be thinking hard.

Papa sat backward on the trunk to watch Daisy for several miles. When he saw she was going to follow all right, he turned around and rode forward, just glancing back once in a while. The cat had given up and gone to sleep on a doll blanket on my lap. Once I saw Johnny almost smile when he looked at the sleeping kitten so I relaxed a little. Maybe he didn't hate cats after all.

Every once in a while, Johnny would roll a cigarette. It was quite a ritual. First he would put the reins between his knees. The sack of Bull Durham and book of papers were in his left shirt pocket. He could draw the book of papers out slowly, open it and pull one off, close the book, and return it to his pocket. Now it was time for the tobacco sack. Equally deliberately he would draw that out and open the top. Then, with three little shakes of his right hand he would salt the tobacco paper, which he held in his left. Never too much, never too little. The shakes were just right. With his teeth he pulled the strings to close the bag. Then he replaced it ever so slowly in his left shirt pocket, leaving the tag hanging out. Next he folded the edges of the paper together, rolled the cigarette in his fingers, touched it to his lips, slid his tongue along the edges, and with his right forefinger and thumb, pressed the edges down. Then putting the cigarette between his lips, he struck a match, lighted it, and took the reins from between his knees in satisfied silence. The cigarette he rolled was small at both ends and fat in the middle, but it looked rather elegant to me. I resolved then and there that as soon as I grew up I'd learn to roll a Bull Durham cigarette. After three of four cigarettes, I had memorized Johnny's movements so I thought I could do it. Later I'd pantomime it sometimes, but always in the dark or when I was sure no one was around to see.

I had been so intent for a while in watching Johnny that I hadn't been looking ahead, and suddenly we were almost at the Riggs ranch. It was nearly eleven o'clock and the sun was bearing down so the ranch looked very inviting.

When we reached the foot of the hill, Johnny stopped the horses and we all piled off the wagon and stretched.

"Do you think we can stay a few minutes?" Mama asked, and I held my breath for Papa's answer.

Papa looked at Johnny. "I guess so. Johnny will want to rest the horses. Won't you Johnny?"

Johnny was leading the horses to the trough and grunted something about "five minutes to water'em."

The door opened at the ranch house above and Mrs. Riggs and Pauline came down the hill.

With them on a little breeze came the most heavenly smell in all the world! Homemade bread just out of the oven!

Mrs. Riggs hugged Mama and me enthusiastically, then we followed her and Pauline up to the big kitchen in the ranch house while Papa and Johnny watered the horses at the corral. After we had been there a few minutes, I whispered in Mama's ear. Mrs. Riggs saw me and laughed.

"I know what she wants," she said. "I'll cut a loaf and we'll all have some."

Mama had always said, "It's not polite to whisper in front of people," but I think she was glad I had this time.

Mrs. Riggs threw back a snowy white flour sack tea towel and exposed five beautiful brown loaves laid upside down on the pine drainboard. She cut thick slices and spread them with fresh churned butter and honey.

Pauline and I each ate two slices, but Mama was too polite to eat more than one. Mrs. Riggs brought glasses of cool water from the olla on the back porch.

We were just swallowing the last bite of bread when Papa called, "Let's go girls!"

Anna Mae and Pauline went down the hill with us to the wagon and this time Pauline let me hold her hand.

The good permanent road to Marble Camp was still being built off to the left of the Riggs ranch. It wound around the foothills for six miles before starting up grade to camp. Papa had said he felt sorry for the road contractor. He had run into solid rock in several places up on the mountain and he'd had to use tons of dynamite and do a lot of work he hadn't figured on.

Johnny turned the horses to the right and we jogged around the Riggs knoll and up the old Apache Pass road, three or four miles in the direction of old Fort Bowie.

The Dickson ranch was on that road higher than the Riggs ranch. Just below it was a corral with a half a dozen horses milling around. There, Papa and Johnny got off the wagon again and fastened another team in front of our horses. It made me uneasy to think we needed four horses to pull our load to Marble Camp.

The night before we left Bowie, Papa had seemed a little worried when he said, "I wish the new road could be finished before you go to camp, Maud. You won't like the trip."

Mama smiled bravely and said, "I guess I can stand it if you can. You've been over the road a dozen times."

Papa looked at her a long time and seemed about to say something else but must have thought better of it.

A half mile beyond the corral the trail suddenly took a turn up the steep mountainside. When Mama saw it she clutched me tight in both arms and said in a horrified voice, "Dana, there's no road!"

Papa just nodded and tried to look matter-of-fact.

"Do you think Alma and I had better walk?" Mama asked anxiously.

Papa looked at her thin shoes and shook his head. His jaw had its determined look. "No I don't. This wagon and these horses have been over this mountain a hundred times and nobody had to get off and walk except to lighten the load. You don't weigh much and you don't know about watching for cactus and snakes. You stay put on that front seat."

From this point on, the trip was hard work for the horses. Papa had untied Daisy and he followed ten or fifteen feet behind the wagon, leading her. At the corral where we got the extra horses, Johnny had thrown a heavy log on the load. One end of chain was fastened around the middle of it and the other was attached to the rear axle of the wagon.

Prince and Nig worked together perfectly as we rose out of the canyon. They each planted their feet firmly and the great muscles stood out on their rumps as they strained to pull the heavy wagon. Once in a while Prince's foot would slip on a rock and Nig's muscles would tense and he'd seem to hold his breath till Prince regained his footing. Then with one accord they'd strain to pull the wagon another couple feet.

Every few feet Johnny would say, "Whoa, Boys," and set the brake and wait while the horses rested and regained their strength for another effort. Sometimes it seemed we waited hours till the horses' sides stopped heaving and they stopped breathing so hard.

When we had been climbing about an hour at this halting gait, Papa called to Johnny, "Let's stop under the next scrub oak and eat our lunch. It's past noon."

Mama had packed sandwiches for us, so as soon as we found a spot that was not so steep, Johnny halted the horses and climbed down. He and Papa put big rocks behind he wagon wheels. I was afraid to let go of the kitten and didn't want to get down till Mama said, "Here, I'll hold it for you."

It was getting cooler now as we climbed and there was a fresh mountain breeze. We could see nothing but the mountains around us now and the deep blue sky above. There was a faint odor of pine in the air. When we were ready to go again Mama started to say something. "Don't you think, Dana—"

Papa anticipated what she had in mind and he stopped her with, "No, I don't, Maud. It's hard walking and I'd feel better if you and Alma rode."

He helped us back on the wagon, untied Daisy from the bushes where she'd waited and pulled the rocks from behind the wheels. The horses seemed to have fresh vigor and for a few minutes we climbed faster.

Mama must have been thinking ahead and worrying about going down on the other side of the mountain. There was nothing to prepare her for the fact that when we reached the summit of that mountain there was another just like it, only higher, on the other side. Papa had thought it best to just say, "It's a long hard trip" without dwelling on any of the details.

I was disappointed when we finally reached the top and could see only that other mountain ahead, and I started to say so. But when I looked at Mama she had such a look of despair on her face that I closed my mouth and just hung onto my kitten and the umbrella handle. I felt as though a big lump was swelling up inside of me.

Now the horses' muscles stood out as they leaned backward to restrain the wagon. Johnny held tight to the reins, giving messages through them to the horses, along with his shouted orders. All the way up he had talked encouragingly to them. "Come on Prince! Whatsa matter Nig! Careful there, watch your step." Then as we started down he scolded them gently. "Not so fast, boys! Slow down, Nig! Watch the feet, Prince! Steady boys!"

When we came to a very steep place going down, Papa pulled the log off the wagon and it dragged behind to act as a brake. He followed close behind the log to move it if it got hung up behind a rock or stump. Mama was clutching my knee.

When we got to the foot of the grade, Papa loaded the log again before we started up. It was only then that Mama relaxed her hold on me but I could still feel the tension in the way she sat so straight in the seat.

Once, though, she remarked, "I had no idea there would be so many wild flowers." Mama did love flowers, and there were all kinds, from tiny blue and yellow daisies to big red Indian Paint Brushes, but I thought she was just trying to act brave and give us something to think about. She was too concerned on that trip to care about flowers.

All the way Daisy trotted along cooperatively. She did hesitate once, and that was when we got to the steepest grade just before we reached the top of the second ridge. She suddenly reared back and planted her feet as if to say, "Enough is enough. I'm not going another step." Papa just stood still and waited for a few seconds. Then she started again, without any explanation.

It was late in the afternoon when we came to the top of the ridge and got our first look at Marble Camp below. The sun was still shining on us, but down in the camp it had already set. Marble Camp sat in the shadow of the mountains. Papa and Daisy reached the top a few seconds after we did.

"I wanted to be with you when you first saw Marble Camp," he said with disappointment. "It would be much better if you could see it first with the sun on it. We'll rest a minute."

He handed the end of Daisy's rope to Johnny and helped Mama down from the wagon. I sat still trying not to wake the little kitten. Papa began enthusiastically to point things out.

"Off there to the right they are building the mill. They're clearing rocks and dirt from the marble deposit. It's right beside the mill. See those derricks?" He pointed at something that looked like two huge toothpicks standing upright. From the base of each, another toothpick reached out.

"Those booms at the base of the derricks will lift the big blocks of marble out of the quarry after they are cut loose, then swing them over onto the stock pile. See those little threads that go from the end of the booms to the top of the derricks? They are really big steel cables."

To the right of the derricks there was one black smokestack even taller than the derricks.

"That smoke stack is eighty-five feet high, almost as high as a ten story building, and there'll be two of them," Papa said with a note of pride in his tone. "Those two building that look alike are our house and the superintendent's house. You are seeing the back side of them from up here. It's quite a little city, isn't it?"

There was a sparkle in Papa's eye as he looked down on the quarry so Mama tried to look impressed. All the while I guess she was remembering the long frightening trip over the mountains and thinking how tired she was and how lonely the camp looked below, and how far away Lorain was.

Papa must have sensed how she felt. "We'd better get along," he said. "We can look the camp over tomorrow, but what we all need now is a warm supper and a good night's sleep. I'll tell you girls this. There isn't anything worse going to happen to you than this trip."

Then he looked at Mama and said softly, "I told you, sweetheart, it's pretty rugged."

And right there on the mountain top with the wind blowing through the scrub oak and pines, with Johnny and me sitting on the wagon silently watching, Papa took Mama in his arms and kissed her as if there was no one within a hundred miles.

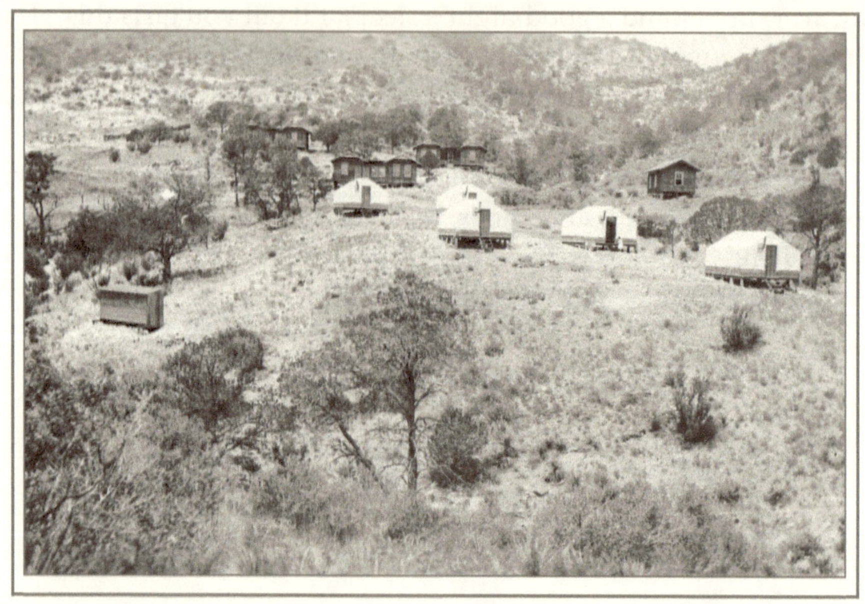

Marble Camp's housing. The building partly hidden by the highest tent house combines Papa's office, the commissary and the general manager's quarters. The house above and to the right is ours, and the one to its left was for the superintendent's family.

3.

Our New Home

Papa helped Mama back into the wagon and Johnny handed him Daisy's rope. At the back of the wagon, Papa grabbed the log and jerked it onto the ground. We started down slowly from the crest of the ridge to camp, the log and chain scraping noisily over the rocks.

The trail was steep, so Johnny drove in a zig-zag pattern. A faint odor of pine smoke hung in the air. As we descended the mountain, ours was the first house we came to. The walls were rough boards topped by a tin roof. In back, the house rested on the ground, and in front it was held up by round wood posts so that is reminded me of a dog sitting down. The posts would be his front legs and they held the house off the ground about four or five feet. The roof was flat in the middle with a gable on each side so that the illusion of the dog was complete, a boxer dog with ears standing up on each side of his head. There was a rough stairway with high steps to the small front porch.

The rest of the camp stretched below our house, and the quarry was off to the right about as far as a long city block. "That's the Quarry Superintendent's house," Papa said, pointing to one between ours and the quarry. It was a twin of ours, except that the ground was slightly more level, so there were not so many steps in the front.

"Ya see that corrugated iron building over toward the quarry" Johnny asked. Mama and I looked where he pointed and nodded.

 "That's the blacksmith shop," he said, as if that were something really important. I'd never heard of a "blacksmith." Probably a colored man, I thought, by the name of "Smith." I wondered what he sold in his shop.

Winding down a trail on the mountainside across from us was a long dark train of something. I pointed it out to Papa.

"That's the burros," he said. "They're bringing wood for the steam engines at the quarry and for our stoves. There are two pack trains that work morning till night, hauling it down off the mountains. "It's a good thing they do, or we wouldn't have any way to cook our food or keep warm, Pet." The pack train interested me. In Lorain we had used coal for heating and gas for cooking, and before we came to Bowie, I had supposed everybody in the world did.

Down below our house on the mountainside was Papa's office and the commissary, both in one building, along with the general manager's living quarters, and below that still were scattered a dozen tent houses with unpainted wood walls about four feet high. Above that, the walls and roofs were of new white canvas. Johnny told us everyone called them "the camp houses." Mama said, "It's a good name. It doesn't look like anybody could do more than camp in them."

Each building in camp had a very tall stovepipe chimney projecting from the roof or from an elbow through the walls, as if someone had bought too many pipe joints and wanted to use them up.

Johnny pulled the horses up to our back porch. Papa tied Daisy to a bush and the two men unloaded our things onto the porch. When

Johnny swung Mama's suitcase over the side of the wagon, he accidentally flipped the canvas off the box under the seat. Before he could replace the canvas Mama's eyes fell on the box. She tuned pale and her eyes got big as saucers as she said in a hoarse whisper, "Dynamite! We were sitting on dynamite on that awful trip." Papa grinned sheepishly but didnt say a word.

Johnny drove away to the barn down below the office, and we stepped into the house. The central room we entered appeared to be a combination kitchen and dining room. There was a crude built-in cupboard with a counter top along one wall. The cupboard doors had wire screen where glass had been in our cupboard in Lorain. The counter top was rough pine boards with huge knots.

"I'll cover it with oil cloth," Mama said. She seemed to have forgotten that box under the seat for the moment and was ready now to make plans for our new home. I think she had expected the house we would live in would be something worse, because her expression changed as she saw the inside.

"Why, this isn't bad at all," she said, running her hand along the filigree on the new Franklin wood stove.

I had no idea, as I looked at the stove, how hard it would be to keep its woodbox full. That would become my job seven days a week, winter and summer. On threatening days the stove needed wood stacked extra high in case of rain, and always beside it, a bucket of kindling chips.

Between the range and the back door was--praise be!--a faucet with running water! I think that was the thing that pleased Mama most.

"Do you mean we have running water in the house!" she exclaimed.

Papa looked as proud as if he had just presented her with a new fur coat. "Surprise," he said with a grin, turning on the faucet so that the water ran into a bucket below. "There's no sink, just a faucet, but we won't have to carry water in from the outside."

"We'll have to get a box there under the faucet to put a wash basin on," Mama said, thinking out loud again. "I'll put oil cloth on the box too and that soap dish we brought will be handy."

She turned quickly to the dining end of the room. The table was made of rough boards. Papa said, "This was thrown together by the carpenters who built the house. Not very good for your linen, is it?"

Mama frowned a little. Then, as she saw concern on Papa's face, she brightened. "That'll need oil cloth too. It looks good and sturdy and it doesn't wobble." She tried to wiggle the table with her hand. There were six wooden chairs and they were all alike, which was the most that could be said of them.

Papa led us to the door on one side of the kitchen. The room we entered was our "living room," the full length of the kitchen and nearly as wide. From the ceiling hung the strangest thing. It could have been a hangman's noose, but it was actually just a piece of rope which operated the ventilator in the ceiling. Mama only gave it a passing glance, but to me it was most amazing to see a rope just hanging there. I hoped Papa could take time to explain it, but Mama seemed so interested in the furniture I hesitated to interrupt. There was a "sanitary" couch. I have no idea where it got its name, but that was what Mama called it. It was a contraption with wings that could be raised to make a bed (not as good as our green divan at home, but at least it did something). I leaned my elbows on the square table that stood in the middle of the room and took a closer look at the kerosene lamp. The rough wood scraped my elbows and I remembered the cool smooth feel of the marble-topped table stored in Grandma's attic.

Mama bit her lip thoughtfully.

"We'll need a rug in here and a bookcase, and with table spreads and our curtains, it won't be half bad. I've never seen a lamp like that," she was pointing at a little glass kerosene lamp hanging on the wall in a tin bracket.

"I bought a lamp for every room!" said Papa. "We can put several on the table when we read at night and maybe you won't miss the gas lights so much."

It was thoughtful of Papa, and it was true about it being nice to have lots of light to read by, but those lamps would turn out to be quite a job. Every other day Mama cleaned the soot out of the chimneys with a piece of old newspaper, then washed and shined them. The lamps had to be filled with kerosene and have their wicks trimmed about once a week. It was hard to trim the wicks so the flame wouldn't go off sideways and make a bad smudge on the glass. Later, Mrs. Riggs showed

Mama how to trim them rounded like fingernails so they wouldn't smoke anymore.

"The bedrooms are on the other side of the kitchen," Papa said, leading the way.

One held an iron bedstead and one straight chair. A door led from that bedroom into a smaller one where there was only an iron cot. I knew that must be my room, and I was remembering my room in Lorain with its pretty flowery wallpaper and ruffled curtains and knick-knacks. I thought the only good things about the rooms were those ropes hanging from the ceiling.

But Mama said, "We can make these bedrooms real cozy. I have an idea for a dresser canopy for our room, Dana. We'll use half of a wooden barrel hoop and hang ruffled curtains from it and put a mirror on the wall in back of the curtains. Oh, you'll see, it will be pretty. But what shall we do for a clothes closet?"

Papa beamed. Mama was taking it much better than he had hoped she would.

"If I put up a shelf and pole for hangers, could you put a curtain around it?" he asked.

Mama nodded, "To match the one on the dressing table." There was a far away look in her eyes as if she could see the whole room completed. I wished I could.

Just then there was a knock at the door--our first caller. A Mexican boy about fifteen years old peered at us from beneath a shock of stiff black hair and twisted the brim of a straw hat in his hands.

"Mees Deekson, she say eef you come now, you can eat right away." Then he added, "She ees a good supper," but the sales talk was not a bit necessary.

"Tell Mrs. Dickson we'll be right there, and thanks for coming to tell us."

The boy flashed a smile and trotted back to the cook tent.

"Let's go! I'm hungary as a bear," said Papa as he was pulling on his jacket.

Mama smiled. We had come here to find Papa an appetite like that.

14.

My Very Own Rock

Mrs. Dickson had left her ranch down the mountain to serve temporarily as the camp's first cook. She heard us coming and called out to come inside the cook tent and eat on her serving table. It was too dark now to eat outside on the rough board-and-sawhorse tables the workmen used, and it had gotten cool, so I sidled closer to the warmth and the delicious smell coming from a huge kettle on the big wood range. Mrs. Dickson was a short, dumpy woman in a brown calico dress. She reminded me of Grandma, except that her weatherbeaten skin was almost the color of the calico. Her hair was twisted in a round little bun on the very top of her head. The big apron she wore was as clean as could be, and she must have just put it on for our benefit. As hard as she worked, it couldn't have stayed white for long. Her face was pleasant and she didn't seem at all put out at serving us so late. "Have some Mulligan Stew," she said, and she poured a steaming ladleful into our bowls.

"I was short of meat for supper," Mrs. Dickson explained "so I just shot a half dozen cottontails and put 'em in the pot. After they was done I added some spuds" — she looked at Mama a little doubtfully and said, "that's potatoes, you know — and a few onions and canned peas. Land sakes, it ain't nothing to make a Mulligan Stew."

"Well," said Mama, "it tastes very good." She failed to add that she never had liked rabbit and she didn't think she'd ever go out and shoot anything if we didn't have a bite in the world to eat. It tasted wonderful to me, and when Mrs. Dickson brought out a raisin pie, I thought, that's funny! Raisin pie tastes just the same in Marble Camp as it did in Lorain!

Mama offered to help Mrs. Dickson do the dishes after we ate, but she said, 'Land sakes, when you cook for thirty or forty workmen all the time, a few dishes for three or four don't mean nothing. Besides, you got plenty to do to get your beds ready to sleep in tonight."

Just then the flap on the tent went up and a broad-shouldered, black-haired man with a trim mustache stepped in and greeted Papa. He was so tall that he had to stoop low to enter the tent, and when he saw Mama he swept off his high-crowned felt hat in a hand with a glittering diamond ring. Except for the ring and his knee-high boots, the man wore workman's clothes but they had the look of being tailored just for him.

"Maud; Alma," Papa said, "I'd like you to meet Mr. Kerr, manager of the camp.

"I'm happy to meet you, Mrs. Milner," he said formally.

He stood as tall and straight as my lead soldiers, and I had a feeling the flap of the tent had raised of its own accord to let him enter. Later, when we knew him better, and he talked of the Tower of London and the marble quarries of Italy and the differences between the way they quarried marble in Vermont and Virginia, we could tell he'd been all those places and he seemed even more impressive.

He was an important man to the marble quarry alright. The whole thing had been his idea in the first place, and he had staked his whole future on it.

As a marble dealer and finisher in Denver, he had attended the St. Louis Fair. Among the displays there were samples of marble from the mountains of Southern Arizona. Mr. Kerr's interest was so aroused that he decided to make a trip to see the marble for himself. He had come back from the territory enthusiastic about his find.

"There's a vein that crops out here and there for ten miles, maybe twenty! Think of it gentlemen! I tell you we ought to get in on it!"

His friends had been carried away along with Mr. Kerr, and before they knew it, The Arizona Marble Company had been formed with a lot of capital— $150,000 to begin — and with Mr. Kerr as General Manager.

I didn't know all that then, but looking up at him there in the tent, it seemed to me I should at least curtsey. It was like standing in the presence of the king, or anyway the Lord Mayor of London. He spoke a few more words to Papa, then I thought I heard his heels click as he turned to leave the tent.

When we got back to the house, I thought it was a good time to ask about those ropes hanging from the ceiling. Maybe Papa would have time to explain them now.

"Oh, they are ventilators," he said, "see!" and he gave the rope in the living room a pull. In the center of the ceiling two wings flew up, exposing the corrugated tin roof above. Papa raised and lowered them several times, and it was like the flapping of a butterfly's wings. It was certainly an elegant contraption, but Mama said, "Humph," and it didn't sound as though she thought much of the idea.

She had Papa shift the boxes around and got out bedding to make our beds. As she smoothed a top blanket, she said thoughtfully, "Dana, let's not go to Bowie til the road is done."

"No, sweetheart," Papa said softly, "you don't have to. It won't be bad when there's a road."

On Johnny's next trip to town, Mama sent for samples of material. Mr. Bunch at the general store sent several and Mama picked out one of a silky cotton material with blue flowers on a white background.

Johnny said when he handed him the slip of paper Mama had given him, Mr. Bunch said, "Thirty-five yards, that beats me! What can that young woman want with so much material?"

The clerk, who was looking over Mr. Bunch's shoulder, said, "Some new-fangled Eastern notion, no doubt. Must be goin' ta curtain that whole camp."

Johnny was a little embarrassed by their comments but he felt a certain loyalty to everybody in camp, so he told mother, "I said if Mrs. Milner ordered a lot of material, she's got use for it. That little woman knows what she's doing." He nodded his head emphatically, then he went on, "Mr. Bunch just began to unwind the bolt, sayin' to himself that some day he'd go to Marble Camp and see what in tarnation Mrs. Milner did with thirty-five yards of material."

Papa and I had to agree that Mama knew how to make a pretty room out of next to nothing at all. As soon as Johnny brought the material, she cut it and opened the sewing machine. She ruffled curtains for the windows and quilted and padded the big packing case for her dressing table. The curtains hung full around the shelves that Papa put up for a clothes closet. She made ruffled spreads out of the same flowered material for the bed and trunk. Johnny told us that Mr. Bunch raised his eyebrows, but said nothing when she sent back for ten more yards of it and twenty yards of another sample for my room.

She ordered a blue rag rug from Sears-Roebuck to match the curtains, and when people stepped into that bedroom, they'd catch their breath to find a room so dainty in a camp so rough.

In my room, she used two orange crates to make my dressing table and covered them like hers. I had a covered toy box in my room and the inside of it was covered with a piece of blue flowered wallpaper from my room in Lorain.

The living room had green curtains that we had brought along, and Mama ordered a cheap rug for that room too. Papa made a hanging bookcase above the sanitary couch for the few books we had brought.

The outside of the house left more to be desired than the inside, and there was nothing Mama could do about that.

The man who had charge of all the building at camp was a Denver contractor. He had heard all about the heat of the Arizona desert, so to make us as comfortable as possible he had invented an outlandish canvas curtain arrangement across the front of the kitchen. The wall on the front of the room was screened, and a series of ropes and pulleys operated the canvas curtains outside. He was very proud of the whole idea and showed Mama how to operate it. Mama examined it rather dubiously. She had a right to be critical because that first winter we nearly froze to death. The contractor failed to consider that Marble Camp was over a mile high and winter weather was more to be reckoned with than summer heat. Occasionally we even got snow. Before the year was out, that screen and canvas were replaced with wood siding and windows. Mama was right about it.

The next morning after breakfast, Mama said I could go outside and look around if I'd stay where she could call me, and if I'd look out for snakes. "Be sure you don't go under the house," she said.

I was disappointed. It would have been a fine place to make a play house in the opening with the house up on stilts like that.

At first I stepped around cautiously, but after awhile, when nothing unusual appeared, I became braver. In front of our house, and on the trail down to the office, were rocks and boulders, a few scrub oak trees, and three beautifully shaped little pine trees. Christmas trees in our own front yard! It was another surprise like the water faucet Papa hadn't mentioned. About a third of the way down the trail, a big rock stood directly in the pathway, and I sat down on its flat top to try it for size. It was just the right height for my short legs. Even Grandma would have approved of it.

Suddenly I remembered what Mr. Hendrix had told us: "Always turn over a rock before you sit down. If there are any scorpions or centipedes you can kill them before they get a chance to bite you." I jumped up quickly and tugged to try to pull the rock over on its side. If I had been able to budge it, and if there had really been any bugs under it, I'm not at all sure what I would have done. Run screaming to Mama, no doubt, but since I couldn't move it, I sat down again.

Down below me, the road stretched to the left for a way beyond the office, then curved out of sight around the mountain. Papa had said the road was only finished a little way beyond the bend, so the completed section I could see from the rock was like a door in a wall that didn't go any place, or a telephone when the wires were broken.

The air was so clear it seemed that I should have been able to reach out and touch the mountainsides around me. Little white veils of smoke rose straight up from the stove pipes of the few finished houses There was that pack train of burros again, winding its way down the mountainside.

High above, and all around me, were the mountains. It was as if we lived near the bottom of a bowl. The one crack in the bowl was the spot where the mountains separated to let the road wind out of camp. I wished I was on top of the ridge. More than that, I wished I could reach out my hand, and give a push to topple a piece of mountain over so I could see out.

The rock was getting a little hard. I must bring a doll quilt next time to pad it. This was going to be a good place to watch what went on in Camp.

15.

The Centipede and the Earthquake

Mr. Hendrix hadn't exaggerated a bit, and our introductions to some of the insect enemies that he had warned us about came in our first week at camp.

I'd always been afraid of the dark, and when I was put to bed alone here in the bedroom at night, strange and scary things seemed to be lurking in the corners. For the first two nights Mama left the light turned low, but on the third night Papa said firmly, "It's time Alma learned to go to sleep without a light, I think, Maud."

Mama murmured something about "It's all so new and strange to her, perhaps —." But another look at Papa's face and Mama said, "I guess you may be right. She has to learn some time."

I cried a little when Mama took the lamp out of the room, and Papa called from the other room where he was reading. "You go to sleep now, Pet. There's nothing to be afraid of. You don't need a light to see to go to sleep."

I felt forlorn and forsaken. In Lorain and even in Denver and Bowie Mama had left a light turned low till I got to sleep.

"We'll leave the door open a little and we'll be right here," Papa called to me. I couldn't see his jaw, but I was sure it had that deter-mined look. I lay in bed looking at the ceiling, my eyes following the cracks in the ventilator wings above my bed in the dim light from the next room. As I watched, I thought I saw one section of the crack above me move. I lay very still and watched till I was sure it moved again.

Then I called out,"Mama, there's a bug in here or a snake or some-thing."

I felt triumphant. There was danger after all and I did need a light to be safe alone in the room.

Mama said, "Go to sleep. You're imagining things."

I kept my eyes on the dark object and just then it moved again. "No, I'm not. Really there is something on the ceiling. It's crawling. Please come!"

There was silence for a second, then Papa said, "I'll settle her," and I could hear him lay down his paper and get up from his chair. He carried the lamp with him when he came in, and the light falling on his face made it look as stern as his voice had sounded.

Mama was close behind him, probably worried about what Papa meant by "settling me."

They took one look at the ceiling where I pointed and Papa said in a tense voice, "Alma, get out of that bed and come over by us. Maud, get the broom and hammer and the dust pan while I keep my eyes on it."

I scrambled out of bed and got back of Daddy while Mama ran to the kitchen. When she came back Papa handed her the lamp and took the things she had brought him. With one sweep of the broom he knocked the centipede from the ceiling into the dust pan. To me it sounded like a falling string of pearls as it landed on the edge of the pan and wiggled over the side to hit the floor and crawl toward Mama and me.

Papa grabbed the hammer and gave it half dozen whacks. After the first one it curled up, but a couple more whacks and it lay still. We laid it on a paper and looked it over. It was big, about eight inches long, and had yellow and black stripes. Mama shivered as she said, "It reminds me of a long fish worm, but it's flatter and has a hard shell like a snake."

Its many legs were like little white bones, not soft like spider's legs.

Mama got a quart jar and right then we started our collection of Arizona fauna to show our relatives in Ohio. Papa put some alcohol in the jar and the next day the centipede had lost all signs of the bruises from the hammer blows, and the sight of it gave us goose pimples.

Mama said, "Lorain had flies and ants, but at least there were none of these dreadful things." Her eyes had a far away look in them as if she was seeing Lorain on Lake Erie where you could pull on your shoes without a single glance to see if an enemy lurked in them.

A few days later we added another specimen to our collection jar.

Up on the mountainside in back of our house, Papa had made me a play house out of one of the big packing cases our furniture had come in. He had put the box on its side and raised the lid for a porch roof, resting it on two posts. Mama brought up two old ruffled curtains that she had brought along, intending to use them for dust rags. She tacked them up at the front of the box and draped them back effectively. An old gunny sack on the floor for a rug and some boxes for dish cupboards and chairs made it a fine place to play. My rocking chair from Lorain was too big to put inside, so we put it on the"front porch."

I played there all morning and, as I sat rocking my best doll, I had my first caller — a black and brown spider with hairy legs that was large enough to fill a teacup. It scrambled over the rocks toward my play house as if I had sent it an urgent invitation to visit. The centipede had sharpened my eyes for bugs and all sorts of strange hazards, and the tarantula looked at least twice as big as it actually was. The San Francisco earthquake of four years before was still recent enough to be talked about often by the grownups. Dire things had been said of the earthquake, and as I looked at this horrible spider, I had a sudden revealing thought.

With a scream, I ran down the mountainside to the house shouting, "Mama, come quick, there's an earthquake up here!"

Without losing a minute, Mama grabbed the broom and bounded out of the back door and up the stony mountainside. As a matter of fact, I think she would not have been at all surprised if it had been an earthquake. Anything at all could happen in a country that allowed a centipede to walk on the ceiling above a little girl's bed!

Papa was just coming home for lunch, and when I screamed he ran up the path as fast as he could. He watched the horrible fuzzy thing while Mama ran to get an empty quart fruit jar. Then he sat the jar down over the tarantula and slipped the lid on.

"We got that fellow alive," he said.

I guess it was cruel, but we put the tarantula in the alcohol with the centipede. It was the only way we knew to kill it without smashing it.

Soon, it lay very still. Papa looked at the jar, then looked at Mama and me, and I guess he was afraid that the collection might not be good for our morale. Anyway, the jar disappeared right after that, and when Mama asked him about it, he passed it off with, "Oh, I buried the things. I didn't think we wanted them around."

Mama seemed relieved and we didn't try to preserve any more insects in alcohol while we were at camp. The flatter we mashed the ones we found, the better we all felt.

16.

A Cowboy's Night Indoors

The quarry was operating at last and the whirr from it was comforting, but at the same time it was beginning to be monotonous. From that very first day in camp when I had discovered my rock, it had been a perfect vantage point for watching what went on in camp. It was like a box seat in a grandstand, but it would have much better if there had been more seats and another youngster sitting on each one.

From my rock I was usually the first person to see Johnny and the wagon come around the bend. As I faced the roadway, the quarry was off to the right and a little behind me. By turning a little, I could see one of the tall derrick booms pick up a three-ton block of marble that had been cut from the quarry. With a complaining grunt and creak it heaved the block out of the hole, swung it lightly over the edge, and laid it gently on the two logs the workmen had placed on top of another block of marble.

Over our house and above me, I could see one of the cables that held up the derricks. Each of the two derricks had four one-inch cables strung across the camp to hold it up. One ran right above our house. It made me a little uncomfortable because I had heard the carpenters talking when they were still building some of the camp houses below ours. It was right after we arrived, and one of them said, "That cable ain't safe. Might snap any time. Eight hundred feet long and there might be a weak spot some place."

"Si! Si! And the house of the Milners, she ees maybe git hit."

"Yep, an' it'll be just like squashing a bug. Smash that house flatter'n a fritter."

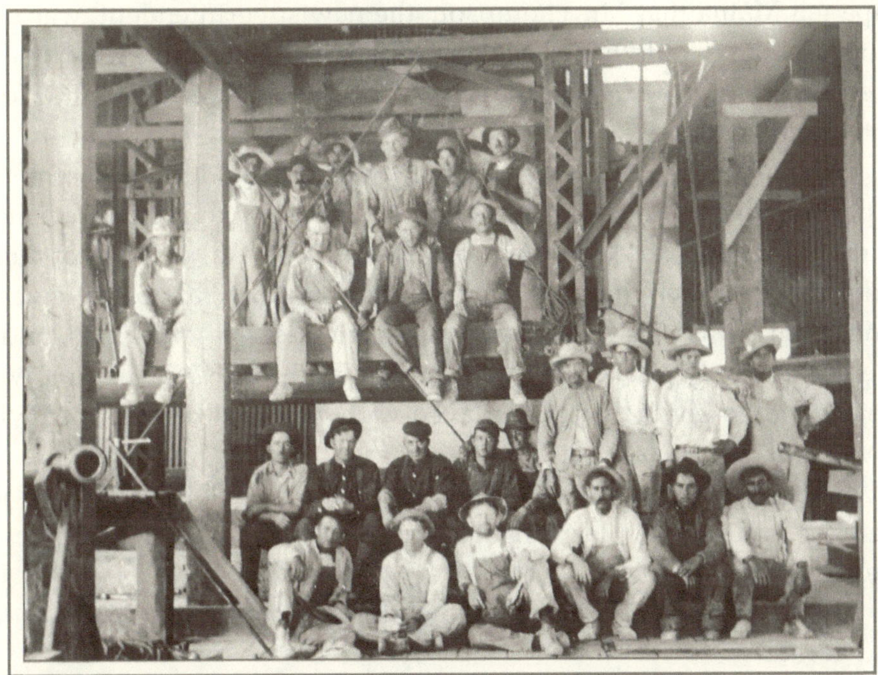

The millworkers and quarry workers photographed at the mill. Sometimes one of them would share his lunch doughnuts with me.

I looked at our house and frowned, trying to think how it would look "flatter'n a fritter." Mama's fritters were pretty flat, almost like pancakes.

When I had told Papa what the men had said, he had just laughed and said, "Oh they figured all those things out. They say it's strong enough to hold ten derricks."

I was reassured, but it had made life interesting to live a little dangerously. "Flatter'n a fritter!" It had great possibilities, but I guess Papa was right because it held up that derrick for more than thirty years after that and never did break.

On this afternoon I was sitting on my rock just hoping something interesting would happen.

One regret I had was that the Thompsons and their four children had arrived in camp when I was not on my rock to watch. I had heard

Papa tell Mama that Mr. Thompson, the new superintendent, was due soon, and that would have been an event in itself, but there was not one overheard word to suggest that there was a Mrs. Thompson and four potential playmates.

When I learned that a whole family had arrived, I raced over to the superintendent's house. I was thrilled and disappointed all at once. Three of the four kids were boys and one of those, Walter, was not much older than a baby! The only girl was Margaret, ten, almost five years older than I was. Still, necessity makes friendships sometimes, and if she was the only girl to play with me, I was the only girl to play with her (everyone knew that girls played with girls and boys played with boys).

Soon Margaret and I were spending a lot of time together as if we were the same age, me learning from her and she greatly enjoying being the older, wiser partner.

But on this day Margaret was helping her mother and I was alone and bored.

The noise from the quarry was irregular. There was a grinding sound above the steady whirring of the drills as the derricks lifted and lowered marble from the quarry to the stock pile. The smoke belched from the stacks and dissolved quickly in the thin air against a backdrop of the mountain. The smell of fresh burning wood hung over the camp. From inside the mill came the constant whirr of polishing as Vermont marble men and laborers from Texas and Missouri put the finish on marble samples to be sent all over the country to advertise the quarry.

I must have been sitting on my rock for nearly an hour when around the bend came a man on horseback.

It was too good to be true, and I jumped up and ran fast down the path to the office to tell Papa. Rushing in the front door I shouted, "Papa, there's a man coming! He's on a horse."

Papa looked up grinning from his ledger.

"Let's see who it is, Pet."

He took my hand and we went outside and down the steps.

A freckle-faced man was unwinding his long legs and climbing down from a tall, lean horse. He seemed young, yet his face was weath- erbeaten. Sitting in the saddle he had appeared short, but as he stood now by the horse, he looked to me like a medium-sized giant. I said, "Goliath" softly under my breath, and then was surprised when he said in a voice that was soft for so large a man, "My name's Bill Shafer, sir. I come from Sulphur Springs Valley over the hill." He pointed at the high ridge to the south of us. And he called it a hill?

He held out a big freckled hand for Papa to shake.

"Glad to see you Bill. I'm Dana Milner. It's been awhile since we've had any company." Papa pulled the office door shut. "Come on up to the house, we'll see what Mother has cooking for supper," he added, looking at me. "We're always glad to have visitors."

In Lorain we would never have invited a total stranger to eat with us, but Papa was getting the same feeling of hospitality that all the West seemed to have.

"Maybe Bill would like to stay all night. You'd like that wouldn't you Pet?"

I nodded enthusiastically, but suddenly I had a disturbing thought. His long legs. They wouldn't fit the bed for company, that sanitary couch in the living room. I had visions of his feet sticking out over the foot like two lean poles turned up at the ends.

I pulled Papa down to whisper in his ear.

He laughed and said, "Alma asked me if our bed was long enough for you, and I think it will do."

"The length of the bed don't matter," Bill said in his soft voice. "They never are long enough anyway, and besides, I'm used to sleepin' on the ground or any old place. When I'm on a round-up or punchin' cattle, all I ask is a sandy spot without rocks. I got my blanket tied to my saddle, carry it everywhere."

We walked single file up the trail to our house. Mama scurried around to get something extra for supper. Papa had a little more work to do and he went back to the office while Bill sat in the living room reading a newspaper that was lying on the table. The papers we got were usually about a week old, but that didn't matter to Bill; he probably hadn't seen one for a month.

Mama and I were in the kitchen getting supper and I had just put the knives around and was laying down a fork when there was a sharp "bang" in the living room. Mama and I hurried to the door to see what had happened, and there was Bill standing in the middle of the room under the ventilator. He looked like he had shrunk a couple of inches, and there was a sheepish grin on his face. A fine shower of dust was filtering down from the ceiling and there was a sprinkling on his head and shoulders. That rope hanging from the ceiling had been too much for him.

It's a funny thing about a dangling rope. Whether it's attached to a school bell, or just hanging from a ventilator like ours, somebody is bound to be tempted to pull it. When it had resisted a slight pull, Bill had given a little jerk and the ventilator had opened with a rush. Seeing the dust begin to come down, he let go of the rope and the wings had fallen with a bang.

"I'm shore sorry, Miz Milner, I wouldn't," — and his voice tapered off ineffectually. The freckles stood out like moles on his red face as he brushed himself off.

Mama laughed. "Never mind!" she said. "someone is always trying those ventilators. We really should take down the ropes."

When Papa came home that afternoon, she whispered to him so Bill wouldn't hear, "Dana, I think we should do something about those things," pointing at the ropes. "Bill Shafer got showered with dust today. He pulled the wings up and let them fall with a bang. He was so embarrassed. My clean house got a coat of dust too," she added ruefully.

Papa climbed right up on a chair, "I'll tie this one up so high no one can reach it. Not even Bill Shafer," he said.

I watched Papa unhappily and dragged one toe slowly back and forth across the boards in the floor. It had been fun to pull down on the rope and run from one end of the room to the other, swinging on it in a wide arc. I had found a way to pull it down slowly so as not to shake down dust. Nobody had ever caught me at it. At least Papa only tied up the living room one. The bedrooms were hardly big enough to get a good running start, but you could hang onto the ropes and swing a little.

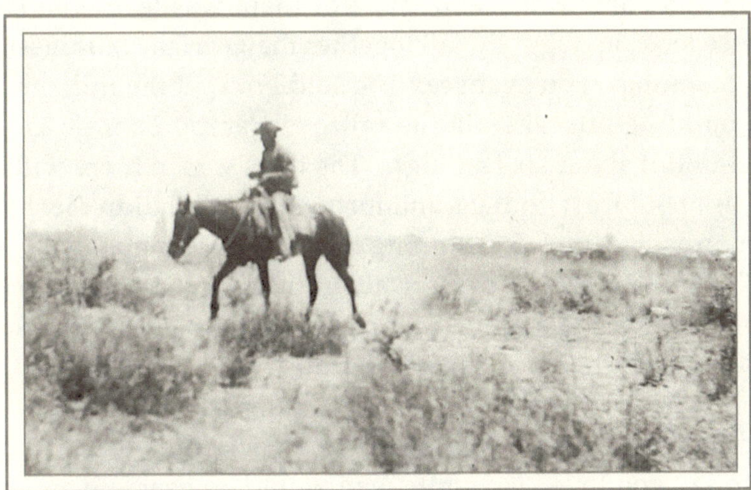

That evening, I was allowed to stay up late to listen to Bill tell Indian stories and about "Early Days" in Arizona. His soft voice and slow drawl made me hang on his words, and I didn't want to go to bed for fear I'd miss something.

He told tales about snakes and coyotes, and he laughed when he talked about them like he wasn't a bit afraid of anything. When he talked about wildcats, though, he seemed to have a lot of respect. He knew a lot about old Cochise and Geronimo, the Indian Chiefs who had carried on the bloody Apache attacks on the whites around Fort Bowie.

Some of the things he told were not particularly good for a five-year-old's ears, and Mama looked at me several times and started to open her mouth to say something. Then she'd change her mind and close it again. One story was about the Indian's dogs.

Bill said, as he leaned back on two legs of a straight chair, "The soldiers was sent to round up Geronimo and his tribe. They brought them to Bowie to wait for the train to take them off to the reservation. They wasn't an Indian in the bunch that didn't have a dog. Some of the dogs was big and some was small, most of them was lean, and some was right nice looking dogs. But all together they was the barkinest, noisiest bunch of animals you ever see. The soldiers kept the Indians in an old adobe building not far from the railroad tracks. There was an adobe wall around it about six feet high. The dogs was in there with 'em and they was about forty Indians and forty dogs." Bill didn't let his fair education prevent him from slipping into cowboy language.

"The Indians stayed in town about three or four nights waiting for the railroad to bring a special car to get them. Seemed like them dogs must a known what was coming, because they howled all night long, so nobody in town got any sleep. When the car finally came, and they loaded the Indians, the dogs stood in a pack in the depot like they'd come to say goodbye. No white man would go near 'em and everyone stood watchin' 'em from a safe distance.

"After the train pulled out, some of the dogs wandered around town lookin' sad, and some walked out o' town on the road to Apache Pass. Their heads and tails was hangin' down and some of the people felt real sorry for them as they watched them mourn for those Indians."

"Couldn't they have taken the dogs along?" Mama asked. "It seems a shame to take even an Indian away from his home and send him to a new place, and then not even let him take his dog along."

"But they was forty of them, Miz Milner! Did you ever see forty dogs in one pile? It's a heap of dogs. And anyway, the town people didn't feel sorry for them for long." Bill was rolling a cigarette almost as deftly as Johnny could. "In a few days they begun to prey on the cattle. First one rancher and then another would find a dead calf. It'd be all torn to pieces with the bones scattered about, and them dogs was as bad as a pack of wolves, after they got real hungry. He struck a match on the sole of his boot and lighted his cigarette.

"They seemed to split up in smaller packs, and some of 'em went over the mountains to live off the cattle in the Sulphur Springs Valley. 'Fore long the cattlemen had to organize a posse and hunt the dogs down. They shot every one of 'em, but not till the ranchers had lost about a dozen young steers and heifers."

I felt sorry about the cattle, but those dogs must have been awfully hungry. You couldn't really blame them. It seemed like it was the people's own fault for not feeding the poor starving things.

After that story, I didn't care if I did have to go to bed.

Mama said, "Come in the kitchen, it's time for cocoa." Cocoa was so good made with canned milk, and Mama made it often; none of us liked to drink canned milk unless it was doctored up.

When our cat went in the living room nobody noticed, but he must have slipped in and crawled on Bill's bed when we were all in the kitchen.

After we finished our snack, Bill said he believed he'd turn in. He said, "I don't need a lamp. I'll just pull off my boots in the dark."

Mama wondered to herself if that was all he was going to take off. She couldn't imagine a man not carrying his night shirt along with him if he might be away from home overnight. In Ohio, all the men wore nightshirts, or so Mama had reason to think. It was just another proof of the ruggedness of the West. No nightshirts! Like as not Bill didn't even own one.

Mama had tucked me in and I lay drowsily listening to the murmur of her voice and Papa's as they prepared for bed.

"E-E-O-OU!" A screech and a howl for the living room broke the silence and I sat bolt upright.

"Help!" Bill shouted. "Help! Mr. Milner! There's a wildcat in here!"

"Mercy!" shrieked Mama, " — a wildcat!"

"Mama, Mama, what is it?" I cried.

"I'm coming, Bill, I'm coming!" Papa strained to make himself heard above the sound of ripping cloth and crashing china, the animal howls and Bill's startled cries.

Mama burst through the door, throwing on her kimono, and Papa followed close behind, pulling on his pants. They lighted the lamp and dashed to the kitchen where Bill was standing in the middle of the room in his union suit. Blood was streaming from his face and he was gasping for breath and daubing at his cheeks with his red bandana handkerchief.

"What on earth happened?" Mama grabbed a kitchen towel and rushed to him.

"Where did it go?" Papa asked, and without waiting for an answer, carried the lamp into the living room.

There, on top of the bookcase sat our cat, his ears back, his hair on end and his tail switching with fright.

He had ripped the curtains to shreds getting up to the bookcase, knocked most of the books off the book shelves, torn the spread off the table, upset one vase, and broken another. And if letting the cat in had been an accident, it was nothing compared to the accidents Tom had from one end of the room to the other. Papa coaxed him down and put him outside while Mama got buckets of warm soap suds and scrubbed and cleaned for half an hour. She had to get clean bedding for the bed. The curtains had to be thrown away the next day as they were beyond mending, and we burned several of the books.

Mama was so mad at that cat she could have killed him, and Bill Shafer shared her sentiments.

Bill said, "I just threw back the covers on the couch, and something flew up and attacked me. I shore thought it was a wildcat."

I spent the next day trying to comfort the cat and tame him down. He seemed to have forgotten how to relax and his tail switched even when he slept.

It was a long time before Mama got the living room back to normal. The scratches on Bill's face would heal in a few days, but I don't think he had any use for even tame cats from then on. With the ventilator knocking dust all over and the cat going crazy, Papa said Bill probably wished he'd slept on the ground in his blanket after all.

All the things, good and bad, that were happening in the house were making it seem like home though. Now it was harder and harder each month to remember just how our house in Lorain looked.

17.

Our First Trip to Town

It was late September and the days were getting shorter. Since June, we had been in camp more than three months when Papa came home at noon one day and said, "Do you girls know anyone who would like to make a trip to the city with me?"

Mama and I shouted together, "We would! We Would!" and hugged each other and then hugged Papa. We had been cooped up in camp so long that we'd have even tackled the trip over the mountains again, but now the road had finally been competed, and the contractor had gathered up his men, his equipment and his losses, and taken them back to Tucson. The road had gone through so much rock formation that the delay had been a disappointment to both the contractor and the Marble Company. But the road — scooped, dynamited, and dug out of the reluctant mountainside by men and horses — was wonderful.

Johnny had been to Bowie over it once, and he came back excited, "Wait till you see it!" he told us. "Makes you think of the Garden of the Gods in Colorado. No more hard pull over the mountains. Prince and Nig will git fat and lazy pullin' that grade. Pretty too. Some places the mountain goes straight up on one side from the road and straight down on the other. Mrs. Milner, you never saw anything like it."

Papa was going to drive us this time and we were to take Colonel and Bob and the light wagon. These horses were the "dress up team," Mama said, but they really didn't even look like a team. Mr. Kerr had picked them for their riding qualities rather than the way they appeared when hitched to the wagon. "Colonel" was salt and pepper grey and stood very still and sedate as we climbed in. "Bob" had a shiny brown coat and proved flighty as all get out. We had hardly rounded the first bend when he shied at a paper fluttering by the roadside. Colonel turned and "gave him a look" like Old Dad Kellum gave his patrons at church that time. Bob acted innocent and lifted his feet and tail a little higher as he trotted along. He was unquestionably a higher spirited horse than Bob, and Papa said, "He's an easier riding horse, but Colonel is more dependable both as a riding horse and when he is fastened in the traces."

The wagon was a light-weight one, black with red spokes in the wheels and fancy red curlycues painted on the side. There was a removeable back seat that had been built by the company carpenter to carry important visitors back and forth to camp, but we didn't use it on this trip.

The days were cool and the nights were very cold now. We didn't need any umbrella to keep the sun off.

It was the first chance Mama had to wear a new hat Grandma had sent her — a wide-brimmed straw hat circled with velvet roses and decked with five elegant turkey feathers. It didn't exactly fit Marble Camp, or Bowie either for that matter, but Mama resolutely took the hat from the shelf and determined to wear it on the trip.

When we were all in our places on the front seat, Papa tucked a lap robe around Mama and me. I felt very important sitting there all dressed up and on my way to town. The Thompson children were standing enviously watching us leave, and I waved at them with unnecessary energy till we rounded the bend.

The road was even better than Johnny had told us. It was a gentle grade, with trestles to bridge five deep arroyos. Big Oregon Pine timbers had been brought to Bowie by long railroad flatcars to construct the trestles. The timbers were held together with great bolts, and a gravel bed was laid over the plank floor of the bridge. Three of the trestles were about twenty-five feet high, but the "Big Bridge," as we called it, was thirty-five feet from the floor to the rock-studded bed of the creek below, a scary distance on a bridge that had no side railings.

Rugged mountains stretched above us on both sides as we rode. In places the slope to the dry creek bed below was gentle, and in other places there was a sheer drop and we rode perilously on a rocky ledge.

All along the way, every quarter-mile or so, we passed stacks of cordwood.

"That's for the traction engine that will take the marble to the railroad," Papa said. "Its steam boiler will burn wood. That's why there is gravel on the trestles, to keep the floors from catching fire from hot falling ashes."

"I wondered why that was," Mama said, tucking the blanket closer around us as a cool wind began to blow, "I thought maybe it was done to keep the horses from being frightened."

Papa smiled. Mama was still worried about the horses. "Well, it probably will help."

Every time we came to one of the bridges, I could feel Mama stiffen a little. The horses' hoofs made a clumping sound like thunder under their feet as we went across. This was Colonel and Bob's first trip over the road, and on the first trestle they did prick up their ears, and it seemed to me they lifted their feet higher as if they were stepping in molasses.

Papa went on, "There will be four flatcars for the traction engine to pull, and each one will carry a big block of marble down to the railroad siding. The traction engine will be here any day now. It might even —!" Here he stopped as though he had thought better of what he had started to say.

As we rounded one bend we passed a small galvanized iron house, and Papa said, "That's a pump-house. There are three more of them and they pump the water from wells in the creek beds. You know that big tank on the saddle above camp?

Mama nodded.

"Well, these pumps work every day to pump water up the mountain to fill that tank with our water supply. It'll take a lot of water for the steam plant at the mill and the traction engine too. Far above us, on a ridge, a lone man was silhouetted against the blue sky. "There's the pumper who takes care of all of the wells," Papa said. "He walks the rounds once a day and sometimes twice." As we watched, the man disappeared behind the mountain.

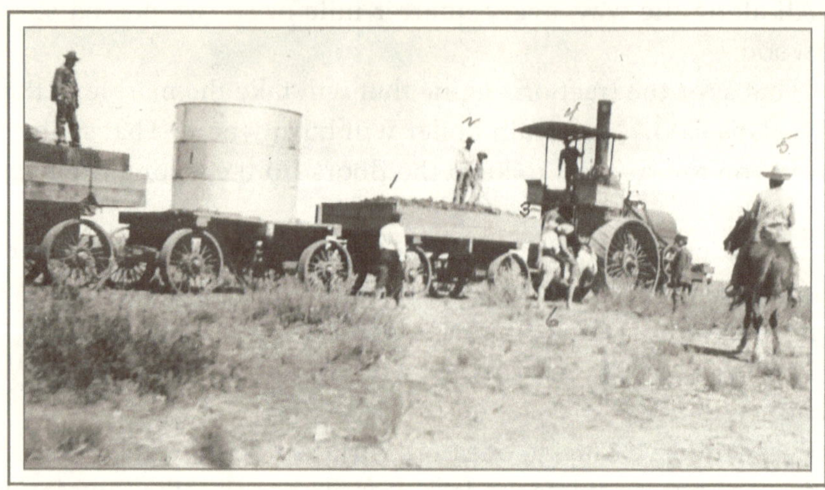

*The traction engine crossing the desert. It often
attracted curious onlookers.*

We were learning a lot as we jogged along, but really we didn't want to think about camp. It was Bowie that was important today. The grade was four miles long to the mouth of the canyon, and we had gone about half way when we heard a strange noise in the distance. Mama turned her head and seemed to be listening even with her eyes. Papa frowned and pulled on the reins to slow the horses down.

Then he looked at Mother and said slowly, "Now, Maud, I was afraid this might happen. That's the traction engine we hear on its way up to Camp for the first time. I hoped they'd wait till we got down off the grade. It will be all right. We'll just find the widest place we can and pull off and let it pass."

This trip was going to be more of an adventure than I had expected. The noise was getting louder and we could see smoke curling above a ridge ahead of us. Papa stopped the horses at a wide spot. "Here," he said as he thrust the reins in Mama's surprised hands and leaped out of the wagon.

Mama looked as though he had handed her a boa constrictor, but she held on to the reins for dear life as Papa stood by Bob and grasped the harness near his left blinder.

"Chug! Chug! Clang!" and a huge top-heavy smoking monster crawled around the bend and crunched into view.

"Whoa, Boys!" Papa soothed as the horses took one look and began to snort and rear on their hind legs. The wagon's front wheels left the ground and Papa had a hard time keeping his footing and holding on to the harness.

The big engine, with four empty flatcars trailing behind, passed us slowly.

As soon as they were passed, the horses put eight feet on the ground again and quieted down.

I glanced at Mama's hands, which were still clenched so tightly on the reins that they were all purple with white spots. I wondered if they'd ever get white again, but I forgot about them as we were able, now that the horses had calmed down, to study the traction engine.

The monster had two iron wheels as tall as a man in back with a smaller wheel in front. Smoke belched from the tall chimney above a vertical steam boiler.

In front of the boiler lay a long round water tank that made the thing look like a small locomotive. A locomotive coming to Marble Camp!

The big wheels, though, were wide where they touched the road, not narrow like a train's. Above them sat a square roofed cab where the engineer and fireman rode.

A boy, probably sixteen years old, sat on the first flatcar and dangled his feet over the side. All at once I wished I could sit beside him. It would really impress the Thompson children if I could ride into Camp on that thing!

Just then the engineer tooted the whistle and there was a mixture of clanking, hissing, and grating of the iron wheels on the rocks and gravel as the crude train slowed down beside a wood pile. The boy on the flatcar jumped up and stood with his hand on the brake of the car, to set it if it was needed. Quickly the fireman climbed down and threw several logs from the stacks by the road, into the firebox as the traction engine continued to roll. As soon as the fireman had mounted the engine again, the boy sat down and waved at us.

The engineer was trying to pick up speed as we stood watching in wonder.

"Mercy, I wouldn't want to meet that thing where there was no wide place to pass," Mama said as Papa climbed back in the wagon. But as she handed the reins back to Papa, for a fleeting moment I had a feeling that she was reluctant to let them go. Papa must have felt it too as he grinned at her and I thought he winked at me as he tucked the blanket securely around us again.

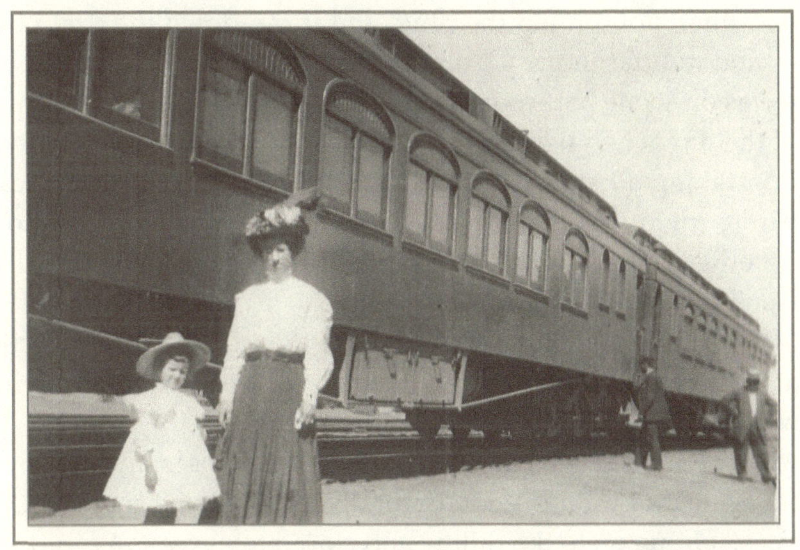

Mama and me at the Southeren Pacific station on one of our trips to Bowie. Don't miss the stylish plume in Mama's hat!

18.

Hindman's Hotel

Although Bowie was slightly downhill from the Rigg's ranch, and the horses trotted at a steady gait, it seemed we'd never get to there.

Papa had telephoned from camp for reservations at the hotel, and when we finally arrived and the porter came to get our suitcases, we felt like we were really back in civilization. Papa took the team to the livery stable while Mama and I got settled in our wonderful room.

We had always taken bathroom plumbing for granted before we went to Marble Camp, but the ugly tin tub in the bathroom on our floor was long enough to stretch your legs out straight, and it looked very inviting.   The water, hot and cold, ran in at the twist of the faucet and ran out when you pulled the plug, and it ran down the drain into real pipes, and not out in the yard as it did at the barber shop.   To be sure, there was only one bathroom for eight or ten rooms, but it was the middle of the day when we arrived and nobody else but me seemed interested in taking a bath.   Of course I had taken a bath getting ready for the trip to town, but one look at the tub and I begged Mama to let me take another.   She laughed and said, "What's struck you to want to be so clean?"

After a little coaxing, she let me fill the tub half full and climb in. That was a good thing because the bathtub was in use at bedtime and I would have been disappointed.

When Papa came back, Mama donned her roses-and-turkey-feathers hat again and we descended proudly to the dining room by the open staircase. I hung on to the railing and closed my eyes so I could imagine the staircase was a circular one and very ornate.

Papa and Mama said the food was good. I was too absorbed by the cut glass vinegar cruet and the crystal finger bowls to notice. Papa left ten cents for the waitress on the snowy white table cloth. I had never seen anybody leave a tip and I thought we must really be rich, throwing money around like that.

The hotel was owned by Mr. Hindman, who made us feel as though we were about the most important people who had ever stayed there overnight. Of course, he made everybody feel that way. The dining room was big as a ballroom, and a landmark between Tucson and El Paso. The floor was polished and the linen spotless. The waiters wore white coats, and the waitresses black dresses and white aprons and caps. Mr. Hindman liked it when people remarked, "This must be a Harvey House?" That was the impression he was trying to give, and the Southern Pacific was pleased to have a restaurant that could compete with eating houses on the Santa Fe up north.

The great migration west was under way, and all cross-country transportation was by train. The Southern Pacific was a main line, and the Bowie station greeted a dozen passenger trains a day. Then the trainmen and most of the passengers got off to eat at Hindman's Hotel.

Trains were to Bowie what teams and wagons were to Marble

Camp — a link with the outside world. I didn't care much for the freight trains.   When they carried squealing pigs or bawling cattle, I felt sorry for the animals and wished I could give them a drink, or at least a kind word as they stopped on a siding at the depot to wait for another train to go by. But the passenger trains! After we ate lunch, Mama and I sat in the lobby of the hotel and waited for a train, any train, to come in. We could tell when it was time for one from the air of activity in the cafe. The waitresses ran around setting tables and putting out pie and doughnuts for the avalanche of customers, and Mr. Hindman came out of his office to puff on his black cigar and look important!

When the train was almost due, Mama and I went outside to wait. Far down the track to the east was a little black speck. The semifores were down so it was not yet "in the block," as the trainmen said. As we watched, the speck got bigger and bigger. The semifore came up to a forty-five degree angle and a passenger train thundered into the station. It ground to a screeching stop with the bell still ringing.

A young Mexican boy in a white coat swaggered out of the hotel carrying a huge Chinese gong in his left hand. In his right hand he held a mallet, and as soon as the train stopped he raised it with a flourish and a loud melodious "Gong-ng-ng" fell on the air, calling passengers to the cafe.

Meanwhile, the fireman scrambled up from the locomotive cab, ran out on the top of the engine, and grabbed a rope hanging from a high swinging joint of pipe beside the tracks. At the same time, he threw a lid back on the top of the engine and swung the pipe around to position. With a mighty pull, he forced the pipe down into the engine connection and opened the valve. He stood with one foot on the pipe and waited for the thirsty steam boiler to get its fill of water. With hands on his hips, he surveyed the station and the crowd.

I watched the fireman till he had the pipe safely connected to the engine, then looked at the swarm of passengers. It was as if a small section of busy Chicago or New York or even Lorain, had suddenly appeared in the depot. Hundreds of people of all sizes, shapes, and descriptions, were milling about. We didn't try to go back into the hotel because the crowd was so dense.

After we had watched the activity for awhile, the conductor suddenly called "Allaboard!" and there was a swish as the people rushed by us to pile on the train. Just then there was the sound of splashing water as it ran all over the engine and fireman. There must have been no way to gauge when the engine had enough.

Mama clicked her tongue, "Ts, ts! That fellow is as wet as a hen. I wonder how he keeps from taking pneumonia in the winter!"

While the fireman had been busy filling the engine with water, another man was filling the coal car from a big bunker by the tracks. "Allaboard!," the conductor called again, and this time he meant business. The fireman, having turned off the water and swung the pipe back to position, slammed the lid on the boiler and climbed back into the cab. The engineer tooted the whistle to call in the brakeman at the other end of the train, and started the bell ringing.

There was a scramble to climb on, as if passengers were sure there was a conspiracy to leave them behind. Mama and I went back inside where the restaurant crew was stacking dirty dishes and scraping doughnut crumbs. There was not enough time between trains to allow for much loafing by the staff.

When we went downstairs to dinner that night, we passed a huge red fire bucket in the hall. Mama turned to take a second look at it and said to Papa, "With all the people in those rooms using kerosene lamps, it's not safe to sleep upstairs. They should have more than one red bucket for water in the hall."

After I got in bed that night, I was afraid to go to sleep for fear the hotel might burn down -- and me in my nightie. But the more I thought about it, the more I thought it would be fun to be carried down a ladder by a man in a red helmet. It would be something to think about as I sat on my rock at camp and wished, oh so much, that something, even a fire or a flood or an earthquake, would happen.

The hotel did not burn down, and the next morning Papa drove the wagon around to the store he called "Solwico" for the things he needed for the commissary. Mama and I walked across the railroad tracks and met him at the store. I hadn't really paid much attention to the store before, but after the little commissary at camp, Solwico looked like quite an emporium.

When we went in that morning, I just sat down in one of the chairs in the shoe department and looked around, thinking what a fine store it was. None of the stores in Lorain had buckets and wash tubs and horse collars hanging from their ceilings. Here, the air was filled with the mingled smell of shoe leather, bolts of cotton cloth, rotting onions, and the vinegar in the barrel at the rear of the store.

There on the counter by me were a shoe horn and three or four button hooks. In an open shoe box was a pair of shoes like Papa had been trying to get Mama to let me wear. They were boy's shoes, wide with metal things at the top to hook the laces under. I had always had black or white kid shoes, but they wore out so fast on the rocks, Papa had been saying he thought I should have sturdier ones. Mama, still living in Lorain with its sidewalks, insisted my feet were too tender for such rough shoes. As I looked in that box, I thought those didn't look so bad. They smelled of new leather and my fingers itched to lace them up. Anyway, it was always nice to get new shoes, no matter what kind they were. I sidled over to the grocery section where Papa was ordering beans and bacon and dried prunes for the commissary. He looked up from his list and smiled at me.

"What is it you've found? Something to wear, I'll bet. She takes after her Mother, Mr. Bunch."

Mr. Bunch looked at me approvingly. So I was to be a potential customer too!

"It's shoes," I answered. "They've got the kind with the little things to hook the shoe laces in."

Mr. Bunch laughed. "Let's go try them on," he said, seeing a chance to make a sale. Mother was still looking over the dry goods. The shoes were too wide, but Mr. Bunch said, "We'll just get a pair a little shorter to make up for the width."

Papa nodded. He knew little more than Mr. Bunch about fitting children's shoes.

He called Mama over to look at them. Her face fell, and when I saw that, I didn't like them so well either. Papa had to sell me again before I was ready to have them wrapped up.

"Lace them up yourself," he said, "see if you can do it. They are high shoes and they'll keep you from getting bitten by snakes and scorpions."

That must have persuaded Mother, for she said with a sigh, "That's right, I guess she'd better have that kind. They look like Marble Camp anyway."

Mr. Bunch wrapped the shoes up and they went in the box with the commissary order. When all the things from Solwico were loaded on the wagon, we were ready to leave for camp. This time there was no dynamite. Papa wouldn't dare because Mama would peer under every stray piece of canvas from now on.

As we drove south, things began to fall into a familiar pattern. There was the Riggs' ranch on the hill. Bread fresh from the oven maybe! Around a Mesquite bush just ahead was "Poor Juan." Beyond the ranch, and to the left, we could see the rock point that jutted out high above Marble Camp. This time we knew what was ahead, including the loneliness we would feel as soon as we rounded the bend into camp.

My rock would be waiting for me and at least I'd have something new to think about. The throngs of people at the depot, the smell of the grocery store, the fireman swinging the water pipe around to the big engine. I'd be rich for a while.

The shoes were the only sour note about the trip. The first time I wore them, they made blisters on eight of my toes, and I cried because I had to curl up my big toe. Mama shook her head and looked disapprovingly at Papa as she said, "I should have noticed they were too short."

Then with a forced little smile, she put them quietly away in their box. When Fidela came to do the washing, Mama got out the shoes and gave them to her for her little nephew. Then she sat down and ordered a pair of sturdy brown girl's shoes from a shoe store in Denver, a store that catered to narrow feet like mine. They cost six dollars, but Mama said, "If she's going to wear that kind of shoes, they've got to fit." She said it grimly as she dotted the "i" harder than she needed to, on one of the words in the order blank.

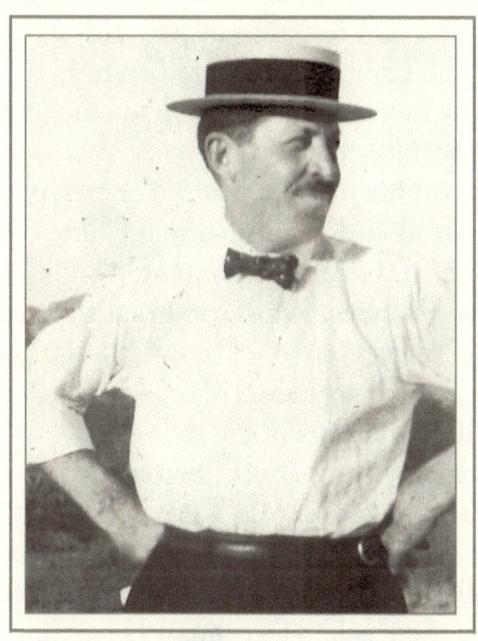

*John Kerr, founder and general manager
of Marble Camp, dressed for the city.*

19.

Mr. Kerr's Mistake

After Mrs. Dickson went back to her ranch, another 'Old Fong"
— not the one we had met in Bowie — ran the cookhouse.
Maybe, to white men, any Chinese cook was just called
"Fong." Old Fong, with one hand on his trusty cleaver and the other in
a lard bucket, believed in quantity for his hard-working boarders rather
than quality.

"Makee plenty buisclit, cookee bean, meat, makee appa pie, alla
time cookee plenty," he said, and that was about the size of it. The men
said the food tasted like it was all cooked in the same pot.

Mr. Kerr ate at the cookhouse with the men for a while, and then one day Papa invited him to have supper with us. I was surprised to hear him unbend and compliment Mama on her cooking as he did. He kept telling her how delicious the homemade bread was and how good the baked corned beef hash tasted.

As he finished off his piece of tart red cherry pie, Mr. Kerr reached for a toothpick from its little hand painted China container by the salt and pepper shakers, and heaved a contented sigh.

"Best meal I've had since we started Marble Camp. Mrs. Milner, I believe you are the finest cook west of the Mississippi."

Mama blushed with pleasure, "Maybe you'd like to eat with us all the time," she said on the spur of the moment.

"I can't think of anything I'd like better," Mr. Kerr answered.

And so it was arranged for Mr. Kerr to take his lunch and supper at our house. His breakfast he still ate with the men at the cookhouse.

We had so little contact with the outside world it was hard to keep track of the days of the week. The camp was running every day, though the office and the commissary were closed on Sunday. When Papa applied for his job, one of Mr. Kerr's questions was, "Do you object to working on Sunday?"

Papa's answer was that he preferred not to, and Mr. Kerr had said, "I guess there's no reason why the office couldn't be closed even though the rest of the camp is in operation."

Sunday morning was my favorite time of the week because, right after breakfast, Papa took down the Bible from the shelf he had built for our few books, and read to me. First he read the scripture as it was written, then he told me the story in language I would understand. He all but dramatized the stories, and they became so real to me that I'd not have been at all surprised to see David stride down our mountainside dragging a lion by its woolly head, or to see Sampson take his stance between the big smoke stacks, extend his arms and push them over with a mighty shove.

One Sunday morning Papa took down the big Bible and said, "time for our Bible story, Alma."

After breakfast I had waited eagerly for him to get shaved and put on his necktie. He always wore a necktie on Sunday, mostly I think to please Mama. I settled myself on his knee and breathed deeply to enjoy the smell of shaving soap that lingered about Papa and mingled with the faint leather odor of the Bible cover.

Papa asked, "What shall it be this morning?"

"Let's have the one about Esther," I replied, "specially the part about the 'fifty cubits high.'"

Papa laughed. When Papa said, "Build a scaffold fifty cubits high," it had an impressive ring to it, and I liked the fact that in the end the villain was to get his just desserts.

Papa had just started to read when there was an imperative knock at the door. Mama, who was washing the breakfast dishes, dried her hands quickly and answered the knock. Without ceremony, Mr. Kerr opened the screen and strode into the kitchen. He was clearly angry and he started speaking as he reached the door of the living room where Papa and I were sitting.

"Mr. Milner," he usually called Papa "Dana," "there's work to be done at the office. I have two important letters to dictate, and that report has to be ready to send to Denver by morning."

As I climbed down from Papa's knee and scampered from the room, Papa said quietly, "I'll be right down if you need me."

Mr. Kerr snapped, "Of course I need you."

"That report is ready for you to sign, Mr. Kerr," Papa said with quiet dignity.

Without appearing to hear what Papa said, or even nodding to Mama, Mr. Kerr slammed out of the house. I wondered what had made him act that way. Papa was not supposed to work on Sunday. I had always stood in awe of the man, and now I was almost afraid for lunch time to come. Then, I knew Mr. Kerr would be coming back up the path to our house to eat.

Mama was very quiet as she went about the work of preparing Sunday dinner. She, too, seemed to be thinking about the way Mr. Kerr had acted. I asked if I might go sit on my rock, and she said, "Uh huh." But when I started out the door she seemed surprised and said. "Where are you going?"

"To sit on my rock. You said I could go."

"Oh, did I? Well, don't stay long," she said, and went back to her work.

Sitting on my rock on Sundays felt very different from other days.

There were no funnies to read because they always arrived in the middle of the week. Funnies, unlike the news, were undated, and it didn't really matter when they came. "The Katzenjammer Kids" or "Grandpa He's a Liar" or "Spare Ribs and Gravy" were good weekdays as well as Sundays, especially with reading matter so scarce.

Mama believed in being quiet and ladylike on Sunday, and she liked it when I sat still for long stretches of time.

That day as I perched on my rock, I looked up at the big fluffy clouds above. Maybe it was the altitude, or it may have been partly the worry about Mr. Kerr being mad at Papa, or maybe it was just the loneliness closing in all around. Whatever it was, I suddenly felt like I was surround by jelly. When I got up and walked back to the house, I had to push the jelly aside with my hands to wade through. When I told Mama about it, she smiled. She had lost her worried look and was humming a little tune as she took the dried apple pie out of the oven. Whatever is was that had bothered her, she must have settled in her mind.

"Get your hands washed." she said, "it's nearly time for dinner. Papa and Mr. Kerr will be coming."

When the two men came in, they were extra polite to each other, but there was an uncomfortable atmosphere in the kitchen. Papa and Mr. Kerr and I sat down at the table while Mama whisked steaming food from the warming oven of the stove and set them on the table. Papa said the blessing and Mama picked up the main dish to pass it to Mr. Kerr.

Mr. Kerr unfolded his snowy napkin and laid it on his lap. As he reached for the dish Mama handed him, she said sweetly, "I'm afraid this is not a very fancy dish for Sunday dinner, sauerkraut and wieners."

She gave a little extra emphasis to the words "Sunday dinner."

If she had slapped his face, Mr. Kerr would not have looked more shocked. He turned pale and his eyes grew big.

"Mrs. Milner, is this Sunday?" he asked. It was almost pathetic to see the big man wilt. He seemed to get smaller as he sat in his place at the table.

He turned slowly to look at Papa. "Dana, I'm sorry.   I didn't know it was Sunday. You know the days are all alike. Why didn't you tell me?"

As I watched the two men, Papa seemed to grow taller as Mr. Kerr shrank. I was glad Mr. Kerr had called Papa "Dana." Now everything would be all right again.

After lunch, we could start over and read about "Fifty cubits high." I might even tell Papa about the way walking through jelly felt. Maybe he'd pay more attention than Mama had.

20.

Mrs. Dickson's Trophy

Mama was always a little envious of Mrs. Dickson's cooking. When we had first come to camp, the men kept talking about their good meals, and Mama overheard one say, "Mrs. Dickson can make a pan of beans or macaroni taste so good I'd keep a job I didn't like just to be near her cookstove." Mama liked Mrs. Dickson but of course that made her feel competitive.

While Mrs. Dickson was still cooking for the construction crew, I went often to the temporary cook tent to visit her. It seemed as though she meant it when she said, "that child is a big help to me."

I could smell her doughnuts frying clear up the hill at our house and I'd run till I got near the tent house. Then I'd slow down and walk in very slowly, as if I just happened to be passing by. Mrs. Dickson would say, "Land sakes, you're out of breath. Here, have a dough-nut." I'd have two or three before I left the tent.

Mrs. Dickson packed lunches for the men and I found that if I arrived at one of the jobs at lunch time and looked hungrily at the dough-nuts in their lunch buckets, they'd say, "Here, girlie, have one of my doughnuts." There were usually several in the bucket.

Mama was a good cook, and she was a little resentful about the way folks raved over those doughnuts. "If I had her recipe," she said once, I'll bet I could make them as good as she does." When I made my next morning call on Mrs. Dickson, I told her what Mama had said. It didn't occur to me that Mama wouldn't care to have that remark repeated.

Mrs. Dickson just laughed and answered, "I'll give your Mama the recipe and she can write it down." Mrs. Dickson was not used to doing much writing.

The next time she saw Mama, she told her what I had said. Mama turned red and tried to apologize.

Mrs. Dickson tucked a wisp of hair in the tight knot on top of her head and said, "Oh, that's all right. Let me give you that recipe right now. Alma shore likes those doughnuts."

Before long, Mama could indeed make them as good as Mrs. Dickson's, but they somehow still tasted just a little different. Mrs. Dickson's plum jam was delicious too, but Mama never could make it quite the same either. Mrs. Dickson's jam was so good I could eat four big slices of bread loaded with it at one time.

She gave Mama the recipe for jam too. "Jest take some prune plumes," she said — there were several plum trees in the yard at her ranch — "and wash 'em and cook 'em with honey instead of sugar. I put in jest about as much honey as I do plums, don't weigh it or nothin', I jest guess. You cook 'em a spell and then you push 'em over on the back o' the stove, and let 'em cool. The next time you build a fire in the stove, cook 'em again. Jest keep a doin' that till they taste right, and then put 'em in the jars and screw the lids on." Mama did just as she said, but I guess she must have missed the moment they "tasted just right." They were good, but not the same.

Mrs. Dickson had raised several children, and she talked about them as if we were well acquainted with them. "Savil says there ain't nobody kin cook like his maw," she'd say, or "You know, Mona, she married her a rich millionaire." We had missed Mrs. Dickson after she quit cooking for the men and left camp to go home to her ranch, and the workers at Marble Camp missed her too when Old Fong arrived to cook. The food was not half as good.

Sundays and holidays were more lonesome than other days. Mama and I still missed getting dressed up for Sunday school and having dinners at Grandma's house. But Mama was beginning to like climbing and she was flattered when Papa said, "You're getting as sure-footed as a mountain goat, Mother!"

She had even ordered material from Sears-Roebuck and made a stout skirt. It was daringly short, hitting her new high boots about half way up. The skirt and boots were all the concessions Mama would make though, as she topped the costume with a frilly shirtwaist and a wide-brimmed Mexican straw hat trimmed with a silk scarf and a big rose. Mama was probably the only woman in the territory who put flowers on a Mexican straw hat.

By this time Papa knew Mama could be trusted to walk and watch out for snakes and little thorny cactus. Experience had been a grim teacher, especially about snakes. She was not likely to forget our experience coming down the mountain ahead of several others on a picnic. That time, a couple of ladies we had met while in Bowie had come up to camp to spend the night and go climbing with Mama and me. We climbed the peak in back of our house early in the morning and had breakfast at the very top.

Mama was leading the way back down the trail when we came to a steep place. She took my hand and we speeded up, almost running for a little way. Below us, in the path, we could see a big flat rock. What we didn't notice was a bed of rattlesnakes sunning themselves there. We came upon them suddenly and there was no way to stop.

"Y-e-e-c-k," Mama shrieked as she grasped my hand and jumped completely over the big rock and the snakes. My arm was nearly jerked out of the socket, but we landed right side up on the trail below.

"Snakes," Mama yelled back at the women behind us, "on that rock! Go around! The women froze in their tracks, and then crept down to peer at the rock from a safe distance above. There were snakes all right. Two big grown ones and little ones coiled in a tangled mass. Mama and I waited below while the women went wide around and looked at them in horrified silence.

When we got back home after watching for more snakes at every step, the women laughed about how funny Mama and I looked, flying through the air, but Mama couldn't see the joke. A snake was a snake in her opinion, and eight or ten in one spot didn't make it funnier.

Papa didn't say anything about climbing for a while, just waited for Mama to say she was ready to go again. But he wasn't afraid anymore that she would forget to watch for snakes.

It must have been a month later, on a lonesome Sunday, that she said, "I'm hungry for a climb again. Let's go over and see Mrs. Dickson."

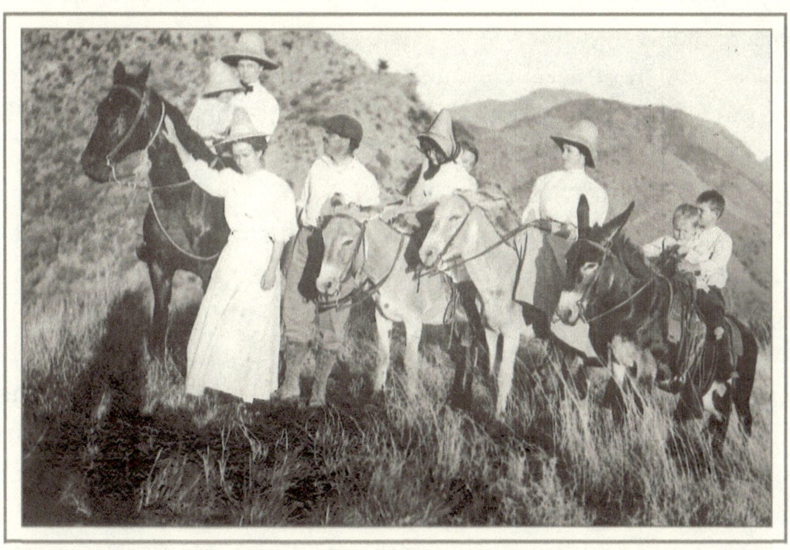

**A group on one of our Sunday picnics. Mama is holding me on
the horse and she wrote on the back of the snapshot that
Mr. Kerr is "flirting with Alma."**

"Fine. I'll go ahead and clear the way," Papa said, smiling. We
knew what he meant. The trail to the Dickson ranch was back over the
two ridges we had crossed on that scary first trip by wagon.

It was surprising how short the walking trip to the ranch seemed
compared to the first trip over the mountains. We hit the lowest points
in the ridges and were there before we knew it.

"Land sakes! I'm glad to see you," Mrs. Dickson called as soon as
we were in earshot. She was dressed in a bee outfit and working with
her hives. Like Mrs. Riggs in the ranch below hers, she kept bees and
her costume would have taken a prize at a masquerade. She had sewed
mosquito netting all around the brim of a large old peaked Mexican
straw hat. The netting was sewn to the neck of a brown, shapeless calico shirt, and the arms of the shirt were tucked into canvas gloves. The
bees knew her well, and were so used to her that she hardly needed so
much protection. "They don't hardly ever sting me," she said. " I jest
wear this outfit as a precaution."

I giggled because she looked so odd and Mama looked daggers at me.

"Come on in and I'll change my clothes. We'll have dinner ready in no time," Mrs. Dickson said, leading us to the front door. She was pulling at her gloves and I hated to have her take that outfit off. It was as funny as a clown's suit.

We could smell a kettle of her Mulligan stew cooking on the stove, and on the kitchen table lay a shotgun. "Something big has been gettin' my chickens. A bobcat I think," she said. "A couple of days ago I found his tracks. Recon' he's gettin' bolder now, and he'll be comin' in the daytime, so maybe I'll be able to git him perty soon. Yesterday the dogs had him treed about dark, but he waited till they weren't watching and slipped down outta the tree and run away. There was jest light enough for me to see him go out of sight up the canyon. Next time I'll have muh gun ready and I'll get him fer shore." She patted the gun affectionately as she took it from the table and stood it in the corner.

"If you do, try to shoot it so it won't hurt the pelt," Mama said jokingly, "I'd like to buy it and have it mounted to hang on the wall."

"Ya cain't buy it, but I'll give it to ya, and I'll be careful how I shoot it." Mrs. Dickson tramped into the bedroom in her sturdy shoes to change her clothes.

In no time she had steaming bowls of Mulligan stew and thick slices of homemade bread on the clean oilcloth of the kitchen table.

"Good thing I made cookies yesterday," she said as she dipped her hand into a large crock and drew out enough to fill a tin pie pan. "I made raisin pie too. Here, have a piece honey, I shore miss havin' you visit me often. It's nice to have people come to see you that like your cookin'." She put a generous fourth of a raisin pie on my plate.

The hike home was not easy because we had all eaten too much, but we reached the house at sunset. As we walked in the door, the telephone was ringing. Mama answered and Mrs. Dickson's voice said, "Mrs. Milner, I got that bobcat fer ya."

"Not really, Mrs. Dickson!"

"Yes, I did, only it ain't a bobcat, it's a lynx. It's got tassels on its ears. That's really the only way you can tell 'em apart. Yessir, I shot it right through the heart. The bullet went clean through, and they was only a little hole where it went in and come out. I used my twenty-two 'cause I figured my shotgun might spoil the skin. The dogs treed him again and I stood right under the tree and fired at him. It wasn't no trick at all. Ya know, he looked so purty up there, I 'most hated to kill him, till I thought about them chickens he'd been stealing. He didn't have no mercy on my old pet rooster. When I thought about that, I got real mad and I pulled the trigger and he come tumbling down. The dogs wanted to tear him to pieces, but I made 'em let him alone. He's shore goin' to make a pretty rug. It's the right time o' year fer his fur to be good. I'm goin' out to the barn now and skin him. I'll nail the pelt to the wall o' the barn like I do skunk skins. When it's good and cured, I'll leave it at the Rigg's ranch for you to pick up."

Mama thanked her again, hung up the receiver, and turned to Papa and shook her head. "What a woman!" she said.

Papa had the lynx skin mounted on felt by a taxidermist in Tucson. There was a double border of tan and green felt scallops around the edge of it, and its glassy eyes stared back at you. It made it a little scary to go in the living room at night. Mama called it a rug, but hung it on our living room wall, and she would have had a fit if anyone had stepped on it.

"I don't believe it would fit our living room in Lorain," she said as she put the last brass-headed tack in the felt mat to fasten the skin to the wall.

I noticed she said, "would," not "will." Mama was talking less about our home in Lorain, and sometimes now she talked about Bowie as though it were the capitol of the world. "When we go to town...," she'd say longingly, and it sounded as though we were going to take a trip to some place important like Lorain or Denver.

21.

The Dentist

It was just beginning to get warm after our first winter in camp, when word came that a traveling dentist was coming up to camp to fix everybody's teeth. I had never been to a dentist and I had no idea, except what Margaret told me, about what "fixing teeth" meant. She said they chiseled holes in your molars and poured in hot lead stuff, and it sounded dreadful, but she should know — she was ten. Margaret was full of case histories too about people who had their jaws broken by dentists who pulled teeth and didn't know what they were doing.

It seemed some people even died with the pain, and most of them yelled and took on awful.

The dentist's name was "Dr. Copp." I remember it because at the time it reminded me of the name of our Dr. Cox in Lorain.

As usual, when someone was expected, I went to sit on my rock to watch.   Margaret came too, and though it was a little crowded, I was glad to let her sit beside me.

The horses that came around the bend were black and sleek and well matched. The buggy, shiny black with swaying fringe around the top, made even our light camp wagon seem big and clumsy. Margaret and I ran down the hill as a fat man in a stylish grey suit stepped out of the buggy at the office. We were a little afraid of him so we didn't go too close, but I was near enough to take a good look at his hands. They were big hands and I whispered to Margaret that I thought they looked strong enough to pull teeth. She nodded, and then we both giggled nervously. Still, I thought his face looked like he was a man who would hate to hurt people and make them yell.

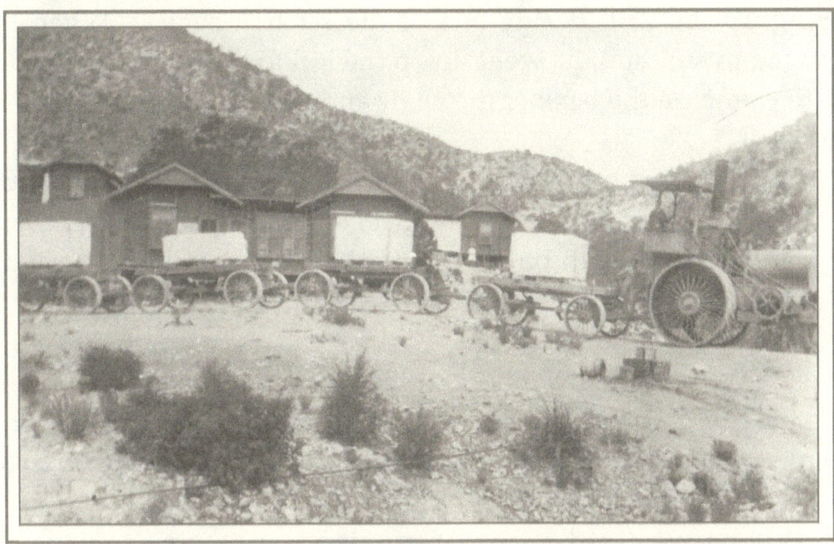

***The traction engine with a full load in front of Papa's office.
(That's me standing in the background between the first
and second blocks of marble.)***

In a few minutes he and Papa came out of the office and Papa directed him up to the Thompson's. We had inched closer and could see the dentist had several fine gold teeth. Margaret wondered if he put them in himself. I told her I didn't think so.

"Mrs. Thompson is expecting you," we heard Papa say.

The Thompson's living room had been turned into a makeshift dentist's office, and since Mrs. Thompson had put up a cot in the same room for him, Dr. Copp would be working and sleeping there till he got his work done. He went to the buggy and lifted out a horrible looking thing that Margaret said was the drill he used for making holes in people's teeth. It had a lot of strings and pipes attached, and a treadle sort of like the one on Mama's sewing machine, only smaller. I didn't see how he could ever sleep in the same room with a thing like that.

Dr. Copp climbed the hill to the Thompson house, and Margaret and I went around and cautiously slipped in through the back door.

With the living room door cracked open, we could see the dentist rigging up the drill beside one of the kitchen chairs. When it was arranged to suit him, he went down the hill to the buggy, to get a head rest to clamp on the back of the chair and a good sized bag of dentist's supplies.

The next morning Margaret and her baby brother, Walter, and I sat on the Thompson's steps and watched Dr. Copp's patients come and go. We kept our ears open but nobody cried out, and it was very disappointing. We could hear the drill and the low hum of voices. Dr. Copp did most of the talking. He kept up a steady stream of conversation, but words we could catch now and then were not about teeth. It seemed to be the quarry he was interested in. Maybe the big chunks of marble being puled out of the ground reminded him of pulling white teeth out of his patients' mouths.

At noon we heard about a man who was coming to have all his teeth pulled. Margaret and I sat on the steps all the rest of the afternoon so as not to miss it. Surely having all your teeth pulled would make a person yell like everything.

Late in the afternoon after work, a Mexican man came from the shacks below and we could tell by the expression on his face that *he was the one*. His wife came with him and she seemed as frightened as he was.

They went inside and, sure enough, after a while we heard moaning and shrieking to beat the band; only it was a woman's voice, and she was really taking on.

Quite a long time later, they came out and the man was holding his red bandana to his mouth. He wobbled a little as he walked.

Dr. Copp followed the man and woman to the door, and we heard him say, "Bring him back in the morning and we'll take out the lowers."

It was the man all right who got his teeth pulled, but the woman had done the yelling. At supper that night, I told Mama and Papa about him wobbling like that and they just looked at each other. Finally Papa said, "Well, Maud, you can't blame Dr. Copp for using whiskey for medicinal purposes. After all, he doesn't give the patients any anesthetics."

Mama nodded, but her lips were pressed together tight.

The next morning the man came by himself, and Dr. Copp pulled the rest of his teeth. The patient didn't make a sound and we wished he'd brought his wife along to liven things up.

After the man left, Dr. Copp came to the front door and looked at us children speculatively. He must have figured he was getting to the end of his available patients.

"Come in, youngsters, and let me have a look at your teeth," he said matter-of-factly.

I had a feeling the sky was falling. Somehow I had no desire to be the one who did the yelling.

"You go first, Alma," Margaret said. It sounded like she was being extra nice to me, but I knew better. Mrs. Thompson came out just then and she said, "Yes, go ahead, Alma." I couldn't think of any excuse good enough to give a grownup, so I went inside and climbed in the chair. What if he had to pull all my lowers or fill some of my teeth with hot lead?

He put a big barber's apron around my neck and fastened it with a safety pin. Then he took a little mirror on a stick and a hooked ice pick and began to poke around in my mouth. I was shaking so I held my knees apart so they wouldn't make a noise knocking. After what seemed like a long time, he laid down his tools and opened his mouth real wide showing his gold teeth.

"Ah! Ha!" he said, and snapped his mouth shut. My heart skipped a beat. It sounded like he'd found trouble all right.

"Keep brushing them, girlie, they look fine," he said as he unfastened the apron and motioned to Margaret that it was her turn.

What a fine morning it was! I skipped out of the chair and flew out of the door.

Going to the dentist wasn't really so bad if you didn't have to lose your lowers.

Margaret's teeth were all right, too, and the next day when the dentist packed up his equipment, we were both sorry to see him get ready to leave. But I guess Mrs. Thompson was glad to have her living room back again.

22.

Music In the Night

The first time Papa ever saw Mama was when she got up to sing a solo in the Methodist Choir in Lorain. The very next Sunday, he asked a friend of his to introduce them, and from that day on Papa's main ambition in life was to marry that Pierce girl. Mama always laughed about it because all the while she had been going several blocks out of her way on the chance that she might run into him near his boarding house.

Next to Papa and me, Mama loved her music, and Marble Camp was about the last place in the world any music lover ought to be.

Papa felt bad about dragging her away from Lorain and her church choir. When she and I were spending that first winter alone in Denver, Mama mentioned in a letter to him that a voice teacher lived near us. Right away, as scarce as money was, he sent her a few dollars extra to take some lessons. Mama didn't waste any time in making an appointment for the first one.

Professor Bund was a fat little fellow with a bald head and very big eyes. I didn't like him very well.   I had to sit on a chair while he had mother sing A-----E-----I-----O-----and so on, up and down the scale, and I didn't see any sense to it. Once when Mama was right in the middle of an exercise, I happened to think she had some little candies in her purse that would help pass the time. I knew Mama wouldn't care at all; she let me get one any time. I opened the purse and was rummaging around when Professor Bund happened to glance in my direction.

"Here, here!" he said, and getting up from the piano stool he strode over to where I was sitting.

He took the purse out of my hands and snapped it shut, looking at me like an owl. I felt as guilty as if I'd stolen a dollar bill. I could feel my face pucker, but when I began to cry softly, Mama put her arm around me and said it was all right. She explained to Professor Bund, "I let her get things out of my purse any time. She knows I don't mind at all." It gave me a warm glow toward Mama, but I didn't like Professor Bund at all after that. I guess the money was gone, because Mama didn't take any more lessons.

At Marble Camp, Mama never complained about not having her piano, but every once in a while she would stop in the middle of her housework and say, "I wonder if Ma is taking good care of my piano." She knew well enough that Grandma wouldn't let anyone lay a finger on it to harm it.

After we had been at camp five months or more, I began to notice that Papa grinned a little when she made such a remark. Once, when she was keeping time to the hymn she was humming, with the rhythm of her dust rag, she stopped and frowned. "I wonder if I'm on key," and Papa chuckled out loud.

It would have been a complete surprise if she and I hadn't overheard Papa's telephone conversation one noon with the man at the freight depot in Bowie. We thought it was just a routine call about something that had arrived for the quarry until we heard Papa say something about "loading the piano carefully," and "will enough men be available?"

Mama whispered, "The piano!" and grabbed my hands and we danced around the kitchen. Papa laughed at us as he hung up the receiver, but I think he was disappointed that it wasn't going to be a surprise.

It was such a thrill to get a package at Marble Camp. Whether it was a pair of black-ribbed stockings ordered from the Sears-Roebuck catalogue, or our piano all the way from Lorain, it was fun to have it arrive. One of the saddest things I remember while we were there was a little formal note that said, "This item is temporarily out of stock. You may re-order in ten days, or we will refund your money." That time the "item" was a bisque-headed baby doll, and I wept with disappointment. Ten days delay sounded like forever. Maybe that was why Papa planned to surprise us. Waiting for things to come was hard.

Johnny made a special trip to town that afternoon for this precious "package," and Mama and I could hardly wait for him to get back the next day. He would leave Bowie early in the morning and the piano would make a heavy load, so it would mean a six or seven hour trip to camp. Everyone in Bowie knew it had arrived. A piano being shipped all the way from Ohio to a rough mountain camp! Who ever heard of such a thing? The party line was busy all the morning, as Johnny was jogging along the dusty road.

Mama started to call Mrs. Riggs but when she lifted the receiver, she heard two ranch women talking.

Mrs. Lawhon said, "It will probably be out of tune and won't be worth two cents when it gets here. That young woman is sure spoiled."

Mrs. Dickson answered, "You're probably right about the piano, but they say he done it without her even asking for it. Ain't she lucky to have such a good man?"

Mama put the receiver down softly and her face got real red. I heard her tell Papa later what she had heard them saying, and he laughed and said, "That will teach you not to listen on the party line, Young Woman."

A few hours after Johnny should have left Bowie, I went out in front of our house to sit on my rock on the mountainside. I wanted to be on hand to see the wagon as it came around the bend.

"Came around the bend!" Those words will always have a thrill to them. Because the road made that sharp turn as it came into camp, it was most exciting to be sitting quietly looking at the clouds and the mountains all around me and to glance just by chance in the direction of the road at the exact moment someone on foot or on horseback, or by team and wagon, appeared. If it was a stranger, he was as surprised as I was, because there were so many bends in the road and nothing at all to warn that Marble Camp was just around this particular one.

Sitting on the rock waiting for the wagon and its important load, I shut my eyes for a moment. If I closed them, then opened them suddenly, I might get a surprise. I didn't dare wait very long as the team and wagon might have come quite a way and I'd have missed part of the thrill. By mid-afternoon Johnny was late, and I went inside to get some bread and butter. When I came out again and sat on the rock to eat, I closed my eyes once more. After a few seconds I opened them, and Presto!, there was the wagon. Johnny was sitting up straight with elbows slightly raised, holding the reins in both hands. It was sort of like driving a team of horses in a circus parade. People were watching him out of their windows. Some of the Mexican workers even came out of their tent houses and stood watching. One little Mexican boy shouted, "L-o-o-o-k, there she ees, the piano for the Milners."

The horses usually found the pull up the grade hard work, and when there was a heavy load on, as there was that day, their heads and tails hung down dejectedly. But just before they rounded the bend, the road leveled out and, though a stranger might not know that camp was around the bend, the horses always knew, and they lifted their manes and tails and sailed into camp at a fast trot. That day they were almost prancing as they came around the bend.

Johnny drove straight to the commissary. He had a few supplies to unload before delivering the piano to our house. As soon as I saw the wagon, I ran down the path. Surely Johnny would let me ride on the seat beside him up to the house. But I was mistaken.

He said, "Better go on home kid, I gotta lot to do before I can git to the piano."

I think he didn't want to divide the honors, he wanted to ride alone up to our house like a fine coachman.

I walked up the hill to the house much slower than I had come down. There was a lot to think about. In the first place, Johnny had spoken sharply to me. Johnny was my friend. I knew he didn't care much about some kids, but he always had that smile around his eyes when he looked at me. Then, besides that, there was something about the piano that worried me. Down at the commissary, they had thrown the big tarp off the wagon and I had gotten a look at what was underneath. I wondered if they had made a mistake. Our piano had been all shiny and polished looking but this one looked like rough boards nailed together. I hated to have Mama see it, but I was afraid to warn her. When Johnny drove up over the rocks and boulders to our back door, half a dozen men appeared at our house to help unload. I don't think anybody asked them to come, but there they were.

Mama stood on the back porch smiling as the wagon came to a standstill. It was at such a tipsy angle that two of the men jumped on the wagon to hold the piano for fear it would break its ropes and pitch out down the mountainside. I watched Mama's face, and her expression didn't change. She just kept smiling. Papa came around the house and he didn't look concerned either. Johnny untied the ropes and the men grabbed hold and strained to lift the thing out. The weight of it made the porch creak.

Mama just stood there looking happy. I couldn't understand it.

Then Papa said, "Get the hammer, Mother."

Mama ran after it, and much to my horror, Papa began beating on it. After some hard taps along the top, the front came off and fell with a loud whack.

There inside, without a scratch on the surface, stood our beautiful piano with its dark mahogany finish and its fancy carved front.

"There's a lot of good lumber in that packing case," Papa said. A packing case – that's all I'd seen! It had never occurred to me that you could put a big piano in a box!

Mama took a square key from her apron pocket and turned it in the lock. As she lifted the lid, one of the men slipped an apple box beside her. She dropped down on the box and ran the scale. The she looked at Papa with her eyes shinning. "It's in perfect tune, Dana," she said disbelievingly.

The men dragged the piano to the living room and Mama dusted it tenderly, just as she dusted our marble-topped table in Lorain. She covered it with a crocheted piano scarf and set a vase of mountain flowers on top of it. It made our house seem almost city-like, and Mama smiled as she went about her work. She sat down and played every little while, and it seemed like she could hardly believe her piano had come.

That night, Mama starred at her own concert, and out on the clean air came the strains of "The Glowworm," "Sing Me to Sleep" and "Just a Song at Twilight."

Papa held me on his lap out on the front porch as Mama sang. It made me kind of homesick, and Papa was awfully quiet. As we watched, one by one, the people below came out in the moonlight and sat on the rocks by their tents to listen. Their lights were out, and except for the moon, the only light in camp that I could see came from the two kerosene lamps Mama was using to see her music.

When she took a breath between songs, the crickets sang an extra chorus. She stopped once in a while and Papa would say, "Sing some more, Mother. It's been so long since we've heard you," and she would open another sheet of music. After a while she closed the piano and blew out one of the lights and Papa carried me in to bed.

As Mama was tucking me in, Papa said, "Mother, the whole camp was listening to you. They are still sitting on the rocks waiting for an encore." Mama just smiled.

The next morning several of the workmen's wives made excuses to buy something at the commissary so they could tell Papa, in broken English, how much they liked the music and "would she do it again?"

Mama gave a concert nearly every night until it got too cold to leave the windows open. After a while some of the people knew her favorites by heart, and it was not uncommon to hear "Sing me to sleep, the shadows fall," down in the tent houses as the Mexican women went about their work.

23.

A Disaster

It was early fall and the quarry had been operating for over a year when Mr. Kerr received a telegram saying we were going to have visitors. The company officials were coming from Denver to look things over.

Mr. Kerr was in a dither. He wanted everything to be just so. Things had not been going too well financially. Operation costs were high and he had to ask for more and more advances to run the quarry. A few orders had been filled, but there was not the demand for native marble Mr. Kerr had expected. Italy still seemed to have most of the market.

"We've got to make a good impression. I want everything to work like clockwork," he said as he ate the last of his pudding at lunch. "I'm especially worried about places for the people to eat. Sleeping is no problem. There happens to be one three-room house empty right now, and I'll have cots put up. Mr. Phipps can use my room."

It would have to be someone pretty important for Mr. Kerr to give up his room, and no wonder. It was at one end of the office and commissary building and was the one luxury spot in camp. The bedroom was large with soft tan painted walls and massive furniture. The bed was a huge brass one with a mattress as fat as a featherbed. The dresser was dark oak with big brass handles on its drawers, and Mama and I were sometimes allowed to slip in when Mr. Kerr was not in camp so Mama could use its big clear mirror to hem the dresses she was sewing.

The dark oak library table held a kerosene lamp with a green bowl and a crinkly glass shade with fringe, the only ornamental lamp the camp boasted. Best of all the furniture was the black leather platform rocker beside the bed.

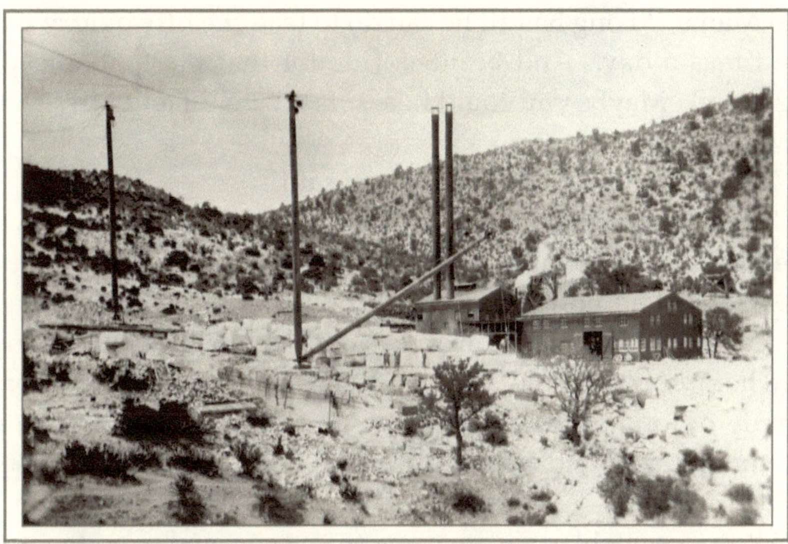

The quarry, booms and marble stack, with the mill and its two smokestacks at the rear.

It was almost as good as a rocking horse, and ingrained in the leather was the good tobacco smell of Mr. Kerr's pipe. There were two Navajo rugs on the floor. It was a man's room all right!

When Mama and I visited the room, I had a special treat rocking in the big tobacco-scented rocker while Mama turned up her hem in front of the mirror.

One end of the room was partitioned off for a real clothes closet and an amazing thing for Marble Camp, a bathroom! There was no tub and the walls and floor of the shower were tin, but the toilet had a fine long brass chain from the high water tank, and there was a conventional lavatory in one corner of the bathroom. "May I pull the chain in the bathroom just once?" I'd beg, and Mama would nod indulgently, knowing herself how citified it made me feel to do it.

It would be a sacrifice all right for Mr. Kerr to give up his room, but he would do it for Mr. Phipps.

The telegram said there would be three men and two women and a young girl.

"I was wondering if you could give them their meals?" Mr. Kerr asked Mama. "Fong has all he can do to feed the fifty quarry workmen three times a day. And besides, I doubt that these people will like Fong's food. Maybe you could take some to board and Mrs. Thompson the others."

"I can feed three of them," Mama said.

"Sure, I'll take part of them," Mrs. Thompson said later when she came to borrow a spool of grey thread.

Mr. Kerr had now been eating at our house for some time and he had been invited to the Thompson's once in a while, so he knew about Mrs. Thompson's cooking too. So everything was settled. Papa laid in a supply of food at the commissary and the company was to pay for everything Mama and Mrs. Thompson used while the visitors were at camp.

All the vegetables we ate came from cans, and even the variety of those was limited. We had only corn, peas, string beans, hominy, tomatoes and sauerkraut, and Mama really had to use her imagination to keep our meals from becoming monotonous.

For this special occasion, Papa telegraphed for a crate of assorted fresh vegetables from Los Angeles. It was timed to come up on the wagons with the visitors. I think Mama and Mrs. Thompson anticipated the vegetables almost as much as the visit of the officials.

As a matter of fact, both of the women were a little frightened about the visitors. They were to come to Bowie by private railroad car, and no doubt they would think even the extra effort Mama and Mrs. Thompson made was very crude.

Mama said to Papa while she was scouring and scrubbing the kitchen, "I'd give anything to have my good things just this once. If only we had the dining room table and chairs."

Papa answered, "Now, Maud, you know they wouldn't fit here. These are good enough for Marble Camp, and besides, those folks will enjoy roughing it. I expect rich people get tired of the fine service they have, and they probably will enjoy your homemade bread and fried eggs fresh from the nest. I'll bet they'll have the time of their lives."

Mama nodded, but she was still dubious.

"At least we should have some fresh vegetables," she said, and that was how it happened that Papa ordered some from the Coast.

A telephone call from Bowie saying the private car had arrived and was in Bowie on a siding sent the camp's two wagons scurrying to town.

Johnny always preferred the heavy wagon, so he drove that one while Papa drove Colonel and Bob and the light wagon. Mr. Kerr stayed in camp to see that everything was shipshape, and Mama and Mrs. Thompson worked fast to do the last minute things. Both of our houses smelled of fresh baked bread, doughnuts, cakes, pies and puddings.

I was so busy dusting and helping Mama that I almost missed getting to my rock in time to see the wagons arrive.

Mama and Papa had talked so much about the importance of the expected guests that I felt sure they would all wear halos or have some other distinguishing characteristics but when the two wagons came around the bend, there were a half dozen tired-looking travelers dressed in dull tans and grays. Why everyone had thought them so special I couldn't see! It was my first discovery that you can't tell by looking at people how much money they have, and that even if they do have a big bank account, they may be eager to make friends and be just folks.

Papa and Johnny drove the visitors to the houses that Mr. Kerr had arranged for sleeping quarters and unloaded them and their belongings. Then they unloaded the groceries at the commissary. Later Papa carried the big crate of vegetables up the trail to a spot half way between our house and the Thompson's and set it on a big flat rock.

Probably the thing that amazed the visitors most of all during their visit, was the big fuss that was made over a mere box of fresh produce. When Papa said, "Alma, get the hatchet and let's see what's in here," I raced home to get it. By the time I returned with the hatchet and the hammer Mama sent along, Mrs. Thompson and four of the Thompson children had arrived and were waiting for Papa to get the lid off the crate, big enough to hold a heaping washtub of vegetables.

The people in the visiting party saw the commotion, and having nothing else to do, came up the hill to see what the excitement was

about. Emma, Mr. Phipp's sixteen-year-old daughter, looked best of
them all. Her shining brown hair hung to her waist, and I'd like to have
run my fingers through it. Papa introduced us all around, smiled and
said, "We ordered some vegetables and we're all anxious to see what
they sent us. If you folks will excuse us, we'll go ahead and open them."

Mr. Phipps said, "Go right ahead. We'll watch."

Mr. Phipps was the largest stockholder in the Marble Company, and
I'll bet it had been a long time since he'd seen a crate of vegetables
opened, if ever. His vegetables all came sauteed or au gratin, or baked
with Italian sauce, and maybe he really wanted to see what a crate of
fresh vegetables looked like.

When Papa had the crate open and pulled back the brown paper,
we all moved up closer to peek in. There were four stalks of celery on
the top, and tucked in beside them were radishes and little green
onions. In each corner of the crate was a head of cabbage. We just
stood feasting our eyes, then Mrs. Thompson reached for a stalk of celery and waved it high above her head shouting, "Look, celery!" It was
like waving the colors in battle. Everyone wanted to have a part in it.
Mama and the Thompson children and I all grabbed the lettuce,
radishes, celery and cabbage and waved them aloft, shouting, "Look
lettuce!" or "What do you know, radishes!" — "As I live, cabbage!"

We laid them out of the crate on newspapers Mama had brought
and dived in for more.

The visitors were drawing closer and grinning from ear to ear. We
were getting close to the bottom of the box when Emma, Mr. Phipp's
daughter, tossed her shining hair, grabbed a head of cauliflower and
waved it aloft shouting, "Cauliflower!"

Perhaps she had been so carried away that she didn't remember
that every day in her world cauliflower, lettuce and cabbage were as
common as sunlight in Arizona. Or perhaps she was making fun of
us. We didn't know which, but it was queer how her joining the game
suddenly dampened the fun. We all looked at her soberly and began
to lay the vegetables back in the crate.

Then Papa said briskly, "Now, we'll divide them up. There are four
of everything for each family. Here, Mrs. Thompson, we'll put yours in
the crate and we'll put ours in a pile on the newspaper."

That night, Mama served lettuce and celery with our supper.   It was the first time I remembered tasting either, and I thought they were very much overrated. I was a little disgusted that we'd all made such a fuss over something that tasted like that.

Most of the buildings, and all of the houses in Marble Camp faced the highest point in the ridge which Mr. Kerr had officially named "The Rocks." Whenever we "took a climb," we had to decide which spot in the bowl of mountains we would aim for. On warm days, or if we got a late start, we'd usually climb to the lower ridges or to the peak in back of Camp, but on brisk days, and when we got an early start, we'd follow the trail to "The Rocks." Actually "The Rock" would have been a better name, because at the very highest point of the mountain a huge square of rock like a giant parcel post package jutted out of the forest of pine and cedar trees.

The trail to "The Rocks" was steeper and a long way for my short legs. I always voted for some lower point. But on days when we got to the summit and walked out to that big rock, it was always worth the climb. The winds coming up the two sides of the mountain met at the top, embraced and struggled in our hair. The thin air smelled fresh and good. The crack of the twigs underfoot was magnified in our ears. We could see a hundred miles in every direction, and if we had brought a visitor along, Papa would say, "Over there is Bowie. You can see the trees and the water tanks. Out there, to the East, you can see San Simon. To the South is Old Mexico. It's ninety miles to the border, but you can see way beyond that."

Mexico was a foreign country and I was always a little uneasy about that part. It was like looking in the enemy's keyhole. Mexico was full of wars and rumors of wars. I had heard Mama and Papa talking about what they read in the papers.

"This is wonderful country," Papa would go on, "the only time the Lord ever pulls the shades down on the view is when He knows the trees and grass need rain, and that's not very often. Maud, do you re- member what a short distance you could see in Ohio?"

On the Saturday while the visitors were there from Denver, Mr. Kerr asked Mama and Mrs. Thompson if they'd mind packing a lunch for all of us to go on a Sunday picnic to "The Rocks." To go climbing was our "trip to Coney Island," or "visit to Aunt Mary's farm," or our "Beach Party," and there was an excitement about it that broke the monotony of days without incident.

Sixteen of us were strung out along the trail that Sunday, besides the two pack burros borrowed from a woodcutter to carry our lunch. Mr. Kerr and the visiting delegation led the way, then Mama and Papa and I, followed by the six Thompsons. It was more fun to go climbing when there was a big party, and for a while the grown folks laughed and shouted back and forth as we climbed.

Mr. Farley called, "Old John there (meaning Mr. Kerr), he climbs like a mountain goat. We can't hope to keep up with him."

Mr. Hughes said, "Oh well, look at his boots. If we had boots like that we could climb easy too."

Mr. Kerr was just ahead of me on the trail. I looked at his boots, heavy brown leather with hooks for the laces part way up and two straps and buckles at the tops. When Mr. Kerr dressed up, he looked like a man in Mama's fashion books, but in his work clothes, he looked as work-a-day as any of the men. The boots were scuffed and worn, and there was not a sign of polish on them. They didn't look like magic boots, but I wondered if there were something to what the men said. Mama had read me a story about a cat with seven league boots, and Mr. Kerr went along in such easy strides that climbing wasn't any effort for him at all. Maybe I could get a pair and they'd be a big help. Still I didn't dare ask him about them. He'd probably laugh at me.

As we climbed, the men stopped talking to save their breath. There was only the scrape of our feet on the rocks and an occasional whippoorwill calling to its mate. The sky was blue and there was not a cloud. On rainy days a cloud sat on "The Rocks" and covered them up, but not today. The weather grew colder as we climbed. When we reached the base of the big rock, Mr. Kerr said, "Let's stop here and rest before we make the last spurt to the top."

Everyone was more than willing, and the Thompson children and I sat down on the rocks beside the path. The quarry below looked like a toy village with smoke rising from the many chimneys as the people began to prepare their Sunday dinners. A skeleton crew was working the Sunday shift at the quarry, and the giant stacks lorded it over the little chimneys as they belched forth heavy grey smoke.

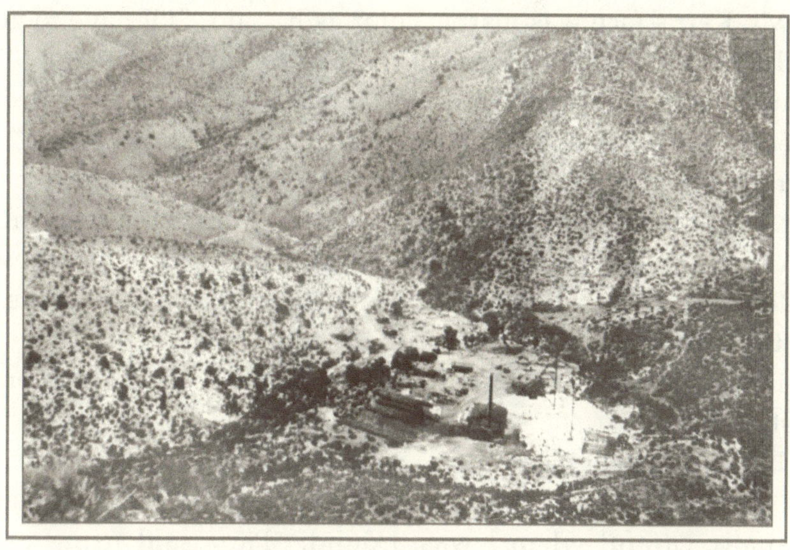

Looking down on all of Marble Camp from a spot high on a mountain trail.

Mr. Kerr had one foot on a log and was resting his elbow on his raised knee as he looked proudly down on Marble Camp. Everything was going better than he hoped.

I was looking at Mr. Kerr and wondering if I'd have nerve enough to ask him about his boots.

Suddenly a look of horror came into his face, and he shouted, "My God, there goes the stack!"

Everyone turned quickly toward where Mr. Kerr was pointing. As we watched in stunned silence, one of the great stacks settled slowly to the ground, trailing smoke as it fell. One of the cables that held it up had snapped and the others had slowed its descent so that the tons of iron went over like a wand on a windless day. The silence was ominous as we all held our breath to wait for what we sensed would arrive later. It was like two separate events — seeing it fall — and then hearing the tremendous booming thud that followed.

Fortunately, the stack had fallen away from the mill and the quarry.

Mr. Kerr's face was marble color as he said, "I'll have to go," and hurriedly took off down the trail.   Then he turned to shout, "No use for the rest of you to spoil your picnic. There's nothing you can do." He added in a low voice that carried on the still air, "Nor I either."

I felt sorry for Mr. Kerr as I watched him scurrying down to the disaster. He had been trying to impress the visitors and everything had been going so well, and now one of the stacks had come down and spoiled everything. It would probably affect the opinion of the quarry that the men would take back with them to Denver.

But worst of all, I thought, was the fact that Mr. Kerr swore when the stack fell.

In spite of rough camp life, very little profanity ever reached my ears. Papa had no patience with anyone who used it, and the men were unusually careful when I was around. Papa said using profanity showed a lack of vocabulary. When I asked him what that meant, Papa said it meant the people just didn't know enough words and that was why he wanted me to get a lot of schooling, so I'd know a lot of words to use and wouldn't have to take the Lord's name in vain.

It was funny about Mr. Kerr! He'd been to college and traveled abroad and could talk well on so many subjects you'd think he wouldn't have to say, "My God, there goes the stack!" He should have been able to think of some fine, high-sounding language in a crisis like that.

It worried me a bit all day, and on the way back to camp that afternoon, I decided I'd talk to Papa about it. There must be some explanation.

After he told me my Bible story that night, I said, "Papa, what made Mr. Kerr swear when the stack fell down?"

Papa smiled a funny way and thought for a minute, then he said, "You know Alma, that was not really swearing. It was almost like a prayer. Like Jesus said when they were crucifying him, 'My God, My God, why hast thou forsaken me?' I don't believe the Lord counted that against Mr. Kerr as swearing. I think he was just breathing a prayer."

I was glad Papa explained it to me, and Mr. Kerr rose in my estimation.   A man with such funny boots! It was nice to know he'd pray like that in public.

24.

Chicken Thief

Fresh meat was scarce, and it was a real occasion when they butchered a calf at the Riggs ranch or the Dickson ranch, and Johnny would stop to get a hind quarter to bring to camp. Papa was the meat cutter, and he passed the meat out to the upper camp and the cookhouse. We'd eat well for a couple of days, then go back to canned corned beef, bacon, and salt pork.

Before we had been in camp long, Mama had told Mrs. Riggs on the telephone one day that she thought we ought to raise a few chickens. Mrs. Riggs said she had some laying hens she could spare, and Mrs. Dickson, who was listening in on the party line, said she had a rooster she could sell us and one old hen that wanted to set. It was late in the season to set a hen, but she said we might try it.

There was such a difference of opinion about which breed of chickens was best. Mrs. Riggs said, "Rhode Island Reds are better for this county." But Mrs. Dickson said, "Nothing like Plymouth Rocks! They lay wonderful in the mountains." Everyone said ours would be half-breeds, and I couldn't see what difference it made. A chicken was a chicken, and any chicken tasted much better than corned beef or salmon out of a can.

We picked out a spot about a hundred feet back of our house for the coop and chicken yard. Papa and I did the building after his working hours. It was my job to hand Papa the tools and help hold the wire and screen in place. The coop was the first thing I'd ever helped build, and I was as proud of it after it was finished as I would have been of a piece of mahogany furniture. On the rare occasions when company came, I managed to coax them out to see the chickens, mostly to get them to admire the coop. Usually they didn't notice how special it was and I had to say, "I helped Papa build this chicken house. Here on the end he let me pound some nails." That impressed them, and I let them go back to admiring the chickens.

It was nearly a year before the smart skunk figured out how to get under than fence Papa and I built. One of the hens had been going around clucking and Mama said that meant she wanted to set. Johnny had stopped at the Riggs ranch to get a setting of eggs and Mama had the nest all ready for the hen. But that night, before Mama could get the eggs under her, a skunk burrowed under the fence and sucked the blood of the setting hen, and before Papa could get there with his shotgun, it slipped out of the deep hole it had dug to get into the pen. Mama was so mad! We could eat the eggs, but it meant we would have to wait until another hen started clucking before we could get a new setting and start all over again.

One hen did take a notion to set before long, and when it was about to come off the nest with baby chicks, Papa said, "Alma, can you help me after work tonight? We'll have to mend the fence before those eggs hatch or else that skunk may try to get in again." Papa had a way of making you feel as though he needed you. We fixed the fence good and tight that time, putting two-by-fours all along the bottom and nailing the chicken wire to them and piling rocks along the sides. Papa carried big rocks and I filled in with smaller ones.

When we were finished, we called Mama out to show off our work, and she laughed and said, "No skunk can get in that yard now."

For a while it looked as if Mama was right. The batch of little chicks came off the nest, and ten of them survived and grew till their pin feathers began to appear. Another hen, setting on eggs Mama got from the Dickson ranch, hatched nineteen chicks from twenty eggs. That was a very high percentage and Mama was proud of that hen and chickens.

One night I was ready to go to bed early because I was to wear a new nightgown Mama had made for me, dainty white nainsook with a square ruffled neck and a ribbon sash. "Like a nightie a princess might wear to bed," I thought. It was Friday, and although Saturday was our usual bath day, Mama let me take my bath early so as to be extra clean when I put it on.

As usual, there was a big teakettle of water on the stove at meal time.   After supper, Mama brought in the wash tub, put it in front of the cook stove and filled it with hot and cold water. We had two wash tubs, one large and one smaller, that hung outside on nails in the wall.

The large one was for washing clothes and taking baths, and the smaller one for rinsing clothes.

A grown person really had to fold up to take a bath, but I wasn't so crowded, and if I shut my eyes I could imagine that I was a princess in a marble bath, the same kind of marble that they were cutting out of the quarry not five hundred yards away from my house. It was an odd thing that with all that marble for the taking, I was sitting in a tin tub!

Mama let me take a bath by myself now, all but drying my back, but she helped me put on my gown. The warm bath had made me sleepy and I could barely keep my eyes open long enough to say my prayer. The nightie felt soft, and I put my nose under the cover to smell the perfume of new material.

Ever since the centipede on the ventilator, Mama had left the door ajar till I went to sleep, but this night she was able to close it as she left the room. She and Papa always read a while before they went to bed but after a while they went to their bedroom too. As the camp settled for the night, the chirp of a cricket or the hoot of an owl was the only sound that broke the stillness. Sometimes one of the Mexican's dogs would bark and all the dogs in camp would join in, but that was on moonlit nights.   This night was dark and the dogs were still.

Suddenly there was a terrible racket up at the chicken house. Papa jumped out of bed and grabbed his pants off the chair by the bed.

"It's that old skunk again," he said. "You light the light, Mother, and I'll see if I can get him this time. Stand in the doorway and hold the lamp high." Papa was jerking his pants on over his nightshirt, "Gotta hurry or he'll be gone."   By the time Mama had found the matches and lighted the lamp, Papa had grabbed the shotgun and streaked up the mountainside.

Mama rushed to the open door and held up the lamp. I clutched at her gown and both of us peered into the darkness, trying to see what was happening up at the chicken coop. We were shivering with excitement, and the coolness of the night air. The chickens were making an awful commotion. It was as if every hen had laid an egg and wanted to tell the world about it. The roosters were shouting too. It sounded like what Mama called "pandemonium."

Then all at once Mama began to scream at the top of her voice. "DA-NA, COME HERE QUICK!" Something had brushed by her and scampered through the open door into the house. I threw my arms around Mama and yelled too, though I hadn't seen or felt anything, and didn't know what we were yelling about. Papa came rushing down the path. He only knew something had happened to Mama and me, that it was more important than what had happened at the chicken coop. The lamp was teetering in Mama's shaking hands.

"Dana, Dana, the skunk! It ran in our bedroom! It touched my skirt as it went by. Oh, what will we do-o-o!"

By that time Papa had taken the lamp and Mama could wring her hands. Papa set the lamp on the table and tiptoed over to the bedroom and closed the door. He usually knew just how to handle an emergency, but not this time.

"If I try to chase it out it'll surely ruin the house and everything we have."

"But, Dana, we can't stay in the house with a skunk in the bedroom!"

It was cold outside by now, but we were afraid to close the door because we wouldn't be able to make a quick getaway in case the skunk "let go." After a while, when nothing happened, we all sat down on the edge of the kitchen chairs to try to figure out what to do. Mama and Papa were talking in whispers so the skunk wouldn't hear.

Finally Papa said, "Well, here goes, I'm going to open the door and see what happens."

He picked up the lamp and tiptoed to the door. Then he waited a second. There was no sound from the bedroom. Cautiously he turned the knob and pushed on the door ever so gently. The skunk was out of sight. It must be under the bed. He set the lamp on the floor just inside the door and got down on all fours. Mama and I scarcely breathed as we peeked around the door. He waited again, then slowly began to inch himself forward, scooting the lamp ahead of him as he tried to see into the shadows. Mama and I were poised, ready to run out of the house at the first sign of danger.

All at once, "Cut, cut, cut, cudaw-cut!"cackled the frightened mother hen as she came flapping out from under the bed and half ran, half flew, out of the bedroom past Mama and me, through the kitchen and out the open back door. As glad to get out as we would have been to get our "skunk" out, she shrieked all the way up the mountain in the direction of a scrub oak tree. Dad hurried to the door with the lamp, but the hen was lost in the darkness. She was still cackling.

Mama and Papa fell into each others arms and laughed. I didn't laugh. I felt sorry for the hen. After a while Mama said, "Alma, you must get back into bed or you'll take your death of cold."

She crawled in my cot to warm me while Papa went back to the chicken yard to see what had happened to the skunk and the chickens. She knew I wouldn't go to sleep until we were all settled down again. This time Papa had time to light the lantern. He was gone quite a while. There wasn't a sound from the chicken yard. When we heard his footsteps coming back, Mama and I sat up and began to shout questions.

"Was the skunk still there? Did it get any of the chickens?"

Papa sort of mumbled and it sounded like "a few." He blew out the lantern and the lamp, which was still burning in the kitchen, and began to get undressed again. Mama went back to their room and they talked in low tones.

Slowly my eyes got heavy and I could feel myself drifting off to sleep, but just then I heard Papa say, "All nineteen of them. Sucked the blood of every one."

I sat up with a wail. "Papa, did that skunk kill *all* our baby chickens?"

Papa hesitated, "Yes, and two of the hens beside. I'm not sure whether it was before our 'skunk' got in, or while we were trying to figure out how to get him out. Anyhow, we'll have a mass burial in the morning. Go to sleep now." Then he said to Mama, "This is dangerous country for chickens."

Mama said, "Only for chickens?" and they both laughed, but not like they really thought it was funny.

I was wide awake again, and I lay a long time planning the funeral we'd have in the morning. We always "said a few words" over birds and animals that died. Since we'd come to Camp, we'd held funerals for a chipmunk, two birds, three baby mice (they died at Papa's hand) and a lizard. I never was sure whether the Almighty would expect us to hold funerals for the chickens we ate; it seemed sort of wicked to chop a chicken's head off and then pray over it. It was very late and I could feel myself getting sleepy again. Just before I drifted off, I thought of something I wouldn't dare tell Mama and Papa. I was really disappointed that the skunk had been only our old hen. I knew it was wrong to wish it, but a skunk under the bed — that would have been something!

25.

High Time for the Wedding

Every morning, the sun came over the mountains, glanced off the white marble by the quarry and began to warm the tin rooftops of the Mexican camp houses below.

Every Monday morning, Fidela Navarette Salinas got up with the sun and climbed from her tent house below to our back porch to do the family wash.

Fidela was the only Mexican I ever saw who had rosy cheeks. Her hair was shoe-polish black and wavy around her plump face, and she had graceful arms and hands that she waved in the air as she talked gleefully of this and that.

Mama tried several washwomen before she found Fidela, and the main trouble with the rest was that she couldn't depend on them. At the least excuse they would fail to show up when Papa had the water hot and everything was ready for them to start the washing.

Fidela was as faithful as her name implied. She even came to wash the day after her baby was born, wagging the little bundle in her arms.

Mama exclaimed, as we peeked in the blankets, "My stars, Fidela, you should be in bed for at least ten days."

Fidela laughed heartily and said, "Oh, ees nothing to have a baby. Is bad to having toot pulled, but the baby, no... When the doctor is pull out the toot you no got nothing. When you born the baby, Caramba! You got the baby and you got the flat stomick." She patted her middle proudly.

Mama always said she had never seen anybody who could get

clothes as white as Fidela. In fact, even the Mexican women ungrudgingly acknowledged her as the best washwoman in the Chiricauhua Mountains.

On Mondays, Papa got up a few minutes early to build a fire under the big blackened wash tub on the mountainside back of our house. When Fidela came, Mama gave her a bar of soap. She cut the soap in tiny flakes and stirred vigorously to dissolve it. When the soapy water suited her, she took two buckets of it to her wash tub on the bench on the back porch. She didn't seem to scrub hard on the washboard. To my eyes, it was more like she was gently coaxing the dirt out.

When we had first come to Marble Camp, Mama hadn't liked to gossip, but before long she was so lonely that she began to look forward to wash day and the choice bits that Fidela always brought along in her broken English. One morning when Fidela arrived, there was an air of importance about her. As Mama handed her the bar of soap, the washwoman said, "Have you hear the news, Miss Milner?"

"No, What is it, Fidela?"

Fidela's cheeks got pinker than usual as she said, "Ees 'bout Maria y Juan."

"Oh," said Mama, "did the baby come?"

"No, no. They going to marry weeth the Priest."

"Get married!" Mama looked at her in amazement. "Why, don't they have four children and another one due any time now?"

"Si, four keeds, that's why the Preist say she got to marry weeth her hosband."

Mama was sorting the laundry into neat little piles. "Do you mean Juan and Maria weren't married before?"

"Si, but weeth Senior Hendrix in Bowie, not with the Priest."

Senor Hendrix, the postmaster, was a Jack-of-all-trades who also performed, with varying efficiency, his duties as coroner, notary, and judge.

"Oh, I see," said Mama, but she sounded doubtful.

Fidela went on, "Anastasia say Maria can wear the wedding dress of her, but ees not beeg enough. Maria say ask eef you can make heem fit. She ees more beeger now as Anastasia."

Mama nodded, "Tell her to bring it and I'll see what I can do."

It was not the first time Mama had made alterations for the Mexican women in Camp, but it was the first time she had let out a wedding dress to fit a pregnant one.

Soon after Fidela went home that afternoon, Maria climbed the path to our house carrying Anastasia's white wedding dress in her arms. It was an elaborate affair of white satin and lace, and I thought it was the most beautiful thing I had ever seen. Mama set to work with a mouthful of pins to let out tucks and seams.

"If I make it shorter waisted, I won't have to cut into it," she said, as she lifted the skirt higher on the waist.

Maria talked matter-of-factly of her approaching wedding as Mama pinned and fitted. "When the Priest come the las' payday, he say eef we no marry weeth heem, we no can stay in the Catholic church." She rolled her eyes at the thought of it.

"But you have four children," Mama said, slipping the skirt of the dress over Maria's head. I couldn't see what difference that made, but Mama seemed to think it was important.

"Si, si, that ees make us to get marry. I tell Father Flores, 'I weesh you wait leetle longer. She ees come the baby, and then I can hold heem and he can see me and Juan marry weeth you.' He is say, 'You wait too long now." Then she added wistfully, "I weesh she is wait. I theenk is going to come the baby before the next pay day."

Father Flores was a hard-working little man in a dusty black robe who came up to Camp twice a month to call on his flock. He came in a battered wagon, driving a pair of old Mexican ponies, and I always watched for him to come around the bend on payday. It was no accident that he always arrived on that day. Mama said probably the fact that he laid claim to a portion of the workers' wages gave the little Priest more influence over his parish in Bowie than he would otherwise have had. The amount he assessed each member was gauged more by the needs of his small mission church there than by his flock's ability to pay. One time, as Fidela scrubbed she said, "We eat nothing only beans thees week. The Priest he need lots of money for make a new fence for the church." Her plump figure indicated that she liked to eat, but she sighed resignedly.

All afternoon on the day of the wedding, I sat on my favorite rock and watched the preparations at the tent houses below. There was great activity as the men carried the furniture out of one tent to make room for the dancing. The air was filed with the pungent odor of tamales steaming in a wash boiler over an open fire. Every once in a while, one woman came to lift the lid and look. Since each tamale was securely wrapped in corn husks, there was no tasting or other testing to be done. She probably only wanted to smell them a little better, but she did it with an air of authority.

Late in the afternoon, the Priest drove into camp accompanied by two other men and a Mexican lady in a bright red dress. Maria came out and greeted them and she and the lady disappeared into her tent house. The two men went to the house that had been cleared of furniture. They carried in several big wooden boxes and some musical instrument cases.

Mama came outside to watch with me. "I wonder what's in those boxes," she said.   I wondered too. Before long, the men brought the boxes out and laid them beside the tent house. They seemed to be empty.

"I don't see how there is room for anything in that small building if they are going to dance," Mama said.

"After the wedding," Papa explained when he got home from work, "they are going to have a puppet show. Those two fellows who came up with the Priest are musicians and puppeteers from Mexico."

"What is a puppy tears?" I asked hesitantly.

Papa laughed, "Puppeteer," he said. "The men make little dolls and animals do things on strings. They do it from behind curtains." I had a vision of lace curtain (Papa said it was behind curtains they did it) and dolls and real live pups and kittens running around stepping on pieces of string.

But Papa had said it was a "show," and a show in Marble Camp was something!

"Can we go, Daddy?" I asked hopefully.

Mama looked horrified. "Mercy, no, all those germs in that tight little room!"

Papa looked at her soberly as he said, "Now Maud, Alma doesn't get to see much. These men are from Mexico, and it should be educational! I think we'll take her. It won't last long, they'll be in a hurry to get to dancing. She can still get to bed early. I doubt if there are any germs in camp that will hurt her."

Papa was trying to answer Mama's objections even before she could think of them. He knew Mama was beginning to worry because I was not in school, so mentioning it being educational was a good point.

Mama had an injured air as she said, "You told me yourself those men were from Mexico, and you know, Dana Milner, that Mexico is full of smallpox and all sorts of things." Mama was still living in Lorain in some ways. Her tone when she said, "of all things," sounded as if she thought anything that came from Mexico was dirty, catching , heathen, and doomed.

Papa smiled tolerantly, knowing he'd get his way.

Just at twilight, the bridal party gathered outside Maria and Juan's tent house.   We stood with the others as the Priest read the service. Maria held the hand of the youngest child, little Juanito, and the other three with their clean faces and slick brushed hair, stood proudly by their mother and father while the whole Mexican population of the camp looked on. No one seemed to think it strange that Maria with her bulging figure, should be standing there in a white wedding dress and white veil, surrounded by her four youngsters, while the Priest conducted the service. The Priest spoke in Spanish, and Juan and Maria's voices were barely audible as they recited the marriage vows. Once tiny Juanito began to wiggle and Maria tapped him sharply on the head. After that, the Priest spoke faster.

As soon as it was over, Papa and I walked up to our house with Mama.

She said, "It will be too stuffy with so many in such close quarters. I think I'd rather stay home." She was still a little miffed.

When Papa and I got back to the tent house, the room was packed with standing people. Fidela, just inside the door, saw us looking in hopefully and she passed the word along.

"Meester Milner and Chiquita Alma they come see our show. Make room for heem," and there was a waving motion as the crowd moved to make a space for us. In one corner of the tent house, two pieces of brown cloth were strung on a wire. The audience stood facing the "stage" in the corner. They pushed me to the front row to stand with the other children. More people were crowding in and the air was stifling with garlic and tequila. Just when it seemed our lungs would burst for lack of air, someone pulled on the ropes that controlled the canvas-covered frames on three sides of the tent house. As the canvas "windows" went up, everybody took a welcome breath of the fresh night air.

There was a whirring sound and a tinpany Edison phonograph began to play a fast Mexican tune. The curtains parted and a tiny ballerina in a shining red satin dress took the stage. I was astonished and the audience in the tent was spellbound as other tiny figures pranced, cavorted, danced, and sang at the end of their strings. If no one had thought to pull up the canvas window frames, it would not have mattered now. We were scarcely breathing anyway.

There was a dancing chorus with dashing caballeros. A beautiful Spanish senorita went to the city to become a great singer. She fell ill and couldn't pay the rent. A sinister man in a black coat and hat came and was mean to her. He made her go out in the cold and snow (confetti from above). It all turned out well because her old sweetheart came and took her back home. He lifted her, flowing skirts and all, and swept her off the stage to great applause from the spectators. The show ended with an exciting bull fight and frenzy of yelling in Spanish on the part of the spectators. This puzzled me a little as I couldn't understand whether they were yelling for the matador or the bull. The matador bowed low as the curtains were drawn, and I could hardly bear it that it was all over. Never had I seen anything so wonderful. Mama really should have come.

As Papa and I walked up the hill in the moonlight, the two puppeteers began to tune up their guitar and mandolin. The dancing lasted till nearly dawn, and all the camp was glad that Juan and Maria had seen fit to follow the Priest's advice and make their peace with the church. Perhaps by the next payday their new baby would arrive and a christening could be held. But it couldn't possibly be as good as the wedding.

When Papa came and knelt by my bed to hear my prayers that night, I had a important question to ask him. It was, "How long will it be till I can get married, Papa?"

He smiled, "Quite a while I hope, Pet. Why?"

"Because I can't wait for my puppet show," I replied.

Papa threw back his head and laughed so hard Mama came to the bedroom door to see what was so funny.

Finally he stopped laughing and said, "They don't usually have puppet shows at weddings, Pet. This was just added because the musicians happened to be puppeteers. Those two men probably saw a way to make some extra money on their trip here to play for the wedding, so they just brought their puppets along."

Usually I could depend on what Papa said, and to believe what he did. But this time I just couldn't quite do it. Anyway, I decided, I am going to have a puppet show at *my* wedding. The wedding wouldn't have been half so good without the puppets.

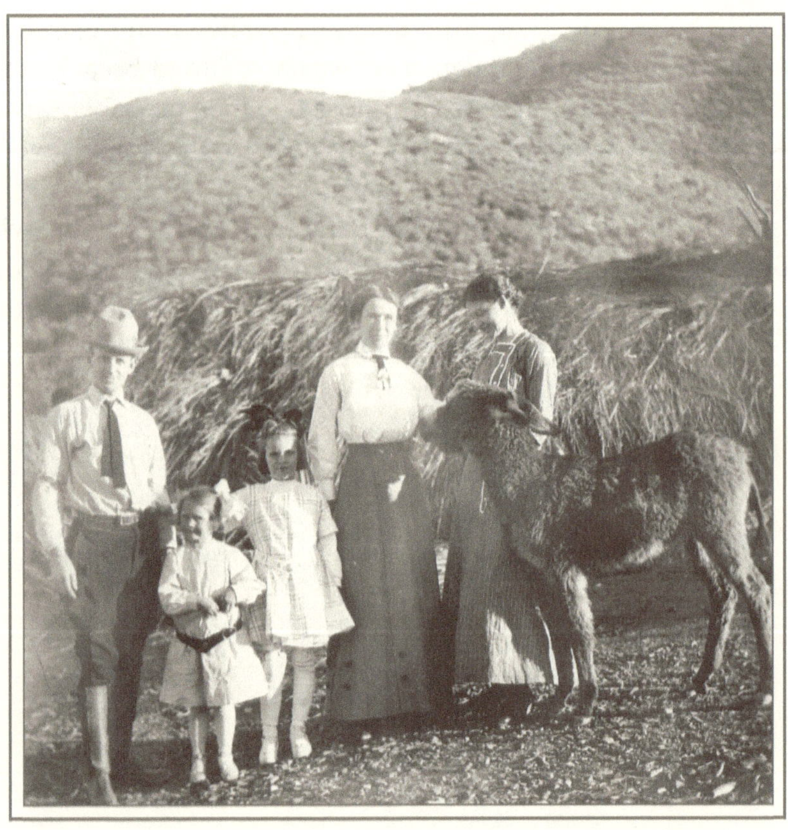

From left, Papa, me, Margaret Thompson, Mama,
Mrs. Thompson and our burro, Daisy.

26.

Daisy's Big Day

After he came home from his office most days, Papa would go to the corral and work with Daisy but, try as he would, he couldn't seem to break her. "I can't understand it," he'd say with a puzzled frown. "I never had a bit of trouble breaking horses on the farm when I was a kid, but I'm having trouble with that burro. She bucks her head off when I try to slip a saddle or bridle on her."

Finally one day after a long session at the corral, Mama and I saw him coming up the path, pleased with himself. "Daisy wore her saddle for a half-hour without bucking," he said. "I'll try riding her next time. I'm taking it slow and easy." It was a week later on a Saturday afternoon that Papa came home from the corral and said, "She's as meek as a lamb now, and I think we'll use her to carry the lunch when we climb the mountain tomorrow."

Most every Sunday Mama packed our lunch and we went on a picnic. Every so often the quarry would shut down on Sunday to clean the big boilers, and when that happened, Mr. Thompson, the superintendent, didn't have to work. This was one of the times, so our two families could picnic together and I'd get to be with all of the Thompson children.

Mrs. Thompson came over to our house that Saturday afternoon to plan the lunch. "I'll make potato salad and we can both take sandwiches," she said. "It takes a mountain of both for my four hungry boys and girls."

"I'll get at a batch of doughnuts," Mama said, poking the fire in the cookstove and pulling her apron off the nail on the back door.

Usually when Mama made doughnuts, she'd pop several of the pieces she punched out of the middle into the hot grease. These were for me and they tasted better than the doughnut rings – much better. Doughnut holes were a stolen treat – dough that should have gone back in the batter to come out properly in rings. They were delicious. I stayed close by in the kitchen to watch and be ready to eat the first hole that tuned brown in the deep fat.

"Not a single one this time," Mama said. There'll be such a big crowd with the Thompsons going that I'll need every scrap of batter. Run outside and play, so you don't even smell them."

I thought it wouldn't hurt to let me have at least one hole, but I did as she said. Later, when I came into the kitchen, there was a heaping mound of sugared doughnuts cooling on the bread board. My mouth watered, but I remembered what Mama had said about needing every scrap for such a big crowd, so for once I didn't taste.

No lunch was complete without coffee cooked over a camp fire, and Papa got out nine tin cups and put them in the blackened five-pound lard bucket we used to make picnic coffee.

I had a very special reason for liking picnics. Mama didn't believe children should drink coffee, but when we climbed on a Sunday, she let me have a cup. She put water in it to weaken it for me, but it still tasted faintly of coffee and made me feel very grown up. At home, most every morning I drained the last few drops from her cup when she wasn't looking, but Papa and I both had the same kind of strong conscience. If someone came in the room and said, "Who took the buttonhook?" or "Where are my spats?" we felt as guilty as if we had swiped or hidden whatever they were missing. It was very uncomfortable to feel so guilty when you really had no idea what they were talking about. So, I always enjoyed the cup of coffee I drank on the mountain, with Mama's blessing.

The next morning, while Mama packed the doughnuts and our sandwiches and pickles in the box with the tin cups, Papa went to saddle Daisy. When he led her up to the back porch, I thought her eyes looked a little red as if she had been out all night, or hadn't been able to sleep for some reason. Papa had a little frown on his face, but this was the day he had set for her debut as a lunch carrier and he couldn't back out now. As they came up the path, Daisy laid one ear back a little, but she didn't pull back on the rope as she had when we made the first trip to Marble Camp. At least Papa had made progress there.

Papa tied her by the house and brought out the box of food with the tin cups and lard bucket, and Mama's everyday forks and spoons.

"You stay back away from her heels, Alma," he told me.

He placed the box on one side of the pack saddle and put an empty box that would hold the Thompson's share of the lunch on the other side. Throwing a rope over the boxes, he passed it under Daisy's belly a couple of times. Papa knew all about knots and he explained to me as he worked.

"We'll use a square knot here, Pet. See, it won't slip." He gave a tug to tighten the rope. Daisy flinched a little and shifted her weight from her left feet to her right. The four Thompson kids had arrived carrying the rest of the lunch and watched as Papa loaded the pack.

"And now we'll..." Papa didn't finish because just then a hen flew out from under our house and went cackling up the hill.

Maybe she had laid an egg or maybe something had frightened her. We didn't know the cause of her excitement, but she did seem in a dreadful hurry.

The pinching of the rope and the cackling of the hen made Daisy prick up her ears and jump. The tin cups rattled loudly in the lard bucket. With a look of fright, Daisy reared back and broke the rope that was holding her. Once free, she took off up the mountain leaping and rattling the tin cups as she went. The more the pack rattled, the faster she ran.

Suddenly she stopped dead still. She hesitated a moment as though saying to herself, "How stupid of me! It's easier running downhill." Wild-eyed, she whirled and charged down upon us. We scattered in all directions as she cut her own path down the mountainside by our house. Then pandemonium broke loose as men ran shouting from all directions in the Camp to chase her.

Papa yelled, "Head her off before she spills the lunch!"

It was no use. Running with complete abandon up one hillside and down another, she scattered tin cups, sandwiches and salad through the bushes and over the rocks. Mama and I stood watching in stunned silence and a horrible thought struck me.

"The doughnuts! She'll spill all the doughnuts!" I yelled. "Stop her, Daddy! Don't let her spill all the doughnuts!"

The panting men behind her were getting winded but Daisy seemed as fresh as ever.

At the foot of the camp in the ravine stood a gaunt scrub tree with only a few leafy branches at the top. Straight out of the side at about burro height stuck one lone, bare, half-dead limb. As Daisy tore madly down the mountain, she made a sharp turn and appeared to be going to dash her head into the tree trunk in her haste. But as she made a desperate leap that limb slid neatly between her and the pack saddle, holding her as if in a sling. There she was, pawing the air and panting her head off. As the men ran up, she laid her ears back and snorted, flailing her legs in the air about four or five inches off the ground.

There was no picnic that day, and as Papa and Mr. Thompson sawed off the limb and let Daisy down, Mama and I watched in disappointment. You could never predict what Daisy would do. When her feet hit the ground, she suddenly melted and became as gentle as a lamb.

The men led her away to the corral and I turned reproachfully to Mama. "You didn't let me have a single hole."

Without a word, Mama went up the steps to our front door. I followed her into the kitchen. She took her apron off the nail on the back door. "Let's make a batch of doughnuts right now," she said as she tied the strings in a neat bow in the back. "Hand me a stick of wood while I stir up the fire."

The next day, Papa sold Daisy to a woodcutter for ten dollars. Mama and Papa and I watched her being led away from the corral, and that was one time I didn't have any regrets. As we turned to go to the house, Papa said, "You know, Pet, I think those little Mexican boys had a good reason for laughing when they told me I could 'buy the burro of Andres.'"

After that, we looked for cups and silverware all over the hill, but we never found a trace. It was funny how they disappeared, but then Daisy hadn't taken any of the trails we used. She had made her own.

27.

Callers

Mama was clearing the lunch dishes from the table one cloudy day when we heard the "clop, clop" of horses' hoofs on the rocky trail in back of our house.

Once the road to Camp had been finished it was not often anyone approached from that direction, and I climbed on a chair to look out of the high transom-like windows above the kitchen stove. Mrs. Riggs was coming down the steep path on a high-stepping horse. She had on a full velvet divided skirt riding habit with a fluffy ruffled collar, and on her head at a stylish angle was a large hat with a white plume. She might have been "the fine lady who rode a cock horse to Banbury Cross" in my Mother Goose book.

Pauline was perched on the saddle behind her. Sometimes she rode in back with her arms around her Mother's waist. Other times, Mrs. Riggs slipped her around and let her ride in front where Pauline could hang onto the saddle horn with both hands. She had been riding with her mother since she was a month old, and she could travel miles over the mountains without complaining.

Papa and Mama ran out calling greetings to them, and Papa lifted Pauline down. It was the first time Mrs. Riggs had ever come unannounced to visit us, though she had come a few times before in her buggy by way of the road. I heard Mama say, "Why Anna Mae, what a nice surprise," but I didn't come out to join the welcome because I was very busy inside.

All the family in Lorain felt sorry that I had so few playmates, so they often sent me toys. I had eight or nine dolls, toy furniture, fancy valentines, and even a few toys for boys.   I liked my things neat and unbroken. Always Pauline left a trail of destruction. She had the strongest little fingers for removing doll wigs, poking in eyes, and tearing off doll dresses without bothering to undo the buttons. She could pull the cover off a book with ease. I was so happy to have her come that I suffered in silence, but I had learned to hide my favorite things before she arrived. The only time anything was ever said to her was once when she picked up a lovely valentine of mine. It opened into a big red fan and it was one of my prize possessions.

Mama was watching that time, and when Pauline said, "How does zis work?" and tore it open with a jerk, my stomach turned over and Mama frowned. When Pauline saw "how it worked" she tossed it aside and began to look for something else to operate on.

Mama saw how my face fell as the fan ripped apart and she said, "Why, Pauline, Alma has had that for months, and hasn't torn it."

Mrs. Riggs just laughed. She used a hairbrush to paddle Pauline's bottom fairly often, but being destructive with toys apparently was not one of the crimes on her list requiring punishment.

"It's just a valentine isn't it?" she said with an indulgent little smile. Nobody said anything more, and I decided then and there that I'd always put away my best things when Pauline came to see me. Of course it was to be done secretly, and Mrs. Riggs was never to know.

Mama has always said this was one of her most embarrassing moments, for I forgot to be discreet this time, and as soon as they all reached the house I came flying out of the living room and said, "Hello, Mrs. Riggs. I almost didn't get my best dolls put away in time." Mama looked horrified and Mrs. Riggs had a frozen smile on her face. Not for anything would Mama have had me say anything to hurt Mrs. Riggs' feelings.

She changed the subject abruptly. "Come and have a bite to eat, Anna Mae. We've just finished, but there is plenty left."

Anna Mae said, "Oh, we brought sandwiches and ate on the way."

"I'm still hungry, Mama," Pauline was pulling off her blue corduroy jacket.

As we entered the kitchen, she ran to the toy box and began throwing the older things I'd left there out with enthusiasm.

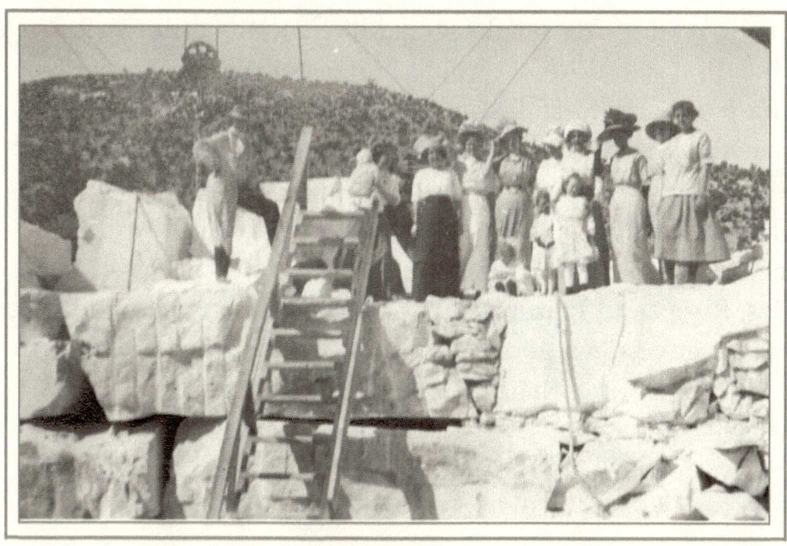

*A group of women sightseers standing at the
edge of the quarry.*

Mother was glad to hear her say she was hungry because I always embarrassed her by wanting to eat when we stopped at the Riggs ranch, and besides it eased the tension I had caused. She gave Pauline a slice of cake and a dish of stewed apricots.

The grown folks all went into the living room to chat and Pauline and I stayed in the kitchen at the table.

As soon as we joined the others in the living room, Pauline began a systematic search for my dolls. I had slipped them hastily under the "sanitary couch." Since Papa was sitting on the couch, the side could not be raised and I knew Pauline couldn't get at them. Putting them there seemed to have been a happy thought, but I knew Pauline would eventually figure it out and wanted to find some means to distract her. Suddenly, with a whoop, she climbed on the piano stool and began to bang a four-year-old's music.

The folks were trying to talk, and the louder they talked the harder Pauline banged. After what seemed like a long while, Mrs. Riggs said, "Pauline, that will do now. You'd better not play any more."

In a panic, I said as fast as I could, "Oh let her play. She likes to play and she doesn't have a piano at home. She's not hurting anything. Just let her play."

Mama, who didn't want her piano mistreated, gave me a "For-goodness-sake, be still child" look.

Mrs. Riggs and Pauline didn't stay long after that, and when they left, Mama gave me a good talking to about contradicting grown-ups and made me sit on a chair. It was not one of my red-letter days.

28.

The Horror in the Privy

Down at the workmen's tent houses there was one privy for every three or four houses, but up on the hill each house had its own. Ours was about a hundred feet up a winding, stony path in back of the house. It was a three holer, and one of the holes was child size, built lower than the others. The walls were the usual one-by-twelve boards, and there was a little screened window near the tin roof on two sides. I wondered why they bothered to put the screen on those windows because the boards soon shrank in the Arizona sun so that they were nearly a half inch apart, and the flies seemed to be snickering at the screened places as they crawled in and out whenever they pleased.

The toilet hole was very deep, and when it was dug, Jacques, the company dynamite man, had been called to do the blasting and break up the rocks.

There were little toilet shacks scattered all around the camp, but not all had children's seats. That was a luxury only ours and the superintendent's house had.

Inside the privy, in a corner by the door, Mama kept a little box of ashes. Every time we "went up the hill" we threw a little scoop of them down the hole.

When we first went to camp, Mama had a stock of old dress patterns, and they were kept in a small box beside the ashes. Later, after we accumulated catalogues that were out of date, Mama tied one by a string to a big nail.

One day one of the workmen stopped at our privy on passing by.

Mama happened to see him, but the outhouses seemed to be public property so we thought nothing of it. However, it wasn't long before another workman came to the little building, stepped in and shut the door. He only stayed a few seconds, and when he left, Mama, who had been watching from a back window, went to the phone and called Papa.

"Dana, there's something odd going on," she told him. "One of the workmen went into our shanty, and after he left, another one came. I wonder why they are coming to ours. There are plenty of others at the quarry."

Papa said he didn't know, but he'd find out. Mama hung up the receiver and went to look out of the window again. Strangely enough, another man was walking up our little trail, looking furtively in the direction of our house. Mama stood at the window with her hands on her hips. "That beats me!" she said with a frown.

From our front window, I saw Papa leave the office and come up the hill. He passed by the house and went on up the little trail. The last man was coming out as Papa arrived at the door. Mama and I saw him say something to Papa, then they both stepped in. They only stayed for a moment or two and when they came out, the man went on in the direction of the Mill and Papa came down to the house.

He had a queer look on his face. It was almost as if he hated to tell us what was going on. "Come on up the hill, both of you," he said reluctantly.

We followed him up the trail, more curious than ever.

As we arrived at the door Papa said, "Step in, both of you, and look down in one of the holes and see what you see."

We did as Papa said. The hole was quite deep, but the sun shone though a wide crack in the walls.

Mama explained in horror, "My Stars, it must be a yard long!"

We could see a centipede stretched out on a piece of two-by-four near the bottom of the hole. It looked to me like a giant string of costume jewelry. It was deep orange with black stripes and a hundred long yellow legs. It made all the other centipedes we'd seen look like miniatures.

Mama and I backed out as soon as we could.

"Go and call the Thompsons, Alma. They ought to see it." Mama shook her skirt as she said it.

Word spread fast, and all day people came one at a time from the Mill and the Mexican quarters, always glancing self-consciously in the direction of our house before they stepped in. They stayed just long enough to take a quick look. That day every man, woman and child in camp must have come to visit our privy. Almost everyone who saw the centipede had a suggestion about how to kill or capture it.

One of the men from the Mill said, "You might bring it up with a wire if you could get it to crawl into a loop."

Jacques said, "We better kill heem. Dynamite ees the best way." Being the company powder man, Jacques thought of dynamite first.

Papa didn't care for that suggestion. At about four o-clock, the people stopped coming, and when Papa came home at five, he and I went up to look. This time the centipede was gone! In the dust outside we found tracks from his many feet as he made his escape. We never saw him again, but we'd all have been much more comfortable if Jacques' suggestion, or something like it, had been taken, even if it had meant building a new privy.

As time passed, the centipede became a camp legend and when the men who had seen it discussed it, it would appear that fishermen held no corner on tall tales.

It must have been a year later when I heard two Mexican men talking about it in English outside the commissary, "Caramba," one said, "she ees the biggest one in the whole world! I see him down there in the hole, and I think Segura! he is big like a snake. Oh Pedro, I weesh you can see him."

Pedro had just arrived so he had missed it.

"You don't believe it!" the Mexican went on, "four-foot long and maybe five inches the body. And the stripes! Oh, Pedro, I am sad you don't see heem. It is only happen one time in your life you see thing like this." Pedro nodded regretfully.

At our house, it was a long time before any catalogue could be read in comfort.

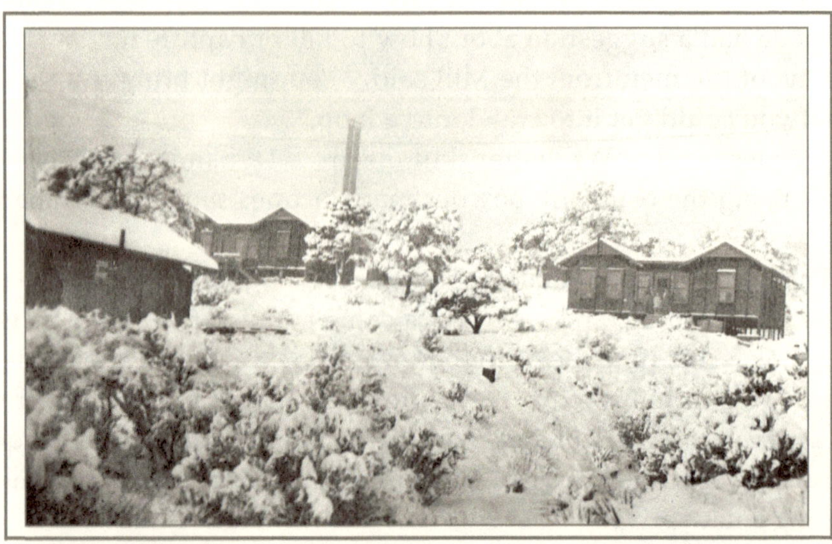

One of our occasional snowy days. Papa, Mama and I are standing on the front porch of our house on the right.

<h1 style="text-align:center">29.</h1>

The Chicken and the Egg

Unlike Papa, Mr. Thompson had always had good health, and his old job was waiting for him in Denver, so there was nothing urgent to hold him at Marble Camp. But it was a shame he couldn't stay because the quarry had just received two big orders for marble, one for an office building in Denver and one for a big bank building in San Francisco. There was an air of hustle and bustle over at the quarry and Mr. Kerr was in gay spirits. He had put the incident of the falling stack behind him because in spite of it, the men from Denver seemed to have taken back a good impression. At least they had put up more money, Papa said, to continue operating the quarry.

After the Denver investors left Marble Camp, it was Emma Phipps I missed most. We children all had chapped, cracked hands and Emma kept talking about it. She was sixteen with very soft hands herself and it seemed to worry her. "Just you wait," she said, "I'll send you something to make them feel better."

We didn't think she'd remember, but she kept her promise. She sent the Thompsons and us each two pint bottles of Frostilla lotion. At the same time, she sent other gifts to each of us children. I don't remember what the Thompson boys' things were, but Margaret and I got beautiful dolls with clothes made in France, and real hair and long lashes. Mine had four petticoats, silk mitts, and a little white straw bonnet. It had a bisque body and China head, and I thought it the most beautiful doll I'd ever seen. Mama put it carefully away in its box and for years we only took it out to look at once in a while, or to show company.

"This is the doll Emma Phipps sent Alma after she went back to

Denver from a visit to Marble Camp," Mama would say casually. The visitors' eyes would pop and they'd say, "My, my!" most impressed. Then to further emphasize the importance of the gift, Mama would add, "Mr. Phipps, you know, is the largest owner of United States Steel stock." Years later, she could add, "He's a United States Senator from Colorado."

Mama enjoyed name throwing, and Papa laughingly said, "There's a little of the snob in your Mother," and he'd pat her indulgently.

I only knew it was a beautiful doll, and Emma Phipps was a pretty girl who kept her promise about hand lotion and things, and she hadn't been mocking us when she held up that cabbage — she just wanted to join in the fun. I decided I'd like to grow up like her some day and ride around in private railroad cars and have long shining brown hair hanging below my waist.

The things Margaret and I shared, and not just the dolls, made us such good friends that it was a shock to me when I found out that the Thompsons were going away. How I hated to see them go!

As Mrs. Thompson hung up the family wash, she told Mama, "Men don't realize how important it is for children to keep up their schooling. Walter doesn't believe it hurts for them to miss, but three of ours are school-age and I know we've got to get back to Denver before school starts in the Fall. As it is, they've missed a whole year."

She jabbed a clothespin into a pair of overalls. "I declare, I should have studied to be a schoolmarm. Our work takes us to such out-of-the-way places!"

With four children, the Thompsons were always doing interesting things. One of the best things they had at their house was an Edison phonograph. There was a stack of records, but they only seemed to play one, "Red Wing." We got up in the morning to the strains of it; we ate lunch to it, and often when we went to bed at night it was the last thing we heard before we went to sleep. It got so Papa would be real cross when they played it, and sometimes he'd speak sharply to me. Then Mama would say, "Don't feel bad, Daddy didn't mean to scold you. He's just mad at that music."

But I hated to see the phonograph loaded on the wagon. "Red Wing" was better than nothing. In fact, I wished with all my might that the Thompsons didn't have to leave at all. Maybe the next Superintendent wouldn't even have any children.

The whole Thompson family had new mail order clothes for their trip back to Denver. It had taken several orders from Sears-Roebuck to outfit them like that. "I declare," Mrs. Thompson had said to Mama, "the children have grown so while we've been here they can't wear a thing we brought along."

The boys had the usual assortment of boys' clothes, knee pants and long-sleeved shirts, and caps with small beaks. Their long black ribbed stockings hadn't been washed yet, so they had no mended holes. Mrs. Thompson always complained that "To wash 'em is to darn 'em," and that "the boys always seem to run a race to see who can get a big hole first in new stockings."

There was certainly nothing about the boys' new things to impress anyone, I thought, but Margaret had a new bright red jumper dress and a ruffle-trimmed blouse with long sleeves. Her high black patent leather shoes had red tops and shiny black tassels that swished elegantly when she walked. Their things were all laid out on the bed when Mama and I went to say our formal goodbyes.

The big washtub was sitting in front of the cook stove in the kitchen waiting for the water to heat so the first of the Thompsons could step in and take a going-away bath. Margaret stood by her mother and there was no denying the triumphant look in her eye. Always there had been a little jealousy among us children about going to town. It was such a treat for me to climb in the wagon with a suitcase full of clean clothes and go down to Bowie to stay overnight at the hotel. With a larger family to take, Mrs. Thompson usually went alone, but Mama and I aways went with Papa.

Standing by her mother, Margaret looked taller than usual and very dignified for her eleven years. "We're leaving tomorrow, rain or shine," she said, which stuck me as most poetic.

Mama had agreed to call me early the morning they left. It was a cool grey day for the middle of September. I laid a doll quilt on my chilly rock and sat down on it to wait and watch. When the last straw suitcase had been put in place on the load, Johnny picked up the reins. I didn't want to appear too interested, as I was at a distinct disadvantage. This time they were sitting up on the wagon going away into no one knew what great adventures, and I was left sitting on a very hard, cold rock with only Mama and Papa and a toy box full of dolls for playmates. I looked at the sky and pretended to be seeing ever so many interesting things.

When Johnny clicked to the horses though, and said, "Lesgo boys," I pulled my eyes quickly back to the wagon and looked the Thompsons over for the last time. As the wagon started down the hill, the children all turned to wave. They were sitting up very straight. I watched as they disappeared around the bend, glad they couldn't see the tears slide down my cheek and splash on the cold hands clasped in my lap.

Mama stood on our porch and waved as they left, then came and drew me gently to my feet with a cheerful, "Now I wonder what the new family will be like. Let's make some candy this morning."

Johnny's trip this time was to deliver the Thompsons to the railroad and to bring back to camp the new superintendent, Mr. Smith, and his family. The train was late arriving in Bowie the next day, and by the time Johnny had the new family and its belongings loaded at Bowie, it was about the time of day he usually arrived in Marble Camp. For three hours I had been sitting on my rock watching hopefully. I had plenty of time to play my game, and I'd shut my eyes and open them suddenly and say, "Oh there they are. Oh, two little girls! How nice!' Then I'd shut them again and let them fly open, "Oh, a girl and two boys, ugh. That's awful! They'll tease us!"

The game didn't prepare me for the sight when my eyes opened on the real thing. On the seat next to Johnny sat a pleasant little lady with slightly graying hair, and in the seat in back sat a boy and Mr. Smith, a tall grey-haired man. The boy was distinctly an "ugh." He must have been about sixteen and looked like he'd have no use for little girls. My heart sank. I was right back to Mama and Papa and my dolls.

The next day Mama and I dressed up and went to call on Mrs. Smith. The two women found a lot of things in common. They compared recipes and talked about religion and politics, and came back to recipes again. I was so bored that I slipped outside to try to find something to do. Like ours, the Smith's house was on stilts in front. As I sat on their porch steps I could see way back under the house. Deep in the shadows I could make out the outline of a chicken. She was crouched but her craw was not quite touching the ground. One of ours, I thought, stealing a nest. Idly, I picked up a pebble and tossed it at her. She blinked the eye that was turned my direction, but didn't move. Suddenly, as I watched, something white dropped beneath her and rolled down the sloping ground under the house toward me. I put out my hand to catch it as it rolled, but before it reached me it came to rest in back of a little rock, and I sat too stunned to move.

I'd gathered the eggs for Mama and Papa ever since we'd had our chickens, but never had I seen a chicken lay an egg. There was something very shocking and yet awe-inspiring about it. My hand closed around the egg. It was warm.

I laid it behind one of the posts that held up the house and went inside to tell Mama what happened.

She and Mrs. Smith were still talking recipes. "I call it Top Hat," Mrs. Smith was saying, "you butter the inside of an oblong bowl and line it with cooked rice. Then you fill the center with ground cooked meat and seasoning. I use leftover roast or steak, and I aways add a little butter. Put rice on top and steam it a half hour. When it's good and hot, turn it out on a platter and pour creamed tomatoes over it. It's a New England dish, and my family loves it."

I tugged at Mama's arm. She frowned at me a little and said to Mrs. Smith, "It sounds delicious. I'll try it. My family is fond of rice," then with a glance at me, "It's getting late and I'd better start supper."

All afternoon I tried to get my nerve up to tell Mama what'd I'd seen and ask her if she' ever seen a hen lay an egg. Something seemed to hold me back. When I was tucked in bed that night and Papa told me my Bible story, I asked him to tell Mama I wanted to talk to her. She came in with her quick step and knelt down by my bed.

"Did you want me, Pet?"

"Mama, did you ever see a chicken lay an egg?" I blurted out.

She laughed and said, "No, I guess hardly anyone has ever seen that."

"I did," I said, "I saw a hen lay an egg under the Smith's house and I caught it in my hand – almost. It was rolling along on the ground and I would have caught it, only a rock stopped it."

Mama said, "You were lucky to see it. Very few people ever see a hen lay an egg." And right then Mama told me a lot of things about life, and how wonderful God made the world, and how good it was to be a part of it."

Even so, it was a long time after that before I could eat an egg for breakfast.

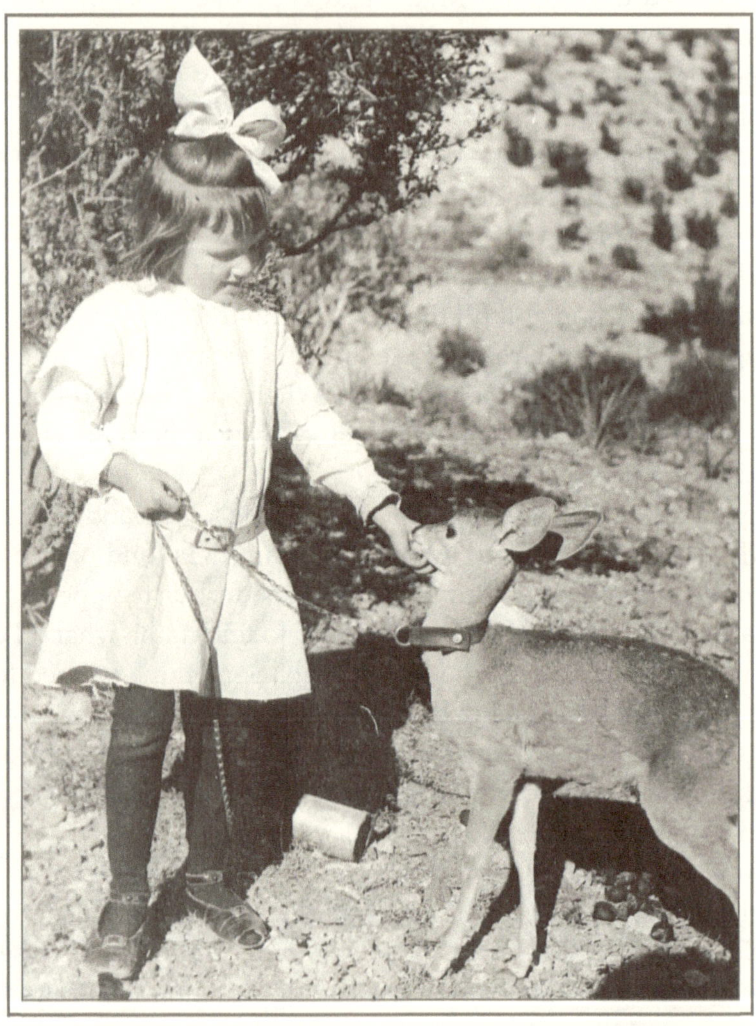

I loved to feed sugar lumps to the camps' pet deer.

30.

The Orphan Fawn

By the time we got up each day, the two burro trains looked like caterpillars twisting along on the rock trails above us near the timber line.

Facing the camp, and below the rocks, were two small ravines. Garcia and Hernandez, the two woodcutters, had each appropriated a ravine for his thatched bear-grass hut. A crowd of ragged children, mongrel dogs, and skinny chickens, surrounded each shack.

Their wives cooked outside in blackened pots over a campfire, and they had none of the conveniences of the Mexicans in the tent houses. There were no outhouses, and the one water faucet in the middle of the Mexican section of our camp would have really seemed like a luxury to the families of Garcia and Hernandez. Each evening, one of the wives would come a matter of four or five city blocks up and down hill, to that faucet for the daily supply of water. In one hand she would clutch a makeshift wire bale that was attached to a square old five gallon gasoline can.

"Why don't those women come together?" Mama asked Papa the first time she saw one come by herself for water.

"There's a good reason," Papa answered, "Garcia has only seven burros and Hernandez has nine, so there's rivalry between them. I guess the women feel it too. As we watched, Garcia's wife ran water in the can and started the long trip back over the winding trail. One shoulder sagged with the heavy but inadequate load of water, which must last her family a whole day.

"It's no wonder those children are always so dirty," Mama said, shaking her head. "Just imagine keeping a family washed and fed on a bucket of water a day." Mama turned on our faucet just for the reassurance of seeing water run into the wash basin underneath. More and more, we were realizing how lucky we were. Just when Mama and I would begin to take things for granted, something like seeing those woodcutters' wives struggling with their heavy water cans would come along and make us feel rich and thankful again.

Garcia's equipment for his burros was no more crude than Hernandez's. Both woodcutters used rope bridles on the animals and simple crossed pieces of two by fours with braces for pack saddles to carry the wood. After a saddle was loaded high with four-foot lengths of wood, a piece of rope was thrown twice over the load and under the burro's belly to secure it. The burros' feet were not shod, and their backs were not well protected from the harsh pack saddle, so that each pack train had to have a couple of the animals in the corral near the owner's shack healing the sores on their backs.

Mama always worried about the burros being mistreated, and she couldn't resist a hint to one of the men once when she saw a burro limping. "Hernandez, I believe one of your burros has a sore foot," she said in a casual tone, as if she hadn't been watching the little burro limping down the trail for the last half hour.

"Si, si, Senora, I work Pico one more day then I give heem the rest and make Gino work. She is no good for work. She is gotta lazy, but Pico got one bad foot. Only one more day an I give heem the rest." He flashed a toothy smile at Mama.

Mama sniffed. The idea of making Pico limp up the rough trail even one more time!

It was a good thing for the camp to have competition between the pack train men, but the fact that Hernandez had more animals made a little trouble for Papa. Garcia loaded his burros higher and tried to catch up with the size of Hernandez's stacks that way. He also had a way of laying the crooked sticks loosely when he stacked the wood so that there were holes in the stack, and it didn't take so much wood to look like a cord. Whenever Garcia came to the office to make his report on the number of cords he had hauled that day, Papa would say, "Come, Garcia, let's go and check it."

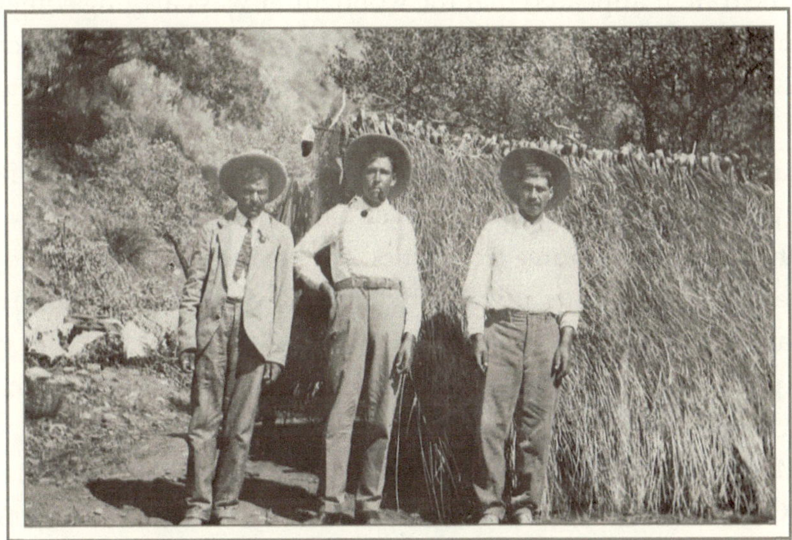

*The two Mexican woodcutters and a friend
at one of their huts.*

Garcia would look injured and say, "Mr. Milner, she is all there. I make theem big cords. I no cheat you."

Papa would nod and say, "Well, let's go see. The company wants me to be sure you give them their money's worth."

Garcia and his dog, Quito, would reluctantly follow Papa up the hill to the big wood pile on the mountain above the quarry. There was a stake in the ground where his wood of the day before left off and the new pile began. If Garcia had been up to his old tricks and stacked it thin, Papa had to make him do it over. Garcia would complain, but he knew he must to get his pay.

When Hernandez came to report, Papa knew everything was as he claimed, and made out his credit slip without question.

When it was time for the burros to start down the mountain trail,

I'd sit on my rock to watch them. One late afternoon, as they wound down the trail, it appeared that the woodcutter was carrying something in his arms. I strained my eyes to see, and when I was sure, I shouted. "Mama, look, the woodcutter is carrying something. It looks like a little burro!"

Mama put her hand up to shade her eyes. "It does look like it. Do you suppose one of the pack train had a baby burro up there?"

When Papa came home from work, the burros were low on the trail, and we could see plainly it was a live animal that Garcia was carrying in his arms.

Papa took me with him to check the load, and we found Garcia excited with his news.

"Meester Milner, these afternoon a gun ees shooting in the mountains. Caramba! She ees shoot close. Somebody is maybe hunt for deer. My leetle Quito he go jump in the booshes and then he come back and jump an' bark and run back in the booshes. I go, and Caramba, there is thes leetle deer. I looking all over but I cannot find the mama. I take so much time for hunt the mama deer, I get home late. My woman she is mad weeth me, but she see the deer and she is like it pooty good. My dog she teenk the deer belong to her. He is home now weeth the deer. I sorry be so late."

Papa said, "That's all right Garcia. It's too dark, just throw the wood off the burros and go home. You can stack it in the morning."

Papa and I watched as Garcia hastily unloaded the burros and started down the trail, leading the first animal by its rope. Suddenly he stopped dead still. The burros were following him so closely that his restraining hand on the first one was not enough to warn them and they ran into each other and reared and bucked as they tried to regain their footing. As Papa and I were wondering why he had stopped, he turned his gap-toothed grin on us and said maliciously, "Hernandez, he no have a deer like thees one. Mañana he hunt in the booshes for little deer." He threw back his head and laughed with satisfaction.

Garcia's dog, Quito, seemed to feel responsible for finding the fawn and he took care of it like a devoted older brother. Garcia let Quito stay at home to keep the fawn company, and each day the pair could be seen climbing around the mountainside close to Camp. They were inseparable. Garcia made a collar for the deer out of an old belt and fastened a short length of chain to it. We could hear them coming as the chain clanked on rocks when they made the rounds every morning for a handout.

"Here they come!" Mama would say as the noise of chain drew near, and I'd run for two lumps of brown sugar for them. We'd open the front door cautiously and go down the steps on tiptoe so as not to frighten the fawn. Even so, the first week or so, he would run away and stand all aquiver, looking questioningly. Seeing the little dog reach up for his sugar unafraid, he'd come back a few feet at a time and flick his ears nervously. Eventually he'd stick his lips way out to nibble the sugar away from my hands and run back to eye us, but after a couple of weeks more he was almost as brave as the dog and came right up to us, even mounting one step of the porch in his eagerness to get his sugar lump.

At night the deer would lead the little dog up a trail to sleep in the bushes. He didn't mind being domesticated in the daytime, but when the shadows began to fall, it was more comfortable up near the timber line.

Each morning from my rock I'd see them bob out here and there on the trails. They had become a part of Marble Camp.

Then one morning the dog came down the trail alone. The fawn had gone back to the wilds. For days little Quito wandered around camp dejectedly looking for the fawn. His eyes were sad, and he made a little whining sound in his throat. He made the usual rounds, but refused his lump of sugar when he came to our door. It was quite a while before he quit his moping and went back up the trail to help with the burros.

Garcia told Papa and me one day at the Commissary, "I am glad Quito ees come back weeth me. He help weeth the burros, but all the time he is still look for the deer. Sometime she stop and listen like she ees hear the deer speak to her, and then she look at me so sad. I weesh

I can find the deer for heem."

We never saw the fawn again while we lived at camp, but about four or five years later Papa and I were talking to some men who had been hunting about five miles from Marble Camp. They had killed a deer on Dos Cabezos Mountain. "Funny thing," one of the men said, "it was wearing a collar much too small for it. In fact the collar was almost buried in its neck. It was a wonder it hadn't choked to death."

Papa and I looked at each other. We didn't doubt that the hunter had shot our pet deer.

31.

Janie McNutt

It was about two o'clock in the afternoon that the quarry's third Superintendent was expected to arrive. I arranged myself early on my rock to wait for Johnny to drive around the bend. Mr. Kerr had said the new family had a little girl, younger than I was, but a little girl just the same.

The Smiths had been gone for a month, and the house next door sat in a film of silence. Even the Smiths had been better than nobody. More and more Mama pulled out scraps of material and made new dresses for all my dolls, and played school and games with me, trying to make up for my lack of playmates. She didn't have anyone to talk to either.

There was one other white woman in the houses below, but she hadn't finished the third grade. She would lie around all day in a wrapper and sip tequila, so she and Mama had nothing in common. Besides, for some reason, there was an invisible wall between our houses high on the hill and the workmens' quarters below.

Sometimes there were cute little Mexican and Mexican-Americans playing beside the tent houses. They always seemed to be having fun. But when I asked Mama to let me go to play with them, she said, "Mercy no, like as not they have runny noses." Or, "no, I'm afraid you'll catch their lice." Once we had seen a Mexican mother picking something out of a child's hair with a fine comb, and Mama was sure she'd been hunting for lice. Even though I didn't play with the children, Mama watched my head. Every time she gave me a bath she looked me over good. I wondered if lice looked like bedbugs.

"I'm not sure where such things come from. Maybe they are just in the air. What a county!" Mama said, and she clicked her tongue. So we stayed up on the hill and I longingly watched the children below having fun together. I didn't see a what difference a little dirt could make.

Johnny rounded the bend with a flourish. If he had only been bringing salt pork, nails, and dynamite, he would have sat slouched on the seat with his hat on the back of his head. But since he carried the new manager and his family, he sat up straight with his hat cocked jauntily over one ear. He was wearing a clean work shirt and his very best sleeve holders, blue ones to match his shirt, and he held the reins high and his elbows out. I looked eagerly at the other people in the wagon. There was a pretty lady on the seat with Johnny and a tall gentleman trying to look dignified as he sat on a sack of beans in back of the seat. But most important of all was the girl who sat between Johnny and the pretty lady.

She was a stocky little edition of her mother. Her hair was bobbed, and her wide jaw and straight cut bangs gave her face a square look, but in spite of the squareness and the sprinkling of freckles across her nose, she looked pretty to me. Her eyes sparkled with mischief and friendliness as they drove by me over the rocks on their way to their house. I noticed her feet dangled like mine had a couple of years ago.

As Johnny drove directly to their back door, I ran into our house and shouted, "Mama, they've come. I'm going to see them unload."

Mama shook her head emphatically and said, "You mustn't go now. Just watch from here. Wait till they get unloaded. It's not polite to go to call so soon unless you are asked."

I wished I hadn't told her I was going. For weeks I'd been longing for a playmate. Here was one made to order, and I had to stand by our house and watch the activity from a distance. It wasn't long though, till the pretty lady saw me and called me over to meet the little girl. Without a glance at our house, I ran to do her bidding.

"We're the McNutts, and this is Janie," she said with a smile. What a beautiful name! It would have sounded good to me if it had been "Claitersnite." "You must be Mr. Milner's little girl," she went on, and I nodded happily. My tongue stuck in my throat. I wanted to at least say, "My name is Alma, and I'm glad you've come," but I couldn't make a sound.

It didn't matter at all that Janie was only four and I was going on seven. She was a living, breathing child who could laugh and cry and run with me and eat bread and jam at tea parties. That afternoon we played together till dark and would have slept together if our mothers hadn't dragged us off to supper at our own homes.

"They are going to stay for a while. You'll have lots of time to play," Mama said as she whisked me into the house.

The truth was, Mama was eager as I was for company, and the next morning she curled her hair with a curling iron and put on a fresh dress to go and ask the McNutts to lunch.

For the next six months, Janie and I were together most of our waking hours.

Her house was across a wide road from the Quarry blacksmith shop. Never had I dared to go close to the shop by myself, but I had gone often with Papa when he went to see the blacksmith about company business. Janie seemed so interested in what went on under the tin roof of the smithy's shop that I didn't like to tell her I was not supposed to go there. In fact, after Janie came to camp, in my eagerness to show her around and to appear to know all about things, I grew a lot more bold than I had ever been.

"What are they pounding over there?" she asked one morning pointing to the blacksmith shop

"Oh, just shoein' horses and things like that," I replied.

"How shoein' 'em?"

"Oh, they nail pieces of iron on their feet. The iron is like a circle only part of it isn't there. It smells awful when they put the shoes on."

Janie wrinkled her freckled little nose. She looked skeptical, and I decided to show her what I meant the next time someone came to have a horse shod. They came often, because the ranchers around found it convenient to "drop over" the mountain to the camp blacksmith shop, and the shop was only busy on quarry tools by spurts. Most of the work for the quarry was sharpening the marble cutters and drills, so shoeing an occasional horse was at least a change. Certainly it was more thrilling than watching them hammer on an old piece of red hot steel to sharpen it.

You were never sure what a horse would do. It took two men

sometimes to hold him still, especially if it was his first set of shoes — real tricky it was, shoeing horses.

One day Savil Dickson, Mrs. Dickson's youngest son, rode a horse over the ridge and down the mountainside to the blacksmith shop.

Janie saw him and raced over to my house to get me.

"There's a man on a horse and he's come to the blacksmith shop," she said.

I glanced at my house to see if Mama was looking, then took Janie's hand, and we ran as fast as we could to watch the horse get its new shoes. Janie didn't know I should have waited to ask Mama's permission to go, and I certainly didn't tell her.

The shop was perched just below the quarry on the side of the mountain above a gulch. They must have run short of windows when they built it, because there was only one, and it was so covered with soot and grease that very little light filtered through. Papa had said it could be that they wanted it dark so they could see the color of the steel when they heated it.

We peered through the big door. It looked different and a little scary without Papa to hold my hand, but I'd never let Janie know that. Now I was playing the teacher's role that Margaret Thompson had, and Janie was playing me as the pupil.

"Look, the man already has the shoes in the fire," I said.

Janie tried to seem uninterested. She always had a knowing little smile when I showed her something strange. It was almost aggravating to show her something colossal and have her appear to be thinking about something else.

The blacksmith looked up. Most of his front teeth were missing and he was the dirtiest man in the world. Grease and soot covered him from head to foot. I'd often speculated as to why he wore an apron, because you could hardly tell where it left off and his clothes began, and certainly his clothes were beyond needing protection. He must have gone to bed at night without ever washing his coal-black face or hands. Papa said once that the men at the cook house complained about sitting next to him because he was so dirty. But he was a good blacksmith and did his work well, and the company couldn't afford to fire him just so they could get a man who would wash his face and hands once in a while.

Savil was holding the horse by the bridle, and the smithy had his back turned to the animal. He had one hoof up between his knees. There were big pincers clutched in his hairy hands, and he dug at the horse's foot, gouging big pieces off the hoof.

"Does it hurt?" Janie asked, still trying to appear unconcerned without taking her eyes off the job the man was doing.

"Papa says, 'no,' only sometimes they burn 'em" I went on, hoping to cut through her show of indifference. "Wait till they put the hot shoe on."

Janie looked toward the shoes glowing hotter by the minute in the forge.

"Let's go now," she said.

But I wanted her to see the whole process and I said, "No, let's stay till they put the shoes on. I don't think they'll burn him this time."

Savil and the blacksmith looked at each other and laughed. Then the smithy stopped laughing suddenly and said, "Say, Almer, how'd ye like to turn that handle and blow the bellows? The fire needs to be a little hotter."

I felt a great thrill inside of me. I was to help the blacksmith by turning the bellows. I had been given a job; the blacksmith needed my help. I looked importantly at Janie and stepped across the dirt floor to the forge. The handle might be hot, so I took hold of it cautiously and turned. There was a whirring sound and the fire glowed redder. I turned faster.

"That's enough," the blacksmith said quickly as he lifted the horse's other hind foot. I walked back to the door by Janie. She was eyeing me with new respect, a girl who could even turn the bellows for the black-smith shop!

The blacksmith picked up a pair of tongs and lifted a shoe from the forge to the anvil. He grasped a huge hammer and gave the shoe some well-paced whacks, quenched it quickly in a big wooden tub of water, and slapped it still burning hot on the horse's hoof.

Steam accompanied a sizzle as the shoe smoldered itself in.

The smell of the burning hoof filled the building and drifted to the doorway where Janie and I stood.

Now I was ready to go, but just then Mama's voice called, "Alma, what *are* you doing over there?"

It was a shame to be called, and then scolded, just when I had demonstrated my importance.

That wasn't the only time I overstepped myself trying to show Janie how superior I was. Once I almost got Papa in trouble over something Janie did. We'd been playing around the chicken house and watching some baby chicks following their mother about. Papa used some white stuff around the coop to keep down the flies.

We had so many flies in the house in the hot weather that often Mama would say, "Here Alma, time to shoo flies." We'd prop the back screen door open and start at the dining end of the room and shoo them out the back door.

We'd repeat the process several times, and by that time there'd only be a dozen left, and Mama could use a home-made swatter on them. It didn't do a lot of good because the outside of the screen would soon be black with flies again, and when we had to open it they'd swarm in. We didn't have any way to fight them except by shooing them out or using fly paper, but Mama always said, "It seems like fly paper just attracts more of them."

The stuff Papa used around the coop was lime, but lime and lye were both white and they looked all the same to me.

That day, playing near the coop, Janie picked up a piece of the lime and put her tongue to it. She barely touched it, but it burned and she began to cry. The word "lye" had a terrible meaning in our family. I'd often heard Mama tell about the time her little three-year-old brother, Birdsall, drank a cup of it by mistake when Mama was a little girl. Grandma was out hanging up clothes and Birdsall climbed on a chair and got the cup off the sink. As soon as he drank it he gurgled and began to cry and Mama ran outside to ask Grandma what was in the cup. Grandma dropped the wet laundry and screamed. "Oh Lord, it's lye!" as she ran into the house.

Dr. Cox came right away and they did everything they could, but the little fellow died three days later. From that time on everyone in Grandma's family had a horror of lye, and Mama had passed on the same feeling about it to me.

When Janie began to cry after touching her tongue to the lime, I ran down to her house as fast as I could to get Mrs. McNutt. On the way I met Mr. McNutt, and I yelled at the top of my voice. "Mr. McNutt, Janie's been eating lye. It'll burn her stomach up like Birdsall's."

Mr. McNutt had no idea who Birdsall was, but he heard me say Janie had been eating lye. He turned white and ran up to Janie who was sitting on the ground by the coop whimpering. I followed him.

"Open your mouth," he shouted.

Janie opened her mouth wide, and all we could see was a little blister on her tongue.

"Did you swallow any?" he asked her. She shook her head no.

"Well go take a big drink of water," Mr. McNutt said, relieved, "I guess you're not hurt."

He left us then and strode down to the office to see Papa. I watched his broad back disappear in the back door of the office and I was frightened. I knew he was surely going to scold Papa about that lye.

I went to our house to be near Mama's protection in case Papa wanted to see me. Sure enough the phone rang. It was Papa's voice and I could plainly hear him say, "Maud, have Alma come down. I want to talk to her."

Mama looked at me quizzically. "What have you been up to child?" she asked.

I burst into tears and sobbed out the whole story.

"There, there," Mama said. She dried my eyes and took my hand firmly in hers as we walked down the trail to the office.

Papa looked real provoked when we came in. "Doesn't that child know the difference between lye and lime?" he exploded.

It was the first time Papa had ever called me "That child."

Mama stiffened. "Well after all, Dana, she's only a little girl, and I doubt if you knew the difference yourself when you were her age."

Papa's face relaxed a little.

"Besides," Mama went on, "she's heard the story about Birdsall so often the she has a horror of lye just like I do. Can't you explain that to Mr. McNutt?"

Papa had to admit that he already had, and that everything was already fixed up.

"Then, what are you making such a fuss about?" Mama asked.

And Papa gave her his sheepish grin and patted me on the head.

Some of the things I did other times earned me spankings, but my usual punishment was to sit on a chair. It was the worst thing in the world to have to sit quietly on a chair with your hands folded. On my rock it was different. There things happened all around me, even if it was only clouds moving or ants walking about, but on a chair staring at the walls, that was dreadful!

As the months went by, things weren't going so well at the quarry, and the McNutts, like the Smiths before them, didn't stay very long.

About a week before they left, Johnny brought them two big wooden barrels on the load. There was a big word stamped on the side of each and I asked Papa what it said. He said the word was "Fragile," and he guessed the barrels were full of dishes. Mama was curious too because she let me go over to McNutts' early the next morning.

When I knocked, Janie came to the door. She had excelsior in her hair and the kitchen was a sight. There were straw and paper everywhere. It was surprising because Mrs. McNutt was usually such a good housekeeper. On the table, cupboard counter, and over part of the kitchen floor were white figurines of every description. There were ducks, dolls, bears, deer, rabbits, chickens, and ballet figures of every imaginable size and shape, and to find such an array in their kitchen! It made you think you had wandered into a gift shop by mistake.

Mrs. McNutt said, "Be careful where you step, child. I wouldn't have one broken for anything."

Mama said she wondered why they had unpacked them when they knew they were leaving right away. Maybe Mrs. McNutt just wanted to see if they were all right, Mama told Papa, "or maybe she just wanted to show off."

Certainly two barrels of figurines had no place in Marble Camp.

As soon as they were all unpacked, Mr. and Mrs. McNutt put the figurines back carefully in the barrels and nailed the lids on. Janie and I watched. The barrels sat in the kitchen till the McNutts were ready to leave camp.

The day they were to go, I sat on my rock alone and watched them load the wagon. There had been something romantic about having two barrels of figurines in camp even though they had been packed away in straw where I couldn't see them.

As the McNutts and their belongings went around the bend, I had the feeling the shade on the window had been pulled down.

As a matter of fact, Mr. McNutt was the last Superintendent the Camp had, and after he left, the work at the quarry was very slack, so the feeling I had was not far wrong. The shades were beginning to fall on Marble Camp.

32.

A Shot at Sunrise

Two quarry workers, Shorty and Big Jim, were like Spare Ribs and Gravy in our funny papers. Shorty was pink-cheeked and roly-poly, and Jim was so tall and thin he had to stoop over when he talked to him. They lived in adjoining tent houses. The camp only worked six days a week now, and Big Jim liked to sleep late on Sunday morning, but Shorty, who liked to hunt, always rose early, cleaned his gun, and spent the morning hunting birds and rabbits.

Big Jim loved nature too much for hunting. Papa said he thought Big Jim would hesitate to shoot at a tomato can for fear he might hit a snake. Mama doubted if anybody's love of nature went that far.

Big Jim teased Shorty often about the tender treatment he gave his gun. The other men said Jim would amble up to the wall where Shorty kept the shotgun lying across spikes driven into the two-by-fours of the tent house.

"Look here, Shorty," he'd say. "There's a little speck of dust on this gun barrel. Better get to work." Shorty would act like he hadn't heard, but when he thought Big Jim wasn't looking, he'd sidle over to the gun and take a look. When Big Jim left, folks said, Shorty would slip his cleaning rag out from under his cot and run it over the barrel just to be sure there wasn't some speck that Jim had really seen.

At about six o'clock one cool fall Sunday morning we were awakened by a "Zing-g-g" on the still mountain air. "Shorty!" I heard Papa say to Mama. "He must be hunting close to camp today." I had just drifted off to sleep again when someone in heavy boots came hurriedly clumping up our front steps and beat on the door.

"Mr. Milner, come quick!" It was Shorty's voice, and I could hear Papa scrambling out of bed in the next room.

"Be there is a minute, Shorty, what's the trouble?"

"It's Big Jim, I shot him! I was cleaning my gun and it went off. I ran into the tent to see if it had hit Jim. At first he didn't move, and then he groaned and--."

I was watching Shorty from my bedroom door and I saw him cover his face with his hands. Papa asked in a low tone, "Is it bad, Shorty?"

"I'm afraid so, Mr. Milner. Hurry! We got to get him to a doctor."

Papa was pulling on his jacket as he ran out on the front porch. Together they ran down the trail to the camp house. Mama and I clung to each other and held a blanket around us as we watched shivering from our front door. Some men had gathered at Jim's tent, and they moved aside to let Papa and Shorty go in. In a minute, Papa came out and ran to the corral. "He's gone to waken Johnny," Mama said, holding me close. We watched Johnny come out of his quarters, hastily fastening the shoulder strap on his overalls. He began to hitch up the big team and wagon as Papa disappeared again in Big Jim's tent. Three of the men came out carrying a mattress and blankets and put them in the wagon bed. They were followed by four men carrying a man on a litter made from a blanket and two poles. As soon as Big Jim was in the wagon, Papa came running up the path shouting to Mama as he ran.

"Get Bowie Central on the line. I have to call the depot."

Mama threw off her part of the blanket, ran to the telephone, and turned the handle for a long ring. Papa came in the house out of breath and took the telephone receiver she handed him. "Hello, Central, give me the depot. We've had an accident here at Marble Camp. Hello, Mr. Lawrence, can you hold the train for a hospital case? A man has been shot. I think we can make Number One. Thanks! We may be there before train time, but I had to be sure."

He hung up the receiver and ran to the wash basin to dash cold water on his face.

Mama was filling our canteen, and Papa looked at her gratefully. "We'll need that, mother," he said as he ran a comb through his hair and grabbed his hat from a nail in the kitchen wall. "I'm going along. Shorty wants to go all the way to Tucson with him, but he's too shaken up to do much till he gets ahold of himself. He'll sit with Johnny and I'll ride in the wagon bed with Big Jim."

He grabbed the canteen, brushed Mama's cheek with a kiss and tore off down the trail to the wagon.

There was something dreadful about a man lying down in a wagon. Standing up, Big Jim was just tall, but lying the full length of the wagon bed, he looked like a giant, and I was glad they were taking him away where we couldn't see him any more. Mama and I stood forlornly in the doorway and Papa turned to wave as the wagon went around the bend. Then I buried my head in the blanket.

When they were gone, Mama and I went into the lonely house. We seemed a long way from civilization today.

Bowie Station held the train for an hour. Papa said the jolting hurt Big Jim so bad that, after they left camp, they had to drive at a crawling pace. The hotel gave them a cot for him, and they loaded him in the baggage car. Papa and Johnny got back to camp late that same evening.

"Big Jim didn't complain all the way to town," Papa said, "just groaned a little if we hit a bump. He asked for water every few minutes, so that canteen was needed all right, Mother."

Big Jim lived three days and the camp was in a daze till we got a telegram saying he had passed away. The bullet had torn his stomach, but the main cause of death was loss of blood.

When we got the word, Papa looked at Mama soberly.

"I know what you are thinking, Sweetheart," he said quietly. "If he had been near a doctor, he might have lived."

Mama nodded slowly, and they didn't talk much all evening. The loneliness and danger of life in Marble Camp seemed to settle over our house like a cloud. I was glad to go to bed each night and snuggle down under the covers. It would be better in the morning when the sun came up and the quarry began to move again.

After Big Jim died, Shorty came back to work, but he couldn't bear to stay. By the third day he came to the office to see Papa. I had come to the commissary for Mama and heard him and Papa talking.

"I thought I'd be able to stay, Mr. Milner, but I can't stand it. If you'll make out my check, I'll go down with Johnny tomorrow. I lie awake at night and hear that shot ring out.

"He was my friend, Mr. Milner. I was always so careful cleaning my gun. I still don't know how it happened. You see why I can't stay?"

"Yes, Shorty," I heard Papa say. "I do.".

The next morning Shorty rode away with Johnny and the camp settled down to try to forget. Two new men came to replace Shorty and Big Jim. When Papa took one of them to Shorty's tent to show him his quarters, he found the gun still on its nails on the wall. He took it to the office for safe keeping, but Shorty never came back for it.

33.

Learning with Aunt Lena

With Mr. McNutt gone, Mr. Kerr had added most of the Superintendent's work to his own. The quarry was running into many difficulties. The price of Italian marble had dropped so low that competition was keen. Italian labor was inexpensive and labor costs in Arizona were high. We were a long way from the marble market and it actually cost more to deliver our quarry's marble to the railroad by traction engine than it did to deliver Italian marble to docks in New York. Ships left our country for Italy loaded with American goods, and Italian marble was shipped back cheaply or even freight-free as ballast in the bottom of the same ships. Papa said they called that "rock-bottom prices."

One night at supper, Mr. Kerr said, "Why, when I called Los Angeles they said the ship captains are glad to have the marble as ballast. They even ask to keep it in their holds all the way from Italy through the Panama Canal to Alaska. Then they unload it for the polishing mills in Los Angeles when they come back down the coast. What kind of competition is that? And with the traction engine constantly breaking down and costing so much to operate, it is a problem all right."

Papa nodded in agreement. "We need better transportation," he said.

The huge traction engine, which steamed and puffed its way up and down the road to camp fired by lengths of cord wood, was not working out. It was often broken down for a week or two at a time waiting for parts. Mr. Kerr was getting wrinkles in his forehead, and he was quick-tempered form worry. It wasn't long after that he received a wire from Denver relayed over Mr. Riggs' telephone lines from Bowie. "Better come up and talk things over," it said.

Papa told Mama that Mr. Kerr had a sick look on his face as he laid the receiver down.

The night before he set out for Denver, he and Papa and Mama had a long talk. I slipped out of bed and opened the door a crack so I could listen. They were all sitting around the kitchen table, and four kerosene lamps threw grotesque shadows on the walls.

"Dana, I want you to stay on, no matter what happens," I heard Mr. Kerr say. "The shut down will be temporary." There was a note of discouraged defiance in his tone. "And I want you here when we are ready to go again."

"I'll stay as long as you like," Papa said quietly. Then he caught Mama's eye and went on. "There's one thing my wife and I have been worrying about though." He hesitated. I guess it seemed like a trivial thing to bring up when Mr. Kerr had so much on his mind. "It's Alma's schooling. She's seven now, and she should have started to school when she was six. We've been thinking about having a tutor come live with us. We could pay her a small salary, and it would be all right if we were sure we'd be here all winter, but we'd hesitate to hire someone if we had to leave camp before the school year was over."

Mr. Kerr said, as he rose to go, "You can depend on staying here as long as you want to. This is only a temporary setback. We'll be operating at full speed in a month or two."

The quarry was his dream child and Mr. Kerr couldn't give it up — yet.

Mama couldn't blame Papa for wanting to stay at Marble Camp as long as he could. It wasn't just that he had regained his health; the salary was very good, and there was no place to spend much money, so we were rapidly building up a nest egg. With the company house, water and telephone furnished free, and no stores nearby to tempt us, about our only expense was groceries and a night at the hotel in town once every month or so.

"Another year," Papa said, " and we'll have enough to buy a small business. It seems a shame to give it up and go hunting for a job somewhere else as long as the company wants me to stay here."

Mama agreed, but she had a faraway look at the thought of getting back to civilization. She and Papa talked a long time after Mr. Kerr left that night. They seemed to agree that I needed to be in school.

It's strange how things sometimes have a way of fitting together. A few days after that, we got a letter from Papa's sister, Lena, who taught school in Lorain. She was not feeling well and she wrote, "It's my stomach. The doctor says I should take a year off from teaching and go on a diet. I've been thinking. Maybe I could come to Arizona and stay with you."

The minute Mama read Aunt Lena's letter, she said, "Dana, there's our answer. If we can get the kind of food she needs here at Camp, let's have her come out and teach Alma. We could afford to pay her a little salary each month, and give her board. Besides, she said wistfully "It would be so nice to have another white woman in camp."

That night Papa wrote a letter to Aunt Lena. Mama smiled as he sat at the library table writing, and said, "You know, Lena has always wanted to come West. I think it might be a good chance for her to meet a nice cowboy."

"Now, Mother, no matchmaking!" Papa grinned at her as he folded the letter and slipped it into the envelope.

When Aunt Lena wrote back she said, "The main thing on my diet is cheese." Mama sent her a letter quick, saying that was, by necessity, one of the main things on our menu. So it was arranged that Aunt Lena should come and be my tutor. She got her principal's approval to be away from Lorain for a year, and he gave her twenty-two school readers and other discarded first and second grade material for me.

On a warm day in late Fall, Miss Lena Milner, with her trunks and hat boxes and the school equipment, stepped off the train in Bowie.

Johnny Kaiser made the trip to town to get her. As a rule there were only two things that kept Mama and me from going to town every time we had a chance. In the hottest weather we sometimes skipped a trip to avoid the slow, miserable ride back up the hill. Then, if Mama knew there was to be dynamite on the load, she refused to ride on the wagon. Papa and Johnny had both tried to persuade her that dynamite was not at all dangerous so long as the caps to set it off were carried in another part of the wagon. Mama didn't believe a word of it.

In describing Aunt Lena to Papa later, Johnny said, "She's a little thing. Sure got a straight backbone. Don't know's I'd care to go to school to her, but she has a nice smile and a pretty face. Kind of woman you like to hold onto her elbow when she gits in the wagon, but you better let go as soon as she don't need your help no more."

Johnny must have thought Aunt Lena had poorer eyesight than Mama. Anyway, he said he didn't bother to cover up the dynamite box when she climbed on the seat for the trip to camp. When she saw the word "Dynamite" on the end of the box she said, "Goodness!" Johnny chuckled and imitated the way she said it. Papa laughed because he knew Aunt Lena could say "goodness" in half a dozen different ways. There was a very pleasant "Goodness!" when she had a nice surprise like meeting an old friend. Then a sad "Goodness" when she heard of a tragedy happening to some old person. And a shocked tone when she heard of something wicked like the husband of a friend having an affair with another woman. This last was a deep-voiced horrified sound with both syllables drawn out.

And then there was the dynamite "Goodness," the most shocked and frightened one of all. With this one she first caught her breath and her eyes popped out a little as she said, "GooooODness," rising to a crescendo in the middle of the word and tapering off to a little hiss at the end. Johnny was hard boiled and matter-of-fact, and though he heard Aunt Lena's exclamation, he pretended not to notice or was too busy with the load to pay any attention. Aunt Lena told us about it first thing and proceeded to demonstrate how she sat down gingerly in the seat and sat so stiff and still all the way to camp that she could hardly get out of the wagon when she arrived. She fell into Papa's arms with a great sigh of relief for not having been "blown to Kingdom come."

Since the manager's house was now empty, Mr. Kerr had said we might use one of its rooms for a schoolroom. Papa had made a desk for me. It had a hinged lid and dark stain. I thought it about the nicest piece of furniture that had ever been built. It was a symbol of what I wanted so very much – to find out about the things in the world outside the rim of our mountains. And, in her suitcases, Aunt Lena had just what it would take to satisfy my craving for new and wonderful things

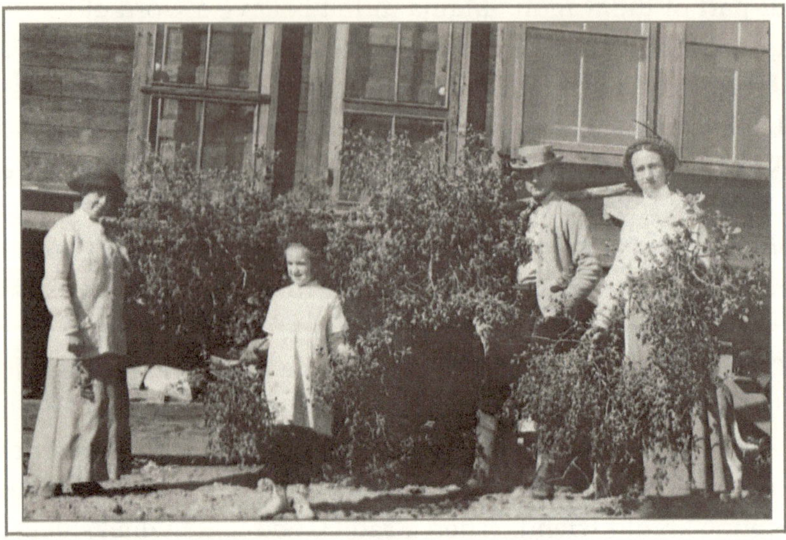

*From left, Aunt Lena, me, Papa and Mama with mistletoe
we gathered before Christmas.*

to think about. If I had books and could read them, I wouldn't be so lonely, even with no playmates. Now there were not even many Mexican children to watch longingly from my rock.

The day after Aunt Lena arrived, she and I went to the schoolroom and set up shop. Papa had made a bookcase out of a couple of orange crates, and Aunt Lena arranged the books she had brought in the order she thought I should study them.

I watched from my new desk in rapt delight. Books and toys from the relatives came more infrequently now. An occasional book from Lorain and a few Mama had ordered from the catalogue had been the only ones I had. After Mama and Papa read them to me a few times, I knew them by heart and there alwas no library to go to for a new supply.

Three monthly magazines were the most dependable things we had to look forward to. Grandma subscribed to the *McCalls* and *Ladies Home Journal* for us, and Papa ordered the *Geographic*. When the *McCalls* arrived, I was allowed to take the wrapper off. After it had been unwrapped and rolled and creased so it wouldn't roll up, I began to thumb through it very slowly, looking over every page and holding back the delight of coming on the paper doll page. When I finally turned to that page, all of the anticipation was over, and the fun of cutting the paper dolls out was all that was left for another month.

The first thing to cut out was the doll itself. Then I'd go outside and sit on my rock a while to make the job of cutting last longer. There was so little to fill up the time of a little girl with a busy mind, and the magazines held very little to be read to a child.

So books lined up in those orange crates were like so much gold. In the next nine months, Aunt Lena took me through all twenty-two of them and sent to Ohio for more. She taught me poems that belonged to the third and fourth grades, too! It would be nice to say Aunt Lena met a wealthy rancher and lived happily ever after. Actually, she went back to her schoolroom in Lorain, strong and healthy, but still unattached. When I thought about her, though, it was as with the wings of an angel.

34.

The Cook's Bad Luck

Old Fong might not have been a very good cook, but the men liked his spontaneous laugh. He was fat and bald-headed, like Fong the cook in Bowie, but they were no relation, as far as we knew. He too clumped about all day in his Chinese slippers. In the evening before dark, he'd climb the trail back of the cook house to sit on a rock and smoke his long, carved Chinese pipe. For climbing he always wore boots a couple of sizes too large for his feet. He didn't bother to lace them up and they flapped along as he mounted the trail.

"Allee time watchee find snake. Snake scary Fong. Flappy boots scary snake. Fong allee time get even," and he'd go off into gales of laughter at his own cleverness.

While the camp was still operating full tilt, on one of Johnny's trips to town, he brought back a friend of Fong's. The visitor, who had only recently arrived from China, spoke no English and was quite deaf. During his visit, Fong took him on his walks in the evening. They'd sit together on a rock and shout at each other in Chinese. Though we were entertained, we couldn't guess a word of the conversation. Mama was really curious to know what they were saying, especially when they would suddenly have a good laugh and slap each other on the back.

"Like as not they are talking about us," she said. Papa grinned at that idea and said he doubted it. "They have plenty to talk about the old country without laughing at any of us in camp."

Fong had a trunkful of Chinese mementoes in his little closet-sized room at the cook house. At the least kindly gesture toward him, he'd open his trunk and draw out a neatly folded piece of embroidered silk or a little box of queer smelling nut meats, and say, "Blingee plesent for you allee way from China. You belly good friend." Then he'd fold his hands and wait to see how pleased we were. If we seemed really delighted with the present, he would close the trunk, but if we were polite but not overly impressed, he would keep drawing out another valuable treasure till we appeared overcome. After each gift he would wait and watch us to see our reaction. We must be impressed before he would close the trunk. I soon learned to get something really good.

Fong had become such a fixture in Marble Camp that we grew to think he'd always be there.

But then Mr. Kerr went off to Denver and production was suspended at the quarry. All but the core-drillers and pumper went on forced vacation, and most of the laborers stayed in Bowie to wait for the quarry to reopen.

"I'm sure it's just a temporary shutdown," Mr. Kerr wrote Papa. "We are trying to enlist more capital."

By that time over a quarter of a million dollars had been sunk by the investors, and it was no wonder they were beginning to balk.

Papa and Mama had been very quiet of late and they talked long after they went to bed at night. I came to believe they didn't think the booms would ever swing again to lift the huge blocks out of the quarry.

Over the ten miles or more of the company's claim, the only activity was an eight-man crew of workmen who began core drilling to establish the color and quality of the marble at different locations. It was like taking inventory of a store's stock. They worked in pairs in several directions from the drilling camp. The cores were about the size and shape of the roller of a rolling pin, and were bored out of solid marble by a hollow drill. Mama used one of them for rolling her pie crust, and she said, "You know, it's better than an ordinary rolling pin because it's so heavy. It's a shame they don't come with handles."

Papa remembered all the wives chasing husbands with rolling pins in the funny papers. "If all the wives in camp had owned marble rolling pins, we'd have been hiring a new crew every few days," he said.

When the men had worked the claim close by, they began to establish camps in hard-to-reach spots on the other side of the mountains to the North. At one location, Whitetail Canyon, the tents and equipment had to be packed in on burros.   With so few men left at camp, Fong abandoned his greasy boarding house and went along as cook for the crew.   He used one tent as a kitchen and slept on a cot right in the tent. The flour, sugar, rice and beans he kept under his bed, and an apple box cupboard at one end of the tent held the dishes and other food.

The men had been away from Marble Camp about a month when they called up from a ranch over the mountain and said their job would soon be done. They'd need a pack train to carry all of the samples and equipment back. Except for the two burros the men had with them, there were no others in camp now. The wood stacked above the quarry should be enough for several years under present conditions, and the burros they asked for would have to be ordered out of Bowie. It would take two or three days for them to arrive at the core-drilling camp.

But the men needn't have worried about bringing back some of the equipment. Two nights before they were finished, Fong was awakened in his tent by something walking across his face. Instinctively he reached up with his two hands to grab it, and soon learned that was a poor decision. I guess skunks smell so strong themselves they can't smell anything else, because the one that climbed on the cot must not have known Fong was there. It "let go" and Fong, the bed clothes, the tent, and the remaining food all came in for a share of the horrible spray.

By this time Fong was wide awake and squealing in Chinese at the top of his voice. The men later chortled gleefully when they told us about it and said part of the words sounded like "Dammey sklunkee! Dammey Sklunkee!'

Fong clenched his fingers around the skunk's neck and squeezed the life out of it, but not before it had bitten him on the palms of his hands. His first screams had brought the workmen scrambling out of their tents, but none of them was willing to go to his aid when the smell began to hit the air. They stood around uncertainly till Fong came staggering out of the tent holding up both of his bleeding hands. The skunk lay dead in the doorway.

When Fong and Garcia came riding the burros back to camp over the mountain late that afternoon, we could smell them coming. They had no saddles and Garcia slid off over his burro's rump as easily as the little Mexican boys had so long ago in Bowie. He swaggered importantly as he told Papa and me how he had taken pity on Fong and guided him down to the little spring near their camp and helped him wash his wounds. Fong moaned and nodded as Garcia talked. The bandages and dressings for possible injuries had been kept in the tent and no one wanted to go in after them. "I tear clean shirt for wrap and hands, and geeve heem overalls and shirt for wear. We bury the clothes," Garcia said, holding his nose.

Papa took one look at the injured hands and said soberly, "We'd better send you to El Paso for treatment for those bites, Fong." Fong rolled his eyes and nodded his head. He was shaking and I wondered if he had been shaking ever since the skunk bit him, or if he was just scared about going to the doctor.

Papa got more groceries ready for Garcia who started right back over the trail with them, canned goods and things that would be easy for the men to cook themselves. As he started to leave, Garcia hesitated, "Mr. Milner, what we do with the cook tent? She is smell awful."

"Tell the men to set fire to it," Papa said quietly. For a horrible moment I thought he looked as though he'd like to do that to the whole of Marble Camp. Garcia slapped the rein against the neck of the burro he was riding and gently pulled on the rope of the loaded burro he was to lead. Papa and I watched him as he started back over the trail.

Meanwhile, Johnny hitched up the team and took Fong to the train. Papa was wise to send him straight to the doctor. His hands did become infected, and Fong was in El Paso for a couple of weeks. Papa said, "Even at that, he'll never know how lucky he was that the skunk didn't have hydrophobia."

When Fong returned, he came only to get his belongings and his trunk full of valuable trinkets.

As the wagon bearing him back to town disappeared around the bend, I thought all of a sudden what a good thing it was that he didn't have the trunk with him in that tent. All those wonderful gifts from far away China would have had to be burned.

35.

Papa's Turn to Worry

It was in the late summer of 1913 that things reversed themselves, and it was Papa who began to worry about Mama's health. For several weeks she hadn't seemed very well and she had a painful abscess that she called a "bone felon" on her right index finger. At night she walked the floor with the pain. All the remedies that came over the party line didn't seem to help at first, but eventually with the help of one of them, the abscess was ready to lance.

It was then that we heard about a doctor who had come to live in San Simon, the first little town east of Bowie, almost on the New Mexico border. Like Bowie, it was about twenty-two miles from Marble Camp, and there was now a passable road from camp directly to it. Papa hitched up Colonel and Bob and drove us down to the new doctor to have Mama's finger lanced. We had misgivings when we drove into the barren yard and up to the miserable little shack that was the "doctor's" home and office. He was a cross-eyed, unshaven little man, and had evidently not intended to practice medicine in San Simon. I doubt if he even had a license, and he had no instruments or equipment that we could see. He sat Mother down on a kitchen chair, though, and put a kettle on the stove to heat water.

Papa and I stood out in the bare yard and waited, as there was very little room for us inside. Mama came to the door and looked appealing at Papa. "Dana, do I have to let him do it?" she asked in a whisper.

Papa looked helpless and answered, "I don't know what else we can do, Maud. We might go to Willcox." Willcox was beyond Bowie to the west and almost fifty miles from San Simon, and Mama shook her head resignedly and went back to the kitchen chair and sat down. The "doctor" soon had the water hot and Papa and I watched from the doorway as he stuck a kitchen paring knife in it for a few seconds to "stertilize" it, he said.

Mama held tight to the chair with her good hand. After adding some cold water, the doctor placed her hand in the same pan of water that he had used to "stertilize" the knife. Then, drawing the hand out of the water, he laid it on the rough kitchen table on an old yellowed newspaper and picked up the knife. He looked hesitatingly at Mama's finger, focusing one of his crossed eyes on the end of it. Then he moved his head so that the other eye could focus on the finger. With a look of panic, Mama gritted her teeth. She flinched as there was a sharp stab of pain, and opened her eyes to see the long gash the doctor had made in her index finger. Papa couldn't stand it any longer and he stepped inside the little room and took her other hand.

I doubt if the man was ever more than a horse doctor, for Mama's finger never did have any feeling in the end, and it was always stiff after that.

After Mama's finger was bandaged, we went on to Bowie and stayed overnight at the hotel.

But the finger healed slowly, and Mama looked pale and thin. Papa had a little frown whenever he looked at her. Finally one day as he soberly watched her clear the table after lunch, he said, "Maud, what you need is a doctor's care, and Alma needs school. I believe I ought to send you two to Denver to spend the winter."

Mama poured hot water from the teakettle into her dishpan before she made any reply. Then she said, "Couldn't we go some place closer? What about Tucson? There are probably good doctors there." But we had never been to Tucson, more than a hundred miles west. Perhaps in the back of their minds Papa and Mama were remembering Big Jim and his ill-fated trip to the hospital there.

The core drilling was over and one by one the men had been laid off, until only four of us — Johnny Kaiser, the teamster, and Mama and Papa and I were left in camp. It was lonely enough when the quarry was operating, and now the dreadful silence may have had a lot to do with Mama's health. I don't think she would have gone off and left

Papa, though, if she had known the quarry would never operate again, and that Papa and Johnny would keep a lonely vigil there all winter.

Papa took us to Bowie to catch the train for Denver not long after that.

The trip to Denver was a little easier than my first train ride there from Ohio, if only because my legs seemed to fit the seat somewhat better now, and Grandma was not along to pull me forward and back. Then too, while it wasn't empty, our Pullman car was less crowded because we were going east. I had noticed when I sat outside the Bowie Station that more passengers seemed to be on the trains to the West than on those going back East. And since Arizona had become a state, even more of them were stopping in our empty part of the world, not just going through on the way to California.

Arizona had gotten to be a state on Valentine's Day in 1912. Papa was first to learn about it by chance when he called Bowie on business, several days before the newspapers telling about it got up to the quarry.

He and Mama seemed pleased at the news. "A state — just like Ohio!" Papa told me. But I wasn't much impressed. I could see we weren't "just like Ohio." I had gone out to sit on my rock and Marble Camp still had no sidewalks or green lawns. I suspected there were still no streetcars in Bowie either.

36.

The Long Winter

In Denver we took an apartment upstairs in a big house across from Wyman Grammar School, and I went to third grade there. "The house is not very stylish," Mama wrote Papa, "but it's good and warm and close to the school."

The time we had spent in Denver before we followed Papa to Bowie had been what they called an "open winter" with only a few inches of snow. There were lots of sunshiny days that year, and when Papa had mentioned Denver, I remembered bright sunshine hitting the Capitol dome on a clear winter day. This time, however, we had only been settled in for a little while when it began to snow.

That was a winter Denver long remembered. Just a little after Christmas the white flakes really began to pile up in earnest. They started hesitantly at first, here a flake and there a flake, but the next morning the streets were silent under a thick white eiderdown blanket. The next day the third porch step of our house was covered, and the following morning snow was banked to the bottom of the windows downstairs and falling fast.

"A bucket of coal apiece a day till it quits snowing," the landlord said as he clumped up the stairs with our hod full. Before long, looking across the street, I could see a sign on the schoolhouse: "Closed till further notice." The windows downstairs were buried in snow. In a lull in the storm, I peered out of our own window to see that all the first floors had disappeared and the street seemed to be lined with bungalows.

But the next morning someone knocked out a snow dam in the

heavens. Banked up by a stiff wind, it mounted rapidly to our second-floor windowsills and began to climb up the glass, cutting our light from the gloomy sky.

The landlord was bringing us skimpier and skimpier buckets of coal, but it wasn't altogether because I was cold that I shivered when Mama reached for a match to light our gas jet. What if it kept snowing and buried the world? Papa had said God sent the rainbow as a promise he'd never send another flood. But what about snow? He hadn't said a word about that.

I had loved making friends in a schoolroom with other children, but now, we were more isolated than at Marble Camp, slowly being shut up in an igloo with no telephone, no newspapers, and no letters from Papa. Loneliness covered us like a blanket. The problem of food was beginning to be serious too. Mama's Marble Camp training was probably the reason we had more cans and supplies in our cupboard than most people, but even she hadn't prepared for such a long emergency as this.

On the morning of storm's seventh day, there was another lull. I cried softly as I looked over the snow which was half way up our lower window pane. "I never want to see any more snow as long as I live," I sobbed. Mama came to comfort me. "Let's see if we can open the window and get a dish full for ice cream," she said brightly. "We have one can of milk left, and sugar and vanilla."

I forgot my tears as we tugged at the window. At first it stuck, then it gave way with a rush and enough snow to fill a bucket fell on the floor at our feet.

Just then we saw the woman next door standing at her window only a few feet away from ours. She was motioning to us and we could see she was saying something about raising the window. We couldn't hear a word. We nodded and tugged it above the snow line till we could hear her shout: "Milk – do you have any canned milk? The baby next door on the other side of the hall cried all night. Poor little thing."

Mama looked at me soberly and said, "We'll have to forget about our ice cream won't we?" I nodded, and she went to the tiny kitchen cupboard to get our last can.

It was a good thing the houses were close together because Mama never could throw anything very far. Papa always teased her about it. "You'd never make a ball player, Mother," he'd say, and Mama always sniffed and said girls weren't supposed to play ball anyway. But now she slipped her arm out the window above the snow and gave the can a toss. The woman next door stretched out her two hands and caught it.

At that very moment the sun broke through the clouds with dazzling brightness and turned the world into a blinding sheet of white. The storm was over, and soon the men came out of their caves to help shovel trenches where the sidewalks used to be.

It was two days before Mama and I could bundle up and put on our rubbers to walk out of our prison and down a snow trench to the grocery. The grocer's shelves had been stripped clean, and things like walnuts and cayenne pepper were about all he had left. He had on a clean white apron, and he said to come back later that day because he hoped the delivery wagon might still arrive.

Groceries got through at last and school reopened, but so much snow had fallen that it seemed to take forever to melt, and the weather was still bitter cold. "I'll be glad when school is out and we can go home to Arizona and thaw out," Mama said one day. Home to Arizona! Always before she had talked about "home" she was talking about Lorain.

When we stepped off the train at Bowie, Papa was there, and Mr. and Mrs. Riggs and Pauline had come to town especially to meet us. The Riggs were riding in a fine new touring car. Mrs. Riggs wore an elegant tan duster and a huge flowered hat tied on with heavy grey veiling.

"Oh, Maud dear!" She threw her arms around Mama. "I never realized how I'd miss those little visits we had until you went away." She dabbed at her eyes with a spotless white hanky.

Mama reached for her handkerchief with one hand and steadied her hat with the other. "It's so good to be back!" she cried, smiling.

Still, there was a lonely summer ahead of us, with the dead silence at the quarry where there was not a wheel turning or a cable creaking.

Papa and Johnny, alone and with time hanging heavily on their hands all winter and spring, had started a garden. They had picked a site on the road two miles below camp where there was a sandy level

spot. The had planted corn, beets, radishes, lettuce, cabbage and wa-
termelon, and both men were full of enthusiasm for their "crops." Papa
had been raised on a farm so no doubt it was his idea. Anything to keep
busy! He and Johnny had spent many hours clearing away rocks and
turning the sandy soil over.

All that sumer, while Johnny and we three were alone in camp, the
men worked at the garden patch every day. Once in a while Mama and
I would go with them. It was a long walk back upgrade, but Papa said
we all needed the exercise, and it was foolish to hitch up the horses for
a couple of miles. Mama was feeling so well again she didn't mind the
walk, but my legs were still pretty short for such a hike.

Never was hard labor more rewarded. The vegetables grew so fast
in the sandy loam of the canyon that we could hardly believe it. In the
cultivated soil, wildflowers also grew, and it seemed as though they
bloomed overnight in the rows between the crops. Papa and Johnny
had to hoe fast to keep the flowers and weeds down.

There was considerable rivalry over who should take the produce
to town. The cabbages were so big and solid and the corn had such a
delicious flavor that they caused a commotion when they were delivered to the store. It was hard to say whether Johnny or Papa swaggered
more when one or the other of them came back to camp from delivering.

"They'll all say they never seen such big cabbages," Johnny would
say with pride.

Or Papa would say, "when I delivered the corn, Mr. Bunch said he'd
like to come up here and see what we did to make corn grow like that."

Money for the vegetables piled up in the bank in Denver, but there
was no denying that Marble Camp had fallen from the days when marble was its main export.

Papa took us climbing to The Rocks on the first Sunday after we
got back from Denver. "I just want you to see what's happening to the
valley," he said. When we got to the top, he pointed off to the north.
"Now look at Bowie, Maud. Different than when we first saw it from
here, isn't it?" Land around Bowie had been thrown open for home-
steading, and families were arriving daily. The valley was dotted with
farm houses. Fences were going up, and wells were going down, and

houses and barns were being built on every section of land as far as the eye could see.

Papa looked it over proudly as he stood on a high rock with his feet wide apart and the wind ruffling his hair. There was such a sense of power and vigor about him that I had a feeling it was Mr. Kerr standing there.

Mama nodded. "It does look like the start of a little city," she said, tucking a wisp of hair in place.

"I think it does. I'd like to be a part of it. Would you mind very much if we stayed here? In Bowie I mean? Maybe later we could start a bank." He was watching Mama eagerly, "Right now I have a chance to buy a half interest in the new general merchandise store that has most of the town's business."

Papa didn't mention that we could go back to Lorain now, if Mama really wanted to.

Mama was looking off toward Bowie. Slowly her eyes followed the train that was puffing toward the east. Then she brought them back from one cleared patch to another in the valley below. In places there was the brown of freshly turned soil, in others, patches of green heralded crops already up. Papa was watching her eagerly.

The wind rushing up to the mountain top from both valleys below, rustled the trees. I could see Mama weighing all the elements of life in Arizona against the old life she had known in Lorain. She looked down on the deserted quarry below. Not a wisp of smoke rose from its chimneys now. The big hole from which the marble had been cut yawned at us. Great white blocks piled on top of each other gleamed in the sunlight. The sun flashed on the long cables holding up the derricks. Nearby a squirrel scolded at the foot of a pine tree. Mama studied Papa's brown face for a moment. She looked off to the north again, where smoke trailed the length of the eastbound train in the valley.

Then she laid her hand in Papa's with a little sigh. "Let's stay and be a part of it," she said softly.

It was the second time Papa had kissed Mama on a mountain top.

37.

Our New Life

On a hot day in August, Johnny came back from taking his turn at delivering the vegetables to town. He climbed off the wagon and handed Papa a little packet of letters. Among them was one from Mr. Kerr. He was on his way to London, and the Arizona Marble Company's quarry would not reopen.

"You will probably want to hunt a job somewhere else," he wrote. "If you succeed in establishing yourself nearby, the Company will pay you a salary to make a monthly trip to Marble Camp. There will be letters and assessments to take care of. Johnny will stay on as guard."

Papa could read Mr. Kerr's disappointment between the formal lines of the note. The quarry had been a dream, but not a profitable one.

Papa left on a trip to Bowie the day after Johnny brought the letter to camp. Mama told me, "He has important business and we'd better not go this time." She walked the floor while Papa was gone, and when I asked her questions, it was hard to get an answer.

"Will Papa be back tomorrow?" She didn't appear to hear. "Will Papa be back tomorrow or not till the next day?" I said it louder.

Mama woke with a start, "Oh, I'm not sure. It may take longer to arrange the details." She didn't say what the details might be.

It did take longer. Papa was gone three days. I missed seeing him come around the bend, and it was too bad. He was almost to the office before I saw him sitting up straight and holding on tight to the wheel of our brand new Ford touring car. With a whoop, I dropped the puzzle picture I was working and shouted, "Here's Papa, and look what he's got!"

Mama hurried out of the house and we rushed down the path to see the new car. There it stood in front of the office with its big brass carbide lights and its shiny black paint, and the water boiling merrily in its radiator! Seldom has any new car received a more enthusiastic welcome. It took a while to examine it, from the gleaming brass radiator to the side curtains under the back seat.

Papa stood proudly by as Mama and I "Oh-h-h-d" and "Ah-h-h-d" over it, and then, like a magician pulling a second rabbit out of a hat, Papa said, "And now do you want to hear my big news?" Mama said with a start, "Oh, yes, what about it, Dana?"

I kept looking at the car. There couldn't be anything better than that to tell us about.

"Joe Shafer and I signed the papers. We now own half interest in "The Bowie Commercial Company." Papa was not given to dramatics, but he almost struck a pose as he said it.

He was right! This news was bigger than the new car. It meant we would be going to live where there would be live people in houses all around us. Now every day we could see the long trains of cars that carried passengers to places even more lively than Bowie. A brand new ice cream parlor had just opened on Main Street — a brand new ice cream parlor complete with wire-legged chairs and tables. It even had fizz water for making sodas. Where in Marble Camp could you get an ice cream soda with real fizz water? I smiled to think of it.

Bowie was coming to life. The afternoon train brought fresh milk in bottles each day from a little dairy in Willcox. Bakery bread arrived twice a week from El Paso.

They were building a new Methodist Church in town, to Mama's great satisfaction. The people coming into the valley had put up part of the money and the Methodist Mission Board had put up the rest. In Ohio, Mama had helped pack missionary barrels to go to the mission churches, and here we were living in the part of the world where the barrels arrived! The church was frame, and had an old locomotive bell hung in a crude belfry. The bell had been donated by the Southern Pacific company, and when it rang, we were never to be quite sure whether a train was coming or it was time for church.

The building had one large room for services and four rooms on the side for Sunday School classes. There was no parsonage, so for a while they'd have to let those four rooms serve as a parsonage during the week and for classrooms on Sunday. Lots of times in the days ahead we were to have a class in the kitchen where the parson's wife hadn't had time to wash the breakfast dishes, and sometimes Papa was to stand watch all night beside a body in the church when there was to be a funeral the next day while the parson's family slept, or tried to, in the next room.

But on Sunday morning I could put on my Sunday best and have a place to go where there were other boys and girls and a teacher for my class, and a lady to play the little organ, and a collection plate to put my nickle in! Only, Mama said I could take a dime every Sunday because we had been away from church for so long we had to make it up by putting more money in the plate.

The flat, sandy streets of Bowie would be much easier on shoes than the rocky pathways in camp. I could take off the heavy leather ones Mama had finally admitted I should wear, and wear thin, "civilized" shoes, as Mama called them, maybe patent leather with kid button tops. In summer, I might even wear white kid slippers for Sunday — the kind without any tops at all.

The new four-room schoolhouse was built of brick, and the school board had hired Eastern teachers. "Two of the teachers are right out of normal school in Indiana, and Alma probably wouldn't have better ones even if we lived in Lorain," Mama said with satisfaction.

There was a new two-story tin building that housed "The Bowie News," a paper run by a most enthusiastic little printer. The upstairs was the family living quarters, and the man and his wife worked day and night promoting the valley through the press. "Jacques" was the printer's name, and he was probably more responsible than any other one man for the way Bowie was growing. He seldom took time to shave, and he charged around town gathering news and "figuring angles." He struck upon first one thing and then another to publicize. "The soil, sandy and rich as all get out," screamed his headlines. Or, "the water 99.44 percent pure. Just like Ivory

Soap." Jacques didn't think the little slivers of redwood floating in the water worth mentioning.

He even inspired the railroad to advertise the valley in its literature in the East. "Make more travel," he said, chomping on his cigar stub, "people and equipment, lumber and hardware, machinery and livestock, no end to the business the railroad can do, or the growth of the San Simon Valley!" He removed the cigar stub and raised it in a sweeping gesture. When Jacques talked like that, you didn't notice the week's stubble on his chin, or the little dirty tan cotton hat he always wore inside the house or out. When the first heavy flowing artesian well was dug, Jacques' joy knew no bounds. He hadn't suspected there were flowing riches under the good, sandy soil he was raving about. "Buy a Hunk of Land," shouted the headlines. "Puncture a hole and you'll have a fortune overnight as H2O comes bubbling out." Jacques did sometimes get carried away. Papa said it took a few men with fanatical zeal to pioneer a new country.

Sometime before, Papa had telegraphed an order for our furniture to be shipped from the warehouse in Denver. Now it was waiting at the depot in Bowie, so it didn't take us long to pack our belongings for the move to town. The furniture we had been using was to be left at camp.

"I might as well be comfortable when I come up once a month," Papa said. "There'll be assessment and tax reports to make from the files, and inquiries to answer."

"Maybe we'll come along sometimes," Mama said nonchalantly as she stuffed a cup into a barrel and tucked some straw around it, glancing sideways at Papa. Papa looked a little surprised, but he answered, "Sure thing! We'll call it our summer home." We'd never thought of returning to camp as a treat before.

Papa had rented a house for us in Bowie, and Johnny was to bring our trunks and gear on the big wagon the next day. The piano would come down later.

Now that we were leaving camp, I felt a little guilty, as if we were deserting an old friend. Early on a Monday morning in September, I went to sit on my rock for the last time.

"Don't go far — we'll be ready by noon," Mama said. The air was still and the sun shone bright on the huge blocks of marble sitting on the stockpile by the quarry hole — as they would for more than a century. The sheer strength of men and machines had wrenched them from the earth. Now they were gleaming, so white it made you squint at midday to look at them.

In every direction there were great chunks of silence.

The smell of smoke from our chimney mingled with the pungent pitch that ran out of the pine trees and hardened like big blisters on their trunks. I took a deep breath. A squirrel ran with its rippling motion from a scrub oak to the Christmas-tree-sized pine nearby, breaking the stillness with its chatter as it ran. I let my eyes travel slowly up the mountain from one trail to another, remembering the things that had happened in the lonely years.

Directly in front of me, up beneath the big "parcel-post package rock," Mr. Kerr was saying, 'My God, there goes the stack!"

Down the winding trail to the right of the Rocks, I could see the Mexican carrying the little fawn as the loaded burros followed him.

Slowly the Sunday feeling of walking through jelly came over me. I hadn't felt like that for a long time. It was one of those long ago Sundays, nearly four years ago, when I was just a little girl and Mama was trying to decide whether to cut my hair or leave it long. I lowered my eyes to the road below. The man was lying wounded in the wagon bed and Papa was climbing in beside him. How could one man be that long? Suddenly I heard the centipede fall with a clatter like a string of beads on the floor by my bed, and I shuddered as the "earthquake" walked into my playhouse uninvited.

My mind hurried to bring all the pictures and sounds back before it was time to go.

At the tent houses below, the people were coming out to sit in the darkness to listen to Mama sing at her piano, and Juan and Maria were standing beside the tent houses, surrounded by their children and friends, while we all listened silently to the Priest reading the wedding service. In a moment now, Papa and I would be going into the tent house to watch the best part of the wedding, that puppet show. I smiled again about that; I'd been very small then. Of course puppet shows and weddings didn't go together. Papa had been right.

As my eyes turned to the spot where the road wound into camp, a succession of teams and wagons, and people on horseback, came around the bend, Aunt Lena sitting up straighter than she needed to beside Johnny; Bill Schafer sitting loosely in his saddle, the dentist in his spiffy buggy. I closed my eyes and was disappointed when I opened them again that Johnny and the piano didn't heave into view. And in back of it all was the ghost of the clanking cables and whirring machinery at the quarry.

I had to come back a long way when Mama called, "Come get a sandwich. We'll be ready to go as soon as we eat a bite." I wasn't very hungry. But the jelly feeling grew thin and faded away quickly as I stumbled up to the house. The thrill of new adventure lay ahead.

Johnny ate lunch with us. "Good samwiches," he murmured.

As soon as he was through, he said a little gruffly, "Got some things to do. See you in town tomorrow." Automatically he reached for his Bull Durham sack and rolled a cigarette. I watched him run his tongue along the tobacco paper to seal it. The cigarette was fat in the middle and pointed on the ends as always. I'd miss Johnny. I looked at him and tried to think how it would seem to be all alone in camp without even Mama and Papa.

He hurried off up toward our empty chicken coop, carrying a shovel, his hat pulled down over his eyes, and one shoulder sagging a little as he climbed.

Our car was parked in front of the office, and we trooped down the trail, each of us carrying last-minute things. Mama had a coffee pot, our newer one, for she said, "the old one will be good enough to leave up here."

I had my arms full of dolls, five of them, and a Billiken. The Billiken wasn't much account. It had a doll's head and a teddy bear's body, and was neither doll nor animal, but it wouldn't be fair to leave it here and take the other dolls. Even a Billiken had a right to see what was beyond those mountains.

As we climbed in the car, Margaret Thompson's words kept ringing in my ears, "We leave tomorrow, rain or shine." Without intending to speak so loud, I said, "We leave today and the sun is shining."

Papa turned to glance at me. "What did you say, Pet?"

"Oh, nothing, I was just thinking."

Papa put down the suitcase he carried and opened the door to the back seat. It was too bad Johnny couldn't be there to say "goodbye." I climbed in and Papa put the suitcase on the back seat beside me.

"Happy, Pet?" he grinned at me. I nodded.

There were boxes on the floor and I had to keep my feet tucked under me. Papa got in the front seat and held the door open for Mama. The door on his side didn't open — it was just made to look like a door.

The car was parked on a slope so that by releasing the brake, and turning on the ignition key, we would roll forward and the car would start without Papa having to get out and crank it. He released the brake and we started down the hill. The car had just begun to gather momentum when we heard Johnny shout. We all looked up toward our house.

He was standing with his feet wide apart holding up the shovel. There was a dead snake draped over it. Part of what he was saying, we couldn't understand, but a few words came through clearly, "rattlesnake — under your house!"

I could feel a little shudder run through Mama. Papa didn't stop the car. He just grasped the wheel more firmly in his strong brown hands. We were under way now and he'd have to crank the engine if it died. No reason to go back just to see a rattlesnake. We went around the bend and I could feel Mama relax. She straightened her hat and sighed.

"As soon as we're settled," she said, "I'll entertain the Ladies Aid." Then, after a pause, "I wonder if we can start a choir." Papa gave her a quick glance as he let the car roll a little faster.

"You start a choir and I'll start a bank, Mother," he said softly.

Was that music coming out of the canyon behind us, or was it only in my head? And what was that tune? "Redwing" maybe?

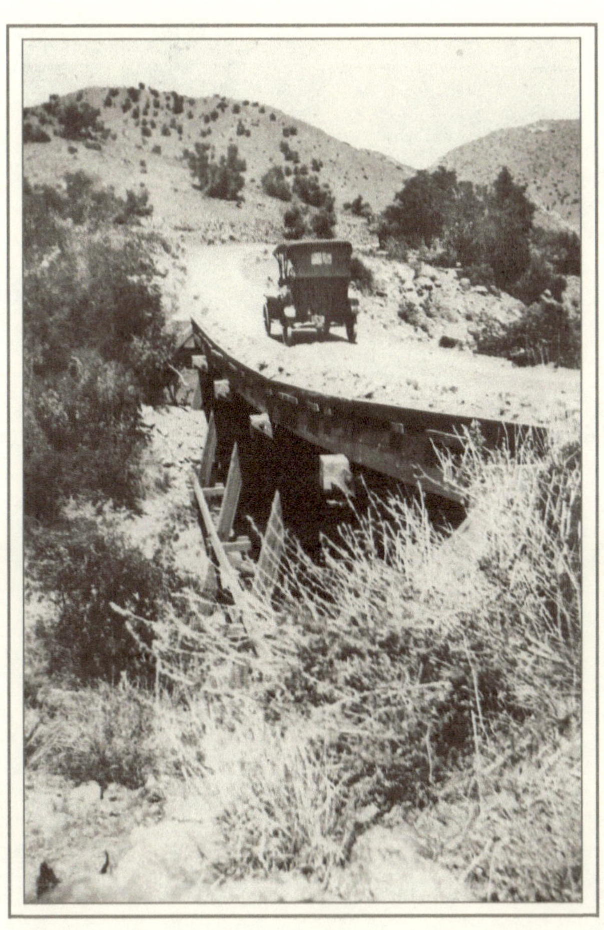

EDITOR'S AFTERWORD

Although this story ends at a natural point, readers might like to know about some things that happened later:

Within a year or two "Papa" — Dana T. Milner — did indeed gather the capital from ranchers and townspeople in Bowie to open the town's first bank and make it a success. Later he moved the family about 25 miles west to the larger town of Willcox and opened the first bank there, a thriving one in cattle country. He served one term in the early Arizona State Legislature and was a civic leader in Willcox until his retirement in the late 1940's. Once, in a town-wide popular vote, Willcox named him "Our Leading Citizen."

"Mama" — Maud (Pierce) Milner — Did help organize a Methodist church choir in Bowie and a church, a library, and a civic center and women's clubhouse in Willcox. She came to love social life in small-town Arizona.

Alma — who was joined by a little brother, Johnny, when she was 11 years old — became the first girl from Willcox to go away to the University of Arizona in Tucson. On a trip back to Ohio when she was a young woman she met my father, Paul MacKenzie Burroway, and they married when she was 24, in 1929, just before the crash that led to the Great Depression. They moved to Arizona in 1931 and the family settled in Phoenix in 1934. With a small initial loan from my grandfather's bank, my father became a successful Phoenix home designer and builder in the years before World War II—the very first phase of the building boom that eventually made Phoenix one of the nation's largest cities.

— Stan Burroway

9 780990 779803